WOMEN NOVELISTS
FROM
FANNY BURNEY TO GEORGE ELIOT

WOMEN NOVELISTS
FROM FANNY BURNEY
TO GEORGE ELIOT

by

MURIEL MASEFIELD

Essay Index Reprint Series

 BOOKS FOR LIBRARIES PRESS
FREEPORT, NEW YORK

First Published 1934
Reprinted 1967

PR
III
.M25

INTERNATIONAL STANDARD BOOK NUMBER:
0-8369-0689-6

LIBRARY OF CONGRESS CATALOG CARD NUMBER:
67-23244

PRINTED IN THE UNITED STATES OF AMERICA
BY
NEW WORLD BOOK MANUFACTURING CO., INC.
HALLANDALE, FLORIDA 33009

2974

CONTENTS

PREFACE

These studies of women novelists have been grouped together not only on account of the writers' sex, but because they represent the development of the natural English novel of life and manners, and provide an incomparable panorama of a century of English society, from 1778 to 1876.[1] Students both of literature and of social history should find their work a fruitful field, and in this book a special feature is made of the period background (so far as space allows), by including short lives of the principal writers and drawing upon their novels for illustrations of new developments in social standards and manners.

Fanny Burney was a pioneer when she set herself " to show the world not what it *is*, but what it *appears* to a girl of seventeen " : her novels provide a rich pageant of the ball-rooms and " public places " of eighteenth century London, with their fine ladies and gentlemen, their fops, wits and blue-stockings.

Jane Austen's dramas of the country gentry at home in Great House, Vicarage or Manor, and the elegant apartments and Assembly Rooms of Bath, are unsurpassed " period " scene and character drawing. Emily Eden continues the same tradition delightfully in *The Semi-Attached Couple* and *The Semi-Detached House*.

The Brontës represent the revival of romance, with its cult of emotion and imagination, which pervaded Europe at the close of the eighteenth century, in reaction from the hard, bright rationality of preceding generations. Charlotte Brontë combined romance with realism in drawing upon her own observation and experience for the material of her novels.

Mrs. Gaskell's pictures of country and country-town life are fragrant with clean, sweet air and old-world charm : she also contributed to the crop of " condition-of-England " novels, bred by the struggles and distress of the " hungry forties."

[1] *Evelina* to *Daniel Deronda*.

Charlotte Yonge represents the mid-Victorian upper middle-class home, with its large family, and particularly the religious earnestness and idealism which followed the Oxford Movement.

George Eliot's best work was inspired by her country childhood, in which the love of the land, and familiarity with country people and their beasts, became with her " a sweet habit of the blood." She also represents the intellectual ferment of the eighteen-fifties, when subjects which had been regarded as beyond speculation were brought into the arena of debate. The contemporary of Charles Darwin, the translator of Strauss's *Life of Jesus*, the friend of Herbert Spencer and George Lewes, she was intensely pre-occupied by the speculative thought of the day, religious, scientific and psychological.

Irish life is pictured graphically by the first novelist to take its society (from landlord to peasant) for her theme— Maria Edgeworth. In her *Tales of Fashionable Life* she also contributes detail to the English social scene.

Scottish life is illustrated by the three novels of Susan Ferrier, the first of which—*Marriage*—Scott was not ashamed to have attributed to him, when it was published anonymously. Her pictures of Scottish castle life in a decaying period excellently supplement Scott's more stirring tales.

M. MASEFIELD.

Charlbury, Oxon., 1933.

I

THE LIFE OF FRANCES BURNEY (MADAME D'ARBLAY)

" At the accession of George III the patricians were yet at the height of their good fortune. Society recognised their superiority, which they themselves pretty calmly took for granted. . . . Here is a whole company of them ; wits and prodigals . . . beautiful ladies, parasites, humble chaplains, led captains. Those fair creatures whom we love in Reynolds's portraits, and who still look out on us from his canvases with their sweet calm faces and gracious smiles—those fine gentlemen who did us the honour to govern us ; who inherited their boroughs ; took their ease in their patent places ; and slipped Lord North's bribes so elegantly beneath their ruffles— we make acquaintance with a hundred of these fine folk, hear their talk and laughter . . . "
" The painters pursuing their gentle calling ; the men of letters in their quiet studies . . . The recorded talk of dear old Johnson ! . . . To have sat with him and Goldy ; to have heard Burke, the finest talker in the world ; and to have had Garrick flashing in with a story from his theatre !—I like, I say, to think of that society."
Thackeray in *The Four Georges*.

Such is the society into which Fanny Burney takes us with the impish pen of her youth, whether she was using it in a surreptitious flutter to add a chapter to *Evelina* after the rest of the household was safely in bed, or to record actual scenes and character-sketches in her diary, with a sprightliness which she " kept prodigious snug " in company. Hers was the eighteenth century world of the beau, the wit and the blue-stocking, of wax candles glancing on satin coats and richly embroidered skirts ballooning over their hoops, of dancing to fiddlestrings, of the concerts, supper-boxes and fireworks of Vauxhall and Ranelagh, of the lordly coach or the humbler sedan-chair and the attendant link-boy at the end of the evening. She had the entrée of the charmed circles of " the Rank and the Literature " in that age of aristocracy and privilege ; her associates were the originals of the portraits of Gainsborough, Romney, Sir Joshua Reynolds, Opie and Hoppner, and of the " conversation pieces " of Zoffany and Devis ; she moved amongst the same

street-scenes as Hogarth. While London's three thousand
Coffee Houses were continual founts of masculine wit
(amongst such of their patrons as were not sunk in cards and
wine), Fanny Burney frequented the routs and *conversa-
ziones* of Mrs. Thrale, Mrs. Vesey, Mrs. Montagu and Miss
Monckton, who provided Boswell with "the finest bit of
blue in London," and where he found that "the fair sex
might participate in conversation with literary and ingenious
men, animated by a desire to please." Better still, she knew
Dr. Johnson, the King of Good Talk, in his own (and in
Mrs. Thrale's) home; she even made breakfast for him, and
he called her "You little character-monger, you!" and
sent her a message as he lay dying—"Tell Fanny to pray
for me."

For five years Fanny Burney endured the misguided
reward of her literary fame by holding the position of Second
Keeper of the Robes to Queen Charlotte. Horace Walpole
complained that she was "royally gagged and promoted to
fold muslins," but the result was an inimitable journal of
court life. And then, having sampled the English aristocracy at the height of its privilege and power, she married
(at the age of forty-one) an émigré from Revolutionary
France—the Chevalier d'Arblay—and with him eventually
shared the fellowship of the ci-devant aristocracy of France
which survived the Revolution to figure in Paris under
Napoleon, bask in the restoration of monarchy under Louis
XVIII and scatter once more during the suspense of the
Hundred Days. She was in Brussels during the Battle of
Waterloo.

Fanny Burney was not born to high estate, hers was the
cachet of the Literature, not of the Rank; her best heritage
was the charm which her father shed on all who came within
his circle. Of Charles Burney, Dr. Johnson said: "Dr.[1]
Burney is a man for all the world to love; it is but natural
to love him," and again "My heart goes out to meet him . . .
I much question if there is in the world such another man
as Dr. Burney."

When Burney was still an impecunious young man,
apprenticed to the musician Dr. Arne, a harpsichord maker
introduced him to Fulk Greville as having "as much music

[1] Doctor of Music, Oxford.

in his tongue as in his hands " and being " as fit company for the prince as for an orchestra." Greville insisted on Burney going to live with him in the capacity of musical companion, a rôle which he filled without suffering any unease in rich and fashionable society, although he had neither the taste nor the means for much indulgence in cards and wine. Eventually both his patron and he married, and Burney became a fashionable music-master in London. In 1751 ill-health obliged the Burneys to leave town, and Frances, the third of their six children, was born at King's Lynn, Norfolk, in June, 1752. When she was nine the family returned to London and within a year suffered a great loss in the death of Mrs. Burney (*née* Sleepe, of French descent on her mother's side).

The bright, clever group of motherless children—of whom Fanny was the only shy one—and their charming father found many friends. Dr. Burney rushed from pupil to pupil, dining on sandwiches and wine in his hackney coach ; and yet, Fanny tells us, he was " always his natural self— gay, facile, sweet." He complained that Mrs. Thrale found him so conversable that he could make no progress in teaching Queeny Thrale music ; his other friends had to find him as best they could, and David Garrick would invade the study where he was breakfasting, served by his adoring daughters, with the hair-dresser busily at work on his head " frizzing, curling, powdering and pasting." When a space had been cleared for the guest amongst a litter of books and papers (Dr. Burney spent his odd moments in translating Dante and later in writing a *History of Music*) he would make him-self at home, once exclaiming : " And, so, Doctor, you and tag-rag and bobtail there, shut yourself up in this snug little bookstall, with all your blithe elves around you, to rest your understanding ? " Garrick's mimicry made many a gay scene for the young Burneys, two of whom he intro-duced to his friends as " two of my children, two of the Burneys." Charlotte, the youngest, whom he called his little Dumpling Queen, recorded with ecstatic energy in a childish diary : " Splitt me ! if I'd not a hundred times rather be spoken to by Garrick in public than His Majesty, G–d bless him ! "

The first visit of Dr. Johnson was one of the most memorable scenes of Fanny's youth, described with verve in a letter to " Daddy Crisp," a retired man of the world, disappointed in literary ambitions, who contributed no little to the education in life and manners which served Fanny instead of regular schooling. Dr. Johnson was wearing his " best-becomes," which consisted of " a large, full; bushy wig, a snuff-colour coat, with gold buttons (or, peradventure, brass) but no ruffles to his doughty fists ; and not, I suppose, to be taken for a Blue, though going to the Blue Queen " (i.e. Mrs. Montagu) " he had on very coarse black worsted stockings."

A duet by Esther and Susan Burney was in progress, and Dr. Johnson seemed to think it was to be seen rather than heard, as he bent so closely over the piano that " poor Hetty and Susan hardly knew how to play on for fear of touching his Phiz ! " Finally, when music should have given place to conversation, Dr. Burney's books caught his attention and he " pored over them shelf by shelf, almost brushing them with his eyelashes . . . and, standing aloof from the company, which he seemed clean and clear to forget, he began, without further ceremony, very composedly, to read to himself." The chagrin of the company still lives in Fanny's diary—" We were all excessively provoked, for we were languishing, fretting, expiring to hear him talk—not to see him read ! What could that do for us ? "

When Fanny was fifteen a step-mother came to preside over the Burney home in St. Martin's Street (once the house of Sir Isaac Newton), and soon there were three families under that friendly roof—a case of his, hers and theirs. The Burneys steered their way with sunny serenity amongst these complicated family relationships ; fashionable and distinguished society still flocked to Dr. Burney's musical evenings, and a guest recorded that she knew no house where conversation was " more pleasantly and desirably managed." There was, however, one rub : although the second Mrs. Burney prided herself upon blue-stocking tastes she looked with disfavour on writing as an occupation for a young, should-be marriageable girl, and under her admonitions Fanny reluctantly made a bonfire of her first attempt at a novel—*The History of Caroline Evelyn*—while her sister Susan stood by with streaming eyes.

Docile and timid as Fanny was—her Father once exclaimed

compassionately, " Poor Fan's such a prude ! "—her talent
was not to be denied its outlet : Caroline Evelyn's daughter
became the heroine of *Evelina*, which was written secretly
at night, and in a feigned hand, lest some sagacious publisher
should recognise the writing as that of the fair copy of Dr.
Burney's *History of Music*. Her brother Charles disposed of
the manuscript to Mr. Lowndes for £20, and requested that
the proofs should be addressed to " Mr. Grafton " at the
Orange Coffee House.

Evelina was published in 1778, when Fanny was twenty-
five, and at once took literary London by storm. Mr.
Lowndes was besieged for copies because " it was so unfashionable not to have read it." There is a pleasing little
scene in the diary describing how Fanny and her step-
mother visited his book-shop and innocently enquired if
he could tell them the name of the author, and he confided
to them that he himself had at first suspected Horace Walpole
—" for he once published a book in this snug manner."
Meanwhile delicious reports reached St. Martin's Street :
Susan had " such a thing " to report to Fanny, who was
hiding in bashful anonymity at Daddy Crisp's country
house—Dr. Johnson himself had got hold of the book and
would " talk of it for ever " to Mrs. Thrale, professing
himself so " ardent for the dénouement " that he could
scarcely wait for the third volume. " Good God ! " exclaimed Mrs. Thrale, aghast that anyone should steal a
march upon her in the discovery of a new author.

When this news reached Fanny she relieved her feelings
by dancing a jig round Mr. Crisp's mulberry tree, and she
wrote off to Susan :—

" I often think, when I am counting my laurels, what a pity it
would have been had I popped off in my last illness, without
knowing what a person of consequence I was !—and I sometimes
think that, were I now to have a relapse, I could never go off with
so much *éclat* ! "

However, further exhilarating tributes were to come :
Sir Joshua Reynolds had not been able to go to bed without
finishing *Evelina*, he would give £50 to know the author,
but was sure he should make love to her—if it were a woman ;
Mr. Burke was said to dote on it and to have sat up all night
reading it. Fanny's cup was full, and perhaps she was

not altogether sorry when the secret of the authorship was revealed by her happy father.

To Mrs. Thrale fell the congenial task of stage-managing Fanny's début in literary London ; it was at her spacious and hospitable white house at Streatham that she was really initiated into fame—" Come, Evelina,—come and sit by me," rolled out Dr. Johnson, and he almost took her into his arms or, as she explains, " one of his arms, for one would go three times, at least, round me," as he charged her to " be a good girl." And so " dear little Burney " came into her own, with Dr. Johnson " grown quite polite " at her side ; and in her other character, as the " very nice observer "[1] in whose company some of her fellow-guests felt uneasy and Gibbon scarcely dared to speak, she made golden use of her opportunities.

In her novel she had drawn a varied range of characters extraordinarily well. Now the same pen—with rather more grandiloquence, unfortunately, at times—set down in a diary, or in long journal-letters to Susan and Dr. Burney, the scenes and personalities of real society. In the dining-room at Streatham she shows us Boswell in the very grip of his inspired obsession, listening to Dr. Johnson with an attention that amounted almost to pain, his ear nearly resting on the Doctor's shoulder, his mouth open as if to catch every syllable that might be uttered ; at Sir Joshua Reynolds' house we sit down to the dinner-table with Burke ; at a " blue " party we see a hostess industriously breaking up the now unfashionable circles into groups, until her guests are driven to sit back to back, and upon this confusion enters Sheridan, with his lovely wife—Elizabeth Linley, from the Linley " nest of nightingales " at Bath—upon his arm, and asks for an introduction to the authoress of *Evelina*.

In 1782 Fanny's second novel *Cecilia* was published, and Burke and Gibbon vied with each other as to which could read it the faster.

In time fame brought strange consequences. Fanny became intimate with Mrs. Delany—Burke's " model of an accomplished woman of former times," whose epitaph, written by the Bishop of Worcester, began, " She was a lady of singular ingenuity and politeness "—and went to

[1] Sir Joshua Reynolds' phrase.

stay with her at Windsor. Here George III and Queen Charlotte would call informally on their old friend, and in Mrs. Delany's drawing-room occurred the memorable conversation in which the King asked Fanny how she came to think of publishing her novel—" what ? what ? " and she stammered out in reply, " I thought—sir—it would look very well in print ! " And then they discussed Shakespeare, and, while showing a considerable knowledge of the plays, the King concluded :—

" Was there ever such stuff as a great part of Shakespeare ? Only one must not say so ! But what think you ? What ? Is there not sad stuff ?—What ?—What ? "

These meetings inspired Queen Charlotte to a great act of patronage towards the young lady who had written novels which even the Princesses might read (with a Bishop's sanction), and Fanny was offered the position of Second Keeper of the Robes to Her Majesty. Her father was enchanted, Fanny herself was not insensible of the honour ; the offer was accepted. Fanny was duly immured at the Queen's Lodge, Windsor in July, 1786, and wrote to her sister :—

" I am *married*, my dearest Susan, I look upon it in that light— I was averse to forming the union . . . but . . . the knot is tied. What, then, now remains but to make the best wife in my power ? "

Fanny Burney's voluminous journal of court life gives us an intimate introduction to the King and Queen in their family circle and to the steady regularity of their routine at Windsor, the personalities of their attendants, and the trials and pleasures of the royal service. We learn to differentiate the six Princesses ; the Princess Royal, dignified, courteous and conscientious, sewing with her own fingers every stitch of the wedding dress in which she was to become the bride of the widower Prince of Wurtemburg [1]; Princess Augusta, lively, friendly, considerate, allowing the hairdresser to take what ornaments he chose from her stock of jewels, feathers and ribbons for the elaborate edifice of her hair, while she gave her attention to talk instead of to her mirror ; Princess Elizabeth, delicate, romantic, *poseuse*, whose rooms were " the most elegantly and fancifully orna-

[1] Some of these particulars about the Princesses are taken from Fanny's accounts of visits to Windsor after her marriage.

mented of any in the Lodge," and who wrote a poem called *The Birth of Love*, illustrated by her own designs; sweet Princess Mary, for whom the sailor Prince William (afterwards William IV) tried to keep sober at her first public ball, but failed in the attempt; Princess Sophia, a pretty child, who would not allow Fanny to carry the basket for Badine, the Queen's little dog; Princess Amelia, so carefully drilled to behave *en princesse* in babyhood, and so pleasingly natural in spite of it. One picture of Princess Amelia, in a terrace procession, is well-known :—

" It was really a mighty procession. The little Princess, just turned of three years old, in a robe-coat covered with fine muslin, a dressed close cap, white gloves and a fan, walked on alone and first, highly delighted with the parade, and turning from side to side to see everybody as she passed."

Fanny was beside Mrs. Delany, who attended in an invalid chair, and the royal family stopped for Amelia to receive the old lady's birthday greeting. Presently the Princess ran behind the chair and put up her face for a kiss from Fanny, solemnly examining her fan and remarking weightily, " O ! A brown fan ! " On another occasion, when Fanny had forgotten the etiquette of appearing in a new dress on royal birthdays both morning and evening, and had answered the Queen's summons in haste in her " usual white dimity great-coat," Amelia put her to shame by exclaiming, " And won't Miss Burney be fine, too ? " But when Fanny did appear resplendent in a new lilac tabby in the evening the kindly King remarked, " Emily should see Miss Burney's gown now, and she would think her fine enough."

The queen is necessarily a central figure. Fanny records her naïve confidences, such as her excitement and pleasure in her jewels as a young Queen and how soon it palled and she longed for the simple, unexacting dress of her girlhood again ; her conscientiousness in taking sample lessons herself from the Princesses' governesses and tutors ; her struggles against the seductions of light literature—" They write so finely now, even for the most silly books, that it makes one read one, and one cannot help it. Oh ! I am very angry sometimes at that ! " Queen Charlotte never spared herself, and was intolerant of weak giving-in to illness or fatigue in those who served her, but she could be considerate in ways she approved : she always sent Fanny away when her hair was being powdered lest the powder should spoil her clothes.

Fanny's gallery of minor court portraits is very varied. Amongst prolix accounts of incidents and conversations which were not really worth retailing in full, character-sketches and scenes of real piquancy and historical interest can be picked out. There are descriptions of days spent at the trial of Warren Hastings : there is Major Goldsworthy, one of the equerries, describing a long day's hunting in the rain with the King, with the offer of a share in the royal jug of barley-water at the end : there is Boswell detaining Fanny at the gates of the Queen's Lodge to plead for some of her notes from Dr. Johnson for his book :—

" Yes, madam, you must give me some of your choice little notes of the Doctor's ; we have seen him long enough upon stilts ; I want to show him in a new light. Grave Sam, and great Sam, and solemn Sam, and learned Sam—all these he has appeared over and over. Now I want to entwine a wreath of the graces across his brow ; I want to show him as gay Sam, agreeable Sam, pleasant Sam : so you must help me with some of his beautiful billets to yourself."

Fanny refused Boswell ; she had imbibed the Court circumspection and was afraid of " a man so famous for compiling anecdotes."

Least pleasant of Fanny's sketches is her senior, the First Keeper of the Robes, Mrs. Schwellenberg, with her broken English, her pet frogs and her jealousy. When she suspected that the equerries preferred Fanny to preside over their tea-table, and took more trouble to make themselves entertaining for her, she asked jealously :

" 'Vell, sleeps he yet with you—Colonel Goldswirthy ? '
' Not yet, ma'am,' I hesitatingly answered.
'O ! ver well ! he will sleep with nobody but me ! O ! I won't come down.' And a little later she added, ' I believe he vill marry you ! '
' I believe not, ma'am,' I answered."

It was Colonel Digby (the " Mr. Fairly " of the Journal) who did very nearly cost Fanny her peace of mind, by indulging too freely in Platonic friendship with her without making his intentions (or lack of them) plain.

Fanny was with the Queen when the King's first mental breakdown occurred, and shared her suspense and sorrow.

B

Later the King, giving the doctors the slip, chased her in Kew Gardens, kissed her on both cheeks and exhorted her not to let Mrs. Schwellenberg worry her—" Never mind her !—don't be oppressed—I am your friend." He then gave her embarrassing details as to the statesmen he intended to dismiss from office when he returned to power—" I shall be much better served ; and when once I get away I shall rule with a rod of iron ! "

There was a touching little scene to follow when Fanny first met the King really restored to health and family life again, and he remarked slyly, " I could overtake you better now ! "

In June, 1791, Fanny gave up her post at court, on account of health. She looked forward to a happy, literary retirement with her father, now organist at Chelsea College, but the great adventure of her life was still to come. At Juniper Hall, near Mickleham, and not far from her sister Susan's home, she became intimate with a colony of French émigrés and soon lost her heart to the Chevalier d'Arblay, who had been Adjutant to Lafayette in the early phase of the French Revolution, when there was still hope of establishing a constitutional monarchy. M. d'Arblay had actually been on guard at the Tuileries on the night when Louis XVI and his family made the escape which ended so wretchedly on the very frontier, at Varennes.

Fanny and her Chevalier made the gallant decision to marry and be content with *le simple nécessaire*. She had a pension of £100 a year from the Queen (by no means certain) and hoped to write again, but it was a bold venture to make at the age of forty-one. The marriage took place on July 31st, 1793, at Mickleham Church. Fanny's subsequent descriptions of the simple life, first in rooms at Bookham and afterwards at *Camilla Cottage*, built on the land of her friends the Locks of Norbury Park, out of the proceeds of her third novel *Camilla* (published 1796), are delightful. All the Chevalier could contribute to the ménage was labour, and he mowed down hedges with his sabre as if he were charging an army, pruned the fruit-trees so drastically that they scarcely survived, transplanted the flowers until they had " danced round as far as the space allows," and grew so many cabbages that they were surfeited with them, despite the fact of wasting a considerable number because they did not realise they were ready to cut.

Fanny d'Arblay's only child, Alexander, was born in 1794. Eventually M. d'Arblay tried to retrieve his fortunes in France under Napoleon, who offered him a military command but withdrew it when M. d'Arblay stipulated that he should not be required to fight against England. They feared this had plunged them in disgrace, but Napoleon gallantly informed Lafayette that he looked indulgently on M. D'Arblay as "the husband of Cecilia." Fanny gives an interesting account of Napoleon at a review in Paris in 1802.

While she was living in France Fanny began a fourth novel— *The Wanderer or Female Difficulties*—which was published in 1814 but had considerably less success than her other books. The d'Arblays had a spell of honour and prosperity at the restoration of the French monarchy, when M. d'Arblay became *Chevalier* once more as an officer of Louis XVIII's body-guard. Then came Napoleon's escape from Elba and his dramatic march on Paris, after Ney had failed to fulfil his boast that he would bring him there in an iron cage. The Chevalier d'Arblay collected all the arms he could and came to say good-bye to Fanny with the war-horse he loved *à la folie* slung with an armoury of weapons. They prayed together, and he left her with a cry of "*Vive le roi !* "

Even at such a moment Fanny was careful to pay all their bills before she joined the Princesse d'Henin and the Comte de Lally Tolendal in their flight from Paris. She shared the suspense of Brussels during the battle of Waterloo, saw the Black Brunswickers march through on their way to death led by their gallant Duke, who "foremost fighting fell," and helped to nurse the wounded in a Church.

After Waterloo M. d'Arblay was in poor health, and they decided to settle in England, and sent "Alex" to Cambridge, where he distinguished himself in mathematics, being tenth wrangler in 1818 and taking a fellowship at Christ's College. In May, 1818, M. d'Arblay died, after nearly twenty-five years of a marriage of which Fanny could write :

"And never was union more blessed and felicitous ; though, after the first eight years of unmingled happiness, it was assailed by many calamities, chiefly of separation or illness, yet still mentally unbroken."

Fanny settled in London and occupied herself in preparing her *Memoirs of Dr. Burney*, cheered by her son and by the attentions of the Princesses Augusta and Mary.   It is grievous to record that there was yet another bitter blow in store for the brave spirit which still shines through the prosy sentimentality of the latter part of Fanny's journal.   In 1837 her son, who had been ordained in the Church of England and was engaged to be married, died after an attack of influenza.   Fanny's own release came three years later, at the age of eighty-eight : she died on January 6th, 1840, the anniversary of the death of the dearest of her sisters, Susan.

II

FANNY BURNEY'S NOVELS

Evelina or A Young Lady's Entrance into the World, 1778. Now to be obtained in Everyman. A beautiful modern edition (illustrated) prepared by Sir F. D. Mackinnon was published by the Oxford University Press, 1930.
Cecilia or Memoirs of an Heiress, 1782. Published in the York Library Series (2 vols.) in 1904.
Reflections Relative to the Emigrant French Clergy, 1793. A pamphlet written with the object of raising funds.
Camilla or A Picture of Youth, 1796.
The Wanderer or Female Difficulties, 1814.
Tragic Dramas, 1818.
Published after her death :—*The Early Diary of Frances Burney* (1768–1778), 1889. (Bell, Bohn's Standard Library, 2 vols.)
The Diary and Letters of Madame d'Arblay (1778–1840). 1st edition published in 7 vols., 1842–1846. Edition in 4 vols., edited by her niece, Charlotte Barrett, 1897. Modern edition by Macmillan, 6 vols., illustrated, 1904. One volume Selection edited by Muriel Masefield (Routledge, Broadway Diaries Series) 1931.

In order to appraise Fanny Burney's achievement in literature it is important to realise how comparatively modern the English novel is. Before the appearance of Richardson's *Pamela* in 1740, there had been good tales, more often in verse than in prose, and there had been character-sketches, but the two were more or less distinct. In fiction high romance had held the field for generations, with some notable exceptions, such as the superlative allegory of *Pilgrim's Progress* (1678), the realistic chronicle of the adventures of *Robinson Crusoe* (1719) and the fascinating, satiric tale of *Gulliver's Travels* (1726). The representation of types of character had been introduced in the prose sketches called *Characters* by Sir Thomas Overbury (1581–1613) and his friends, but it was only on the stage that story and character were satisfactorily blended into a unity.

The form Richardson chose for *Pamela* and *Clarissa Harlowe* was a series of letters, and this forced him to develop some personality in his heroines. A girl who writes a minute history of all the throes and vicissitudes of her beleaguered virtue or her much-tried heart must betray her feelings, and even something of her mind ; she necessarily becomes more than a pretty lay figure to be draped with adventures and misadventures. Richardson, as it were, inserted little panes of glass over his heroine's hearts and allowed his readers to peep through.[1] Directly that element of analysis of the feelings was introduced into fiction the novel no longer depended on strange happenings and high-flown romance ; characterisation was mingled with story, and the novel proper came to birth.

Richardson's was a feminine type of novel, and the tear-fall of his heroines was excessive ; his greater successor, Fielding, jibbed at *Pamela* and began his career as a novelist by parodying it in *Joseph Andrews* (1742). Fielding, however, promoted still further the abandonment of the marvellous for the real ; in *Tom Jones* he did not so much tell a story as exhibit a series of scenes from the lives of his full-blooded characters. Fielding was followed by Smollett in an equally robust style, but *Roderick Random* (1748) and *Peregrine Pickle* (which Lydia Languish bids her maid fling under the toilet when she hears her aunt and Sir Anthony Absolute at the door) fully justify the remark that Smollett's heroines " are regarded by his heroes rather as luxuries than as ladies," and that the heroes themselves are " not merely libertines, but often behave like selfish ruffians."[2]

Sterne achieved a more modern form of art in *Tristram Shandy* (1760), with its recognisable portraits of actual people, but his pen was dipped deep in sentiment and caricature, and still deeper in coarseness. This latter quality, in fact, was almost invariably associated with the novel—*The Vicar of Wakefield* (1766) was an honourable exception—and Macaulay was not exaggerating when he wrote that " most of the novels which preceded *Evelina* were such as no lady would have written ; and many of them such as no lady could without confusion own that she had read."

Macaulay's opinion gives us the measure of Fanny Burney's courage in invading a field which had hitherto been chiefly

[1] See Arthur Ransome's *The Art of Story-Telling*.
[2] Andrew Lang.

commanded by men of the world and which had such an unsavoury reputation. Later in her life Queen Charlotte said of her " her character is too delicate to suit with writing for the stage. . . . It is too public and hazardous a style of writing:" but Fanny had already made an equally bold and hazardous venture, and her personality suffered for years from the necessity of demonstrating in her manners that a girl need not necessarily be brazen and fond of publicity because she wrote novels. Her own claim was modest:

" I have only presumed to trace the accidents and adventures to which a " young woman " is liable ; I have not pretended to show the world what it actually *is*, but what it *appears* to a girl of seventeen ; and, so far as that, surely any girl who is past seventeen may safely do ? "

In doing this Fanny Burney brought about a literary revolution : the novel was freed from the reproach of coarseness (hitherto considered a practically necessary ingredient of humour) and the natural story of life and manners came into its kingdom. Perhaps no one appraised the refreshing qualities of her work better than Dr. Burney, who, after his first reading of the book, pronounced on its heroine : " Evelina is in a new style, too, so perfectly innocent and natural." Of other scenes he admitted they were " pure vulgar to be sure," but he added that " the girl's account of public places is very animated and natural, and not *common*."

Natural : that was the great achievement. After the innumerable attempts on Pamela's virtue, related in all their sensual detail, the sobs of Clarissa, the roystering and swagger of Tom Jones, Roderick Random and Peregrine Pickle, the caricature of Tristram Shandy, men and women alike—from Dr. Johnson, Burke and Gibbon to the " tonish misses " of society—found it extraordinarily refreshing to read of the naïve embarrassments of an unsophisticated young girl at her first balls, of the " mortifying situations " into which her vulgar relations thrust her at one " public place " after another, and the unfailing manner in which the hero, Lord Orville, rose to the occasion " with a politeness which knows no intermission."

With Fanny Burney, as with Charles Dickens, the way to get the best from her work is not to subject her novels to strict literary analysis and criticism, but to follow her characters

into the society of their class and their day. Her canvas is
not so wide as that of Dickens, who " had the key of the
streets," but it is wider than that of Jane Austen or of Charlotte
Brontë. Mrs. Thrale, who knew her world, is a trustworthy
witness, and she wrote of *Evelina*, before she knew the name
of the author :

" There's a great deal of human life in this book, and of the
manners of the present time. It's writ by somebody that knows
the top and the bottom, the highest and lowest of mankind."

It is true that the uneasy stir of industrialism and democracy,
so soon to transform English society, found no place in *Evelina*,
but that was because it did not yet ruffle the smooth surface
of life in the drawing-room, the ballroom and the public
place. Fanny portrayed what she knew and had seen,
either in musical, literary and fashionable circles or in the
household of the wig-maker next door. Occasionally she
exaggerated to make a good tale : Dr. Burney himself thought
that the horse-play of Captain Mirvan was overdone,
especially in the episode of the monkey.

The reader who takes up *Evelina* for the first time will
probably find the opening letters (Fanny adopted Richardson's form for her first novel) dull and pompous : those who
have a period sense will nevertheless appreciate the flavour
of the stately phrases and circumlocution. By Letter X
Fanny has set the stage by an explanation of Evelina's situation at the opening of the story, and the book comes to life
with the girl herself writing from Queen Ann Street,
London :—" This moment arrived. Just going to Drury
Lane Theatre. The celebrated Mr. Garrick performs
Ranger. I am quite in extacy." Evelina's zest for life is
at once apparent, in the comments she dashes off on her
return :—" I could hardly believe he had studied a written
part, for every word seemed to be uttered from the impulse
of the moment. . . . I would have given the world to have
had the whole play acted over again. And when he danced—
O how I envied Clarinda ! I almost wished to have jumped
on the stage and joined them." Just so, no doubt, had Fanny,
Susan and Charlotte Burney often felt as they watched
Garrick from the box he had offered them.

In all her embarrassments Evelina showed a fearless
and independent judgment, in fact it is often this which

causes her difficulties. At her first ball she unknowingly
defies convention by refusing to dance with a fop because
she thinks him ridiculous, and then accepts the hand of the
delectable Lord Orville. A typical scene follows : the
fop persecutes her all the evening with enquiries as to how
he had given her such offence as to warrant the insult,
Evelina is put to confusion, and Lord Orville comes to the
conclusion that, despite her beauty, she is but " a poor,
weak girl." This opinion is repeated to Evelina by officious
friends.

Evelina's second ball is the best of Fanny Burney's ball
scenes. In Sir Clement Willoughby we have the ballroom
bully of the day to perfection—well-born, immaculately
dressed and correspondingly self-confident, to the pitch of
insolence. Evelina tries to protect herself from him, and
also to gain time, in the hope that Lord Orville may ask her
to dance again, by telling him that she is already engaged.
Suspecting this to be untrue, Sir Clement gives her no peace,
and a long and lively dialogue follows, in this vein :

" ' What an insensible ! ' continued he, ' why, Madam, you are
missing the most delightful dance in the world ! The man must
be either mad or a fool—which do you incline to think him yourself ? '
. . . ' Pray, what coat has he on ? '
' Indeed, I never looked at it.'
' Out upon him ! ' cried he ; ' What ? Did he address you in
a coat not worth looking at ? What a shabby wretch ! '
How ridiculous ! I really could not help laughing." (*This
irresistible impulse to natural laughter in Evelina was often her undoing*)
" which, I fear, encouraged him, for he went on—' Charming creature !
—and can you really bear ill-usage with so much sweetness ? . . .
For my part, though I am not the offended person, my indignation
is so great that I long to kick the fellow round the room !—unless,
indeed—it is a partner of your own creating ? ' "

Even when he has forced the tormented girl to dance with
him his raillery continues, only varied by extravagant personal
compliments. Evelina is reduced to childish distress :

" ' I wish you would say no more to me, Sir. . . . You have
already destroyed all my happiness for this evening.'
' Good Heaven ! What is it I have done ?—How have I merited
this scorn ? . . . '
' If I have offended you,' cried I, ' you have but to leave me—
and O how I wish you would ! '

'My dear creature,' (said he, half-laughing) 'why, where could you be educated ?'

'Where I most sincerely wish I was now !'

'How conscious you must be, all beautiful that you are, that those charming airs seem only to heighten the bloom of your complexion !'"

And so the scene moves on to an excellent climax, when Evelina is rash enough to let her eyes rest on Lord Orville at yet another sally about the defaulting partner, exclaiming—" I wish *his* presence, Sir, could awe *you* !" Sir Clement seizes his opportunity, calls to Lord Orville as he passes by and presses Evelina's hand upon him, with profuse apologies for his " usurpation." Lord Orville lives up to his Grandisonian character by murmuring to the now weeping Evelina—" Be not distressed, I beseech you ; I shall ever think my name honoured by your making use of it." Nevertheless, he sees no reason to withdraw his opinion that she is but a poor, weak girl.

Evelina's embarrassments in fashionable society prove to be negligible compared with those which beset her when her wealthy, but vulgar, grandmother from France arrives and eventually insists on taking her under her wing. Now we are introduced to Fanny Burney's most famous low comedy characters. Madame Duval's brother, Mr. Branghton, who keeps a silversmith's shop on Snow Hill, his family and their lodger, Mr. Smith, who apes the fashionable beau and only achieves what Dr. Johnson described as " a fine varnish of low politeness," all betray incomparably lively vulgarity whenever they open their mouths. Any page about the Branghtons or Mr. Smith yields a harvest of graphic phrases. One which society London quoted with delight, even to Fanny herself (to her embarrassment at Sir Joshua Reynolds' house), is Miss Branghton's ecstatic cry to her sister—" Lord, Polly ! Only think ! Miss has danced with a lord !"

We see young Branghton, between whom and Evelina a match is actually proposed, swell with patronising pride as he says to his father outside the Opera : " Lord, Father, make no words about that, for I'll pay for the coach that Miss had," and " Sir, if you please, I beg that I may treat Miss." Even more vividly we see his odious smirk, if not nudge, when he says to Evelina, " I suppose, Miss, aunt has told you about you know what ?—hasn't she, Miss ?"

Mr. Smith excels himself when he offers Evelina a ticket
for the Hampstead ball and persists in believing that her
attempt to refuse is all due to coyness. When she goes so
far as to refuse to dance, after her grandmother has taken her
to the ball against her will, he is startled into giving her
encouragement he had not dreamed of when he set out—
" I assure you, there is nobody so likely to catch me at last
as yourself." After a long dose of such company, Evelina
finds she views Sir Clement Willoughby with less distaste,
he has at least the power of effectually silencing Mr. Smith,
who sits lost in envious admiration of clothes which he knows
must have cost thirty to forty pounds. This welcome
restraint upon the party wears off, however, when Madame
Duval gathers spirit to " give the beau a trimming." Evelina
saw that " every one, who before seemed at a loss how, or
if at all, to occupy a chair, now filled it with the most easy
composure." When Sir Clement actually showed signs of
embarrassment, Mr. Smith resumed his expression of
satisfied conceit and young Branghton became rude and
familiar once more.

Perhaps the most outstanding feature of *Evelina* is the
series of pictures it gives us of the " public places " of
eighteenth century London at the zenith of their popularity
and fashion. The string of names which can be collected
within a third of the book calls up a world. We sample
Ranelagh, Vauxhall and the Pantheon and their distinctive
entertainments : in the company of the Branghtons we go
further afield to White-Conduit House, Marybone Gardens
and Kensington Gardens ; there is talk, too, of Cox's Museum,
Don Saltero's at Chelsea, George's at Hampstead, Foote's
and Sadler's Wells.

One of the best of these scenes in public places is the
evening at Vauxhall on which Miss Branghton venturesomely
proposes to her sister, " Lord, Polly, suppose we were to
take a turn in the dark walks ! " Evelina's attempt to hang
back is silenced with a contemptuous—" O, dear, I thought
how uneasy Miss would be without a beau." Miss Branghton
pays for her rash experiment by being forced to walk up and
down the dark walks at a breathless pace between two young
men, until rescued by her father, and Miss Polly has a similar
experience. Evelina herself is caught by the hands and

soon surrounded by a ring of disputants all claiming to be her companion, until Sir Clement Willoughby, exclaiming " Heaven and earth ! What voice is that ? " scatters the smaller fry and tries to take advantage of the situation himself.

Only a little less alarming is the adventure of Marybone Gardens. Startled by the explosive conclusion of the story of Orpheus and Eurydice as set forth in fireworks, Evelina is separated from her party in the crowd, and soon terrified by numerous facetious offers of protection from insolent gallants. Rushing blindly up to the two women nearest at hand, she cries, " For Heaven's sake, dear ladies, afford me some protection ! " only to find herself arm-in-arm between two hoydens who shout with laughter at every word she says. Her relief is intense when she sees Mr. Brown, Miss Polly Branghton's young man, who is good-naturedly looking for her : but Mr. Brown proves a broken reed, as the women annex him too, and soon he is anxiously complaining, " Lord, ma'am, there's no need to squeeze one's arm so ! " In this wretched plight Evelina suddenly sees Lord Orville looking at her with indignant astonishment. By now her own party is close at hand, and she has no wish to introduce them to him and no need to appeal for his help. At the same moment a still more anguished cry goes up from the unhappy Mr. Brown, " Goodness, ladies, you hurt me like anything ! Why, I can't walk at all if you keep pinching my arms so ! " The women laugh uproariously, even the Miss Branghtons are betrayed into titters, and Lord Orville turns sorrowfully away.

At the theatre and the Opera similar mortifications, and even dangers, are thrust upon the luckless Evelina. The Opera scene with the Branghtons is particularly good : their ignorance of the difference between theatre and Opera as to prices and dress is devastating, and Evelina's torments in full evening dress in the two-shilling gallery and the imprudence of her attempt to escape are most graphically described.

We are forced to the conclusion that London was a dangerous and unpleasant place for the woman who was not carefully protected, and also in possession of some knowledge of her world, and sufficient self-confidence to act upon it. In *Cecilia* there is a striking instance, when, after Mr. Harrel's suicide at Vauxhall, Mrs. Harrel and Cecilia realise the impossibility that "two ladies could go to town alone, in a hackney coach, and without even a servant, at near four o'clock in the morning." Even a walk in the streets in broad daylight on a fine day was almost an heroic enterprise ; when the Miss Branghtons had walked from Holborn to Queen Ann Street they were obliged to brush their coats and dry their shoes.

The high spirits in which *Evelina* was evidently written carry it to a happy conclusion just in time—had Lord Orville had to exclaim even once more " Good God ! Do I see Miss Anville ? " as the innocent Evelina was revealed in yet another comprising situation, both his patience and the reader's might have been exhausted.

Fanny Burney's second novel, *Cecilia*, is not as good as *Evelina*, although it contains the strongest dramatic scene she ever wrote—that of the evening at Vauxhall on which Mr. Harrel collects a strangely mixed company in a supper-box, and, when all but the bewildered ladies have been well primed with champagne, leaps the barrier and rushes into the shrubbery to shoot himself.

The plot of *Cecilia* is clever, and the girl herself is lovable, with the same refreshing spirit which pleases in Evelina. When she is persecuted at a masquerade by a man dressed as the Devil, and the White Domino who comes to her rescue asks her if she knows her tormentor, she replies " I hope so, because there is one man I suspect, and I should be sorry to find there is another equally disagreeable." There is, however, less sprightly dialogue, and the long series of ingenious incidents which embarrass the heroine become wearisome and unnatural before the end of the book.

Cecilia presents quite a good gallery of minor characters (rather too many, in fact), but there is no low comedy equal to that of *Evelina*. Mr. Briggs, Cecilia's miserly guardian, who keeps her waiting at her first visit while he counts over his things from the wash, is trenchantly drawn. Fanny does remind us now and again of the reverse side of eighteenth century pageantry in dress and manners. No doubt the free use of powder and pomade had its abuse (Mr. Smith complained that the Miss Branghtons left his sitting-room " so greasy and nasty "), and uncombed wigs must have been particularly objectionable. Probably the fop in *Camilla* who applied jessamine drops to his hands during a ball, and then spirted lavender about him, had his reasons !

As regards style, *Cecilia* supplies some particularly well-contrasted examples of the grandiose language of Fanny's descriptions and formal speeches and the unaffected, lively dialogue she can write for a character-part. Mrs. Delvile, for instance, is described as having eyes which " though they had lost their youthful fire, retained a lustre that evinced their primeval brilliancy." As to character, Cecilia found her

" sensible, well-bred, and high spirited, gifted by nature with superior talents, and polished by education and study with all the elegant embellishments of cultivation."

Mortimer Delvile gave proof of " the elegance of his education and the liberality of his mind" by addressing Cecilia in these terms :—

" Resent not my presumption, my beloved Miss Beverley, but let the severity of my recent sufferings palliate my present temerity ; for where affliction has been deep and serious, causeless and unnecessary misery will find little encouragement ; and mine has been serious indeed ! Sweetly, then, permit me, in proportion to its bitterness, to rejoice in the soft reverse which now flatters me with its approach."

It is like a plunge into reality to pass from such exalted passages to Mr. Briggs scolding Cecilia for failing to pay him a visit he was expecting :—

" Waited for you three days, dressed a breast o' mutton o' purpose ; got in a lobster and two crabs ; all spoilt by keeping ; stink already ; weather quite muggy, forced to souse 'em in vinegar ; one expense brings on another ; never begin the like again."

If Fanny Burney had not had to conform to the vogue of the three-volume novel *Cecilia* might have been more nearly equal to *Evelina* ; as it is, the vacillations of the lovers under Mrs. Delvile's high-flown appeals are absurdly prolonged.

In Fanny's third novel, *Camilla*, a deterioration is obvious. Horace Walpole called it " the deplorable *Camilla*," and wrote to Hannah More that Fanny Burney had " reversed experience " ; she had known the world and penetrated character before she had stepped over the threshold, but now she had seen so much of it she had little or no insight at all. Nevertheless, *Camilla* has some good contributions to make to the rich panorama of society which Fanny Burney offers us : it deserves to be rescued from oblivion for the sake of its fops and beaux, with their " air of fashion easy almost to insolence," and of Mrs. Arlbery, a worthy successor to Mrs. Selwyn of *Evelina*, with her gift for *trimming* and *cutting up* " impertinent fools of lords." It has, too, interesting side-lights on the fashionable cults of *sensibility* and *elegance*, which survived into Jane Austen's day. Jane Austen herself is kind to *Camilla* : in a letter written to her sister in 1796, she says of a new acquaintance " there are two traits in her character which are pleasing, namely she admires *Camilla*, and she drinks no cream in her tea."

In the passage on novels in *Northanger Abbey*, introduced by " ' Oh, it is only a novel ! ' replies the young lady ; while she lays down her book with affected indifference or momentary shame," *Camilla* is classed with *Cecilia* and *Belinda* (by Maria Edgeworth) as works which display " the greatest powers of the human mind and the most thorough knowledge of human nature." That *John Thorpe* found it " the horridest nonsense you can imagine " reflects no discredit upon it !

It is more difficult to find any palliation of Macaulay's severe verdict on Fanny's last novel, *The Wanderer or Female Difficulties*, than of Horace Walpole's on *Camilla*. Of *The Wanderer*, Macaulay wrote that " no judicious friend of the author will attempt to draw it from the oblivion into which it has justly fallen." It is the story of a friendless, penniless girl who escapes from France during the Revolution. Only here and there does a flash of Fanny's early vivacity break out, or a characteristic touch, such as the remark of a young man who explains " I always say *à propos* when I am at a loss how to introduce anything." Here, too, however, there are crumbs of interest for the students of manners and social standards.

It must be admitted that once Fanny Burney lost the lively spontaneity of youth there was little to take its place. She could observe, and—until five years of court decorum and the responsibility of fame made her self-conscious in her style—she could mimic and narrate uncommonly well ; but she had not the originality or insight which amount to genius. It has been suggested that her style suffered from imitation of Johnsonian prose, which was particularly unsuitable for a society novel. There are, however, plenty of long words, abstract nouns and deliberately balanced phrases in *Evelina*, which was written before she was steeped in Johnsonese : from the first, it is only in dialogue that her high spirits really run away with her. We must bear in mind that in her age and society to write too simply was to be " inelegant," if not slovenly. Remembering this, our period sense is pleasantly tickled, and we are only the more deliciously conscious of Lord Orville's satin coat and lace ruffles when he presses for an early wedding-day in these terms : " Suffer therefore its acceleration, and generously complete my felicity by endeavouring to suffer it without repugnance."

In *Cecilia* there is a larger proportion of grandiloquence to lively dialogue than in *Evelina*, in *Camilla* elaboration of style encroaches still more upon art. There is no sentence in the first two novels as bad as this from *Camilla* : " Where opinion may humour systematic prepossession, who shall build upon his virtue or wisdom to guard the transparency of his impartiality ? " In Fanny's last work—*The Memoirs of Dr. Burney*—the style is execrably sententious and wordy.

It is as a photographic character-monger, a show-woman of a period and a class, that Fanny Burney excels. Nowhere, for instance, can we find a better gallery of fops and beaux to illustrate the traditions built up by Beau Nash, the Macaronis and the Dandies than in Fanny's first three novels. *Evelina* gives the vapid type in Lovel, the insolent and licentious in Sir Clement Willoughby and Lord Merton, the paragon in Lord Orville, the pseudo article in Mr. Smith. In *Cecilia* we have in Mr. Meadows an example of the vogue of the *ennuyé*. In Mr. Harrel there is a hint of Macaroni[1] fashions, since Mr. Briggs complains of his wearing " a bit of a hat won't go on a man's head," and carrying a watch no bigger than a sixpence.

We are first introduced to Mr. Meadows in the talk of the voluble Miss Larolles, who tells Cecilia that he is " the sweetest dresser in the world," and it is a great thing to be

---

[1] The Macaroni Club was founded, in opposition to the Beef-Steak club, by a party of young bloods who returned from a tour in Italy in 1772. They had their own fashions in dandyism, which lasted until about 1786.

spoken to by him, although he makes all the ladies angry by taking no notice of them. When Cecilia asks whether their anger is in honour of himself or his coat, Miss Larolles exclaims, " Why, Lord, don't you know all this time that he is an *ennuyé* ? . . . One is never affronted with an *ennuyé*, because one always knows what it means."

Fanny draws Mr. Meadows uncommonly well : perhaps the best example of his pose is when Mr. Harrel's suicide is talked of, and, although he was there at the time, he gives quite a brilliant exhibition of absent-minded indifference.

Camilla offers a prince of *ennuyés* in Sir Sedley Clarendel, who is all the more effective because he is by no means empty-headed (and even capable of being startled into stopping runaway horses !), although, in Mrs. Arlbery's phrase, he " labours harder to be affected than any ploughboy for his dinner." Lounging superbly in the ballroom, in an attitude calculated to show off his figure to advantage, he is summoned to join Mrs. Arlbery's circle, but excuses himself as being " ineffably tired." Eventually, he approaches with " magnificent tardiness," just in time to tilt up the chair on which Mrs. Arlbery intended to sit and lean his elbow on the back of it. She is enchanted with his impertinence, and murmurs to her neighbour, " It is quite irresistible—so conscious and so piquant ; I think, General, it is a little like my own."

In *Camilla*, too, we have an example of the effrontery with which the dandies made audible comments on the ladies as they sauntered in the ballroom without deigning to dance : even the traces of small-pox and other misfortunes in the appearance of Camilla's sister Eugenia are not spared.

If Fanny Burney's pictures of the fops and dandies of her day are thought exaggerated, there is supporting evidence in Maria Edgeworth's novels of fashionable life, and in the description of the English dandy in the late eighteenth century by the great French Romantic Chateaubriand, who wrote :—

" The dandy betrays the proud independence of his character by keeping his hat on his head, lounging upon a sofa, and stretching out his boots in the faces of the ladies seated in admiration before him. He rides with a stick, which he carries like a wax taper, paying no attention to the horse which he happens to find between his legs. . . . It is said that he can hardly know whether he exists, whether the world is about him, whether it contains ladies, or whether he should greet his neighbour."

The type must have survived well into the nineteenth century, as Bulwer Lytton says of one of the characters in his *Henry Pelham*, which was published in 1828, that " he gave offence too universally not to be sought after."

A delightful study of that admired eighteenth-century quality *sensibility* could be compiled from Fanny Burney's novels, with corroboration from her diary. Perhaps the best example is the cultivated timidity of Indiana Lynmere in *Camilla*, and its evident success. Having been carefully taught " to nourish every fear as becoming," Indiana takes advantage of hearing a cow low when she is walking with the handsome undergraduate Melmond ; conveniently supposing that it is a savage bull, she goes into a paroxysm of shrieks and palpitations. Every one of these " rendered her, in the eyes of the Oxonian, more and more captivating." Loth to soothe her, his ecstatic ejaculations form a chorus to her screams—" What lovely timidity ! " he exclaims, " what bewitching softness ! What feminine, what beautiful delicacy ! How sweet in terror ! How soul-piercing in alarm ! "

Evidently Mary Wollstonecraft was not too caustic when she complained (in 1792)[1] of woman's cultivated fragility, designed to give her " natural protector " an opportunity to " guard the lovely trembler—from what ? Perhaps the frown of an old cow. or the jump of a mouse."

The time was growing ripe for Jane Austen to contrast sense with sensibility, and Fanny Burney prepared the way for her. When *Camilla* was published by subscription the name of Miss J. Austen, Steventon, was in the list of subscribers. It is pleasant to hear, too, through Caroline Austen-Leigh, of Jane Austen's reading *Evelina* aloud at Steventon. She chose a chapter about Mr. Smith and the Branghtons, and Caroline thought it as good as a play. It is even possible that the title of *Pride and Prejudice* was suggested by Fanny Burney's dissertation on these words (printed in capital letters) at the close of *Cecilia*. Of all the honours so liberally accorded to Fanny Burney's work, none were more pregnant that these : but Fanny certainly deserved well from the supreme mistress of the novel of life and manners, to whom she was certainly one source of inspiration, and upon whom her mantle fell.

[1] In *A Vindication of the Rights of Women.*

BOOKS ABOUT FANNY BURNEY

N.B. Books especially recommended are marked **, those only a little less helpful or interesting *.

Madame d'Arblay. Macaulay. (Critical and Historical Essays.)
Fanny Burney and her Friends. L. F. B. Seeley. (Seeley & Co.) 1890.

**Fanny Burney. Austin Dobson. (English Men of Letters)* 1903. The only book giving detailed literary criticism of the novels. (*N.B.* See also Prefaces to good editions.)

Juniper Hall. Constance Hill. (John Lane) 1904.

The House in St. Martin's Street. Constance Hill. (John Lane) 1907.

Fanny Burney at the Court of Queen Charlotte. Constance Hill. (*John Lane*) 1912. Constance Hill's three books give very attractive pictures of three main phases of Fanny Burney's life. The descriptions of her homes, and the illustrations by Ellen G. Hill, are pleasing.

Fanny Burney and Surrey. S. W. Kershaw. 1911.

Dr. Johnson and Fanny Burney. Introduction and Notes by *C. Brewster Tinker* (*Andrew Melrose*), 1912. A collection of all the passages in Fanny Burney's works which refer to Dr. Johnson.

The Keeper of the Robes. F. F. Moore. (Hodder & Stoughton) 1912.

Fanny Burney and the Burneys. Brimley Johnson. (Stanley Paul) 1926. This book contains hitherto unpublished portions of Madame d'Arblay's diary, of which the most interesting describe a journey in France and a visit to Madame Campan's fashionable school. It also gives letters written by members of the Burney family, including Susan. Preface and notes by Brimley Johnson.

The Story of Fanny Burney. Muriel Masefield. (Cambridge University Press) 1927. This small book is intended to supply a background for the *Diary and Letters* and includes extracts from them.

The Diary and Letters of Madame d'Arblay in *Broadway Diaries* series. Biographical preface and notes by *Muriel Masefield*. (*Routledge*) 1931.
This selection from the *Diary and Letters* in one volume is useful to those who do not wish to read the 4–7 volumes of the various full editions.

III

THE LIFE OF JANE AUSTEN

On the 17th December, 1775, the day after the birth of his second daughter, the Rev. George Austen wrote from Steventon Rectory, Hampshire :—

" We have now another girl, a present plaything for her sister Cassy, and a future companion. She is to be Jenny, and it seems to me as if she will be as like Harry as Cassy is to Neddy."

Such was the first report of Jane Austen's birth, prophetic in so far as there cannot have been a more devoted and happy companionship than that of the Austen sisters, and Henry was probably the brother who matched her best in wit and temperament. Her intellectual heritage was good : her father had been a scholar and later a fellow of St. John's College, Oxford, where he was known at one time as " the handsome proctor," and according to his wife " classical knowledge, literary taste and power of elegant composition he possessed to the highest degree." Mrs. Austen no doubt felt competent to pronounce on these qualities, as her father was a fellow of All Souls' and one of her uncles a Master of Balliol, celebrated in the University for his wit. Both families—the Austens and the Leighs—had an honourable history behind them : the Leighs of Stoneleigh Abbey (a fine place in Warwickshire, which Jane visited in 1806) had been devotees of the Stuart cause, and perhaps from them descended to Jane the zealous loyalty which led her to write in the margin of her schoolroom copy of Goldsmith's *History of England* various pungent comments in favour of the Royalists, including the exclamation on Cromwell and his party, " Oh ! Oh ! The Wretches ! "

Jane was the youngest but one of the family, her only sister, Cassandra, being two years older. They were evidently a lively, clever, good-humoured group of young people ; some of the charades and conundrums of their youth survive to show how naturally they took to such games of wit, in which both mother and father gave them a lead ; no doubt Jane had many an actual scene in her mind when she described the game of speculation in Mansfield Park, with Henry Crawford's pre-eminence in " all the lively turns, quick resources and playful impudence that could do honour to the game," and the Watsons learning *vingt-et-un* from the equally confident Tom Musgrave.

As they grew up the Austen brothers brought varied experience into their sisters' lives. James, the eldest son, who was ordained and in time succeeded his father at Steventon Rectory, was heir to his uncle, Mr. Leigh-Perrot (whom the Austens visited at Bath) and eventually took the name of Austen-Leigh. His son, Edward Austen-Leigh, was the author of the *Memoir* of Jane Austen which was the first account of her life to be published (1869), and one of his daughters, Anna Lefroy, was a very dear niece, whom Jane advised in the composition of a novel, which the young author had not the heart to finish after her aunt's death. The second son, George, was mentally deficient and any references to him there may have been in Jane's correspondence were probably cut out by her sister Cassandra. Edward Austen was adopted by wealthy, childless relations, Mr. and Mrs. Knight, of Godmersham House in Kent and Chawton Manor in Hampshire, and took their name. They sent him on the " Grand Tour of Europe " which was the fashionable completion of a young man's education. He inherited both the Knight estates, and so two " Great Houses " were added to the gallery upon which Jane could draw for her pictures of the life of such places as Barton Park, Mansfield Park, and Kellynch Hall. The next brother, Henry, was probably Jane's best-beloved ; from references in her letters we gather that he was clever, animated and witty, very likely in the vein of Henry Tilney and Henry Crawford. He was first in the army and then a banker, and Jane owed various visits to London to him. The remaining two brothers, Francis and Charles, immediately above and below Jane in the family, were in the navy, and both rose to the rank of Admiral.

The Austen family circle was further enlarged by the frequent exchange of visits with uncles, aunts and cousins.

One of Mr. Austen's sisters, Mrs. Hancock, and her husband, were intimate friends of Warren Hastings, whose son was sent to Steventon Rectory for part of his education ; his death in boyhood was a great grief to the Austens. Mrs. Hancock's only daughter, Elizabeth, was often at Steventon, and always to the fore in promoting theatricals in the barn and other inspiriting projects. She completed her education in France, and in 1781 married a French nobleman, the Comte de Feuillide. If only for her sake the Austens must have watched the course of the French Revolution with anxious interest. The Comtesse and her baby came to Steventon when they had to leave France : unfortunately, the Comte returned to try to save his property, and he was then accused of conniving at the escape of a royalist friend, and was sent to the guillotine, in 1794. Elizabeth de Feuillide made Steventon her principal headquarters, and at the end of 1797 she married Henry Austen, although she professed herself loth to give up " dear liberty and dearer flirtation." She must have brought a breath of keen life and novel experience into the Rectory, and probably something of her spirit is preserved in Jane Austen's livelier heroines.

Jane Austen's was mainly a home education. As a small child she was sent to school at Oxford with her sister Cassandra chiefly because she could not have borne a separation. The two little girls moved with the school to Southampton, where Jane nearly died of a " putrid fever " (presumably typhoid). After this, the sisters were taken home, but later on they spent two pleasant years at the Abbey School, Reading ; probably, however, the most valuable education that Jane imbibed was in her own home. In her teens she wrote a vivacious *History of England from the Reign of Henry IV to the Death of Charles I* by " a partial, prejudiced and ignorant historian," of which the racy, satirical style is a good earnest of the quality to come in the novels. At seventeen, she produced a skit on contemporary romantic novels called "*Love and Freindship* " (even as late as 1805 ' ie ' and ' ei ' were a problem to her, and she began a letter " My Dear Neice ") dedicated to " Madame la Comtesse de Feuillide." It is excellent farce.

Meanwhile as full a social life as bad roads and the limitations of carriage horses allowed in a country neighbourhood opened out to the Austen sisters. Dancing was a great feature of their youth, and Jane once professed that she " could just as well dance for a week together as for half-an-hour." Nor was dancing the only art of the ballroom in which she played a lively part ; she owned with gallant frankness to the enjoyment of flirtation, and even to a partiality for other girls who were not above indulging in that art—" Miss looked very handsome, but I prefer her little, smiling, flirting sister Julia." After watching another couple at the time-honoured game she wrote : " But *they* do not know how *to be particular.*"

Her own chef-d'œuvre in flirtation was carried on with Mr. Tom Lefroy, an Irishman, nephew of the Rector of Ashe, whose wife was a friend—older than herself—for whom Jane had a loving admiration. Writing for her sister Cassandra's benefit in January, 1796, she says :—

" You scold me so much in the nice long letter I have this moment received from you, that I am almost afraid to tell you how my Irish friend and I behaved. Imagine to yourself everything most profligate and shocking in the way of dancing and sitting down together. I *can* expose myself, however, only *once more*, because he leaves the country soon after next Friday, on which day we *are* to have a ball at Ashe."

On the Friday in question, she wrote :—

" At length the day is come when I am to flirt my last with Tom Lefroy, and when you receive this it will be over. My tears flow as I write at the melancholy idea."

In other letters she declares she " does not care sixpence " for Mr. Lefroy, and in any case he wears such a light coloured overcoat that she could not accept him unless he promised to give it away. However, she was evidently interested in news of him nearly three years later.

Probably no one was much the worse for such ebullitions of high spirits on Jane Austen's part, she had wit and good taste to keep her heart under control, and neither she nor her heroines are to be taken literally in their aspersions on themselves. However, such merry evenings may have given rise to the reported opinion of Mrs. Mitford (mother of the author of *Our Village*), that Jane Austen was " the prettiest, silliest, most affected, husband-hunting butterfly she ever remembered."

In appearance Jane Austen seems to have been attractive, with a rather tall, slender figure, a quick, springy step, a glow of health and animation with a brunette's complexion, bright hazel eyes and brown hair curling round her face. She was not without genuine *affaires de cœur* : one admirer was a Cambridge don (named Blackall), who fled from further temptation (so Mrs. Lefroy understood), because he would lose his income as a fellow of his College if he married. Later he was presented to a living and did marry, and Jane wrote of his bride :—

" I could wish Miss Lewis to be of a silent turn and rather ignorant, but naturally intelligent and wishing to learn, fond of cold veal pies, green tea in the afternoon, and a green window-blind at night."

Cassandra Austen told her niece Anna Lefroy that when the sisters were staying in Devonshire, probably about the year 1799, they met a man of great gifts and charm between whom and Jane there was certainly a mutual attraction. He was eager to see her again, but before this could be accomplished, they heard of his death. Another family tradition is that a suitor nearer home, favoured by her relations, proposed to Jane in the year 1802, and that she first accepted him and then almost immediately withdrew from the engagement.

Cassandra Austen was engaged to be married about the year 1795 : her fiancé (Thomas Fowle) went abroad and died in the West Indies in 1797, shortly before his return to England was due.

We cannot know what impression her *affaires* made upon Jane Austen, and whether, as has been suggested, a loss or disappointment in love partly accounts for the long gap between her two groups of novels. Her sister destroyed all her more intimate letters, and cut passages out of some of those which she preserved, and in those that we can read, she never admits that her zest for life was dimmed by any depression. She writes gallantly of her pleasure in small things, declaring that even the purchase of a sponge-cake was interesting to her, and after a rather dull ball she wrote :—

" I had a very pleasant evening, however, though you will probably find out that there was no particular reason for it ; but I do not think it worth while to wait for enjoyment until there is some real opportunity for it."

Re-visiting a ballroom of her youth, when she was thirty-three, she wrote :—

" It was the same room in which we danced fifteen years ago. I thought it all over, and in spite of the shame of being so much older felt with thankfulness that I was quite as happy now as then."

If Jane Austen had not sampled the pleasures and piquancy of society so whole-heartedly her novels would certainly have been the poorer.

At Steventon, three of the novels were written. Jane's first attempt at fiction, *Elinor and Marianne*, in the form of letters, was revised in 1797–98 and re-christened *Sense and Sensibility*. *Pride and Prejudice*, originally called *First Impressions*, had been written in 1796–97. Her father offered it to a publisher on completion, but he refused even to receive the MS. on approval ! In 1798 *Northanger Abbey* was begun, but for the present no further attempt to publish was made.

In 1801, Mr. Austen resigned the living of Steventon, in which his son James succeeded him, and retired to Bath with his wife and daughters. Tradition says that Jane fainted away on hearing of the decision. At Bath, Henry Austen, acting for Jane, sold the MS. of *Northanger Abbey* to a bookseller for £10, but it was laid aside in a drawer and not published. It is possible that some time during the first years at Bath, Jane wrote *The Watsons*, which she left unfinished : otherwise she wrote nothing more until after the return to country life at Chawton, in 1809.

In 1805, Mr. Austen died, and after a move in Bath and some visiting, Mrs. Austen and her daughters settled in Southampton, sharing a roomy house with the Francis Austens. In 1809 a final move was made, to Chawton Cottage, on the Hampshire estate of Edward Knight, within a short walk of Chawton Manor where he and his family came into residence from time to time, although Godmersham in Kent was their chosen home.

Two years after the move to Chawton Cottage, Jane, now aged thirty-five, experienced a revival of literary activity. *Sense and Sensibility* was given a final polish and published, at the author's own expense, in 1811, and Jane set to work upon *Mansfield Park*. Her first novel met with no spectacular success, such as that of *Evelina*, or of Charlotte Brontë's first venture, *Jane Eyre*, but *Sense and Sensibility* was sufficiently well received for a publisher to be willing to undertake the risk of launching the newly revised *Pride and Prejudice* in 1813.   There is a pleasing account in one of Jane's letters of a visit she paid to her brother Henry in London soon after this, on which they went to two exhibitions of pictures and she amused herself looking for portraits which she could fancy to be Jane Bingley and Elizabeth Darcy. She failed to find one that would satisfy her ideal of her favourite Elizabeth, and concluded, " I can only imagine that Mr. Darcy prizes any picture of her too much to like it should be exposed to the public eye.   I can imagine he would have that sort of feeling—that mixture of love, pride and delicacy."

During this year (1813), Mrs. Henry Austen (formerly de Feuillide) died : Edward Knight had also lost his wife, another favourite sister-in-law of Jane's, in 1808. These were sad losses, following on that of Jane's friend, Mrs. Lefroy of Ashe, who had been killed by a fall from her horse in 1804, and they left their mark on Jane.

Mansfield Park was published in May, 1814, and by November, Jane was able to report that the first edition was all sold.   In the autumn of 1815, Henry Austen had a long, serious illness during which Jane nursed him devotedly, and her own health suffered in consequence. During his convalescence at his house in Hans Place, his physician, who also attended the Prince Regent (afterwards George IV), told Jane that the Prince was a great admirer of her novels, and had a set of them kept at each of his residences. This led to the librarian of Carlton House calling upon her on the Prince's behalf, and it was intimated that she might dedicate her next novel to His Royal Highness. Accordingly *Emma* appeared duly dedicated to royalty in December, 1815. The Prince had some claim to good taste in literature, but when Jane received his thanks for " the handsome copy " of *Emma*, she remarked dryly that he was merely commending the publisher's part in its production.   She received suggestions from his librarian that she should take as her next hero a clergyman of an enthusiastic type, or, failing that, try her hand at an " historical romance illustrative of the House of Coburg " (in celebration of Princess Charlotte's marriage). Both suggestions were refused in Jane's best vein of light raillery.

Meanwhile the anxiety about Henry Austen's health was followed by that about his financial affairs, which Jane felt keenly, and in 1816 he was declared bankrupt.

A picture of the daily life at Chawton Cottage may be built up from Jane's letters and from accounts left by the various nephews and nieces who were now old enough to appreciate their aunt's inspiriting friendship. One of them deplored that Cassandra and Jane took to caps and considered themselves middle-aged before they need have done : but evidently there was always a bright welcome and stimulating companionship to be had at the Cottage, although the lack of a carriage now curtailed the Austens' social round, except when the Knights were at Chawton Manor. Caroline Austen-Leigh, a daughter of James by his second wife, has left an account of the sisters' daily routine as she remembered it. Jane usually began the day by practising the piano before breakfast, and it was her particular duty " to make the breakfast," the household supplies of tea, sugar and wine being under her charge. The morning was generally spent in the drawing-room ; when visitors were there it was often dedicated to needlework, and both sisters sewed for their poor neighbours. If the family was alone, Jane might, perhaps, write at the desk in this family sitting-room. Edward Austen-Leigh adds the details that she wrote on small sheets of paper in order to be able to slip them under the blotting-paper if she was disturbed, and that she objected to having a creak in the baize-covered door between kitchen and front door remedied because it gave her timely warning of the advent of visitors. Another niece recorded seeing her sometimes jump up from her place in the family circle with a smile and go across to the little mahogany writing-desk for a minute or two to make a note.

After lunch, according to Caroline, the sisters usually went out walking, perhaps to shop or change books in Alton, or to stroll in the grounds of the Manor. The long evening would be given to needlework, reading, writing and talk, and when Jane needed a rest from these employments, she would recreate herself with cup and ball ! She was also expert at spilikins ; Edward Austen-Leigh wrote that " none of us could throw spilikins in so perfect a circle, or take them off with so steady a hand. Her performances with cup-and-ball were marvellous. She has been known to catch the ball on the point above a hundred times in succession."

All through Jane Austen's letters there are charming allusions to her brothers' children, singly and in groups, and a number of letters are addressed to them. Fanny Knight, her brother Edward's eldest daughter, was almost like a younger sister to her, and all her zest and sympathy were at her service and Anna's when they wanted advice, whether on love affairs, literary efforts or dress. One of the last letters she wrote at Chawton was to a small niece, Cassandra, in printing letters and written backwards to make an amusing puzzle of it. Amongst the tributes she received as an authoress none is more pleasing than the verses addressed to her by Edward Austen-Leigh, then a schoolboy at Winchester, when the secret of the authorship of *Sense and Sensibility* and *Pride and Prejudice* was revealed to him, some time after he had read them.[1] Recording his delight in discovering " that you made the Middletons, Dashwoods and all," he continues :

> " And though Mr. Collins, so grateful for all,
> Will Lady de Bourgh his patroness call,
> 'Tis to your ingenuity really he owed
> His living, his wife, and his humble abode."

Jane Austen's happy relations with all these young people are evidence that she cannot have been alarmingly sharp and sarcastic, in spite of a few strictures upon neighbours in her letters which have been picked out as caustic to the point of heartlessness.

In 1816, *Persuasion* was written (but not given a title), to be laid aside and eventually published after Jane's death by Henry Austen, bound up with *Northanger Abbey*. Jane's health, already tried by her anxieties on Henry's behalf, began to fail seriously in 1816, and by 1817 she was an invalid to the extent of spending much of her time resting on two chairs (leaving the sofa for her mother), taking her exercise first in short walks with rests between and then in a donkey-chair. Sometimes she was unable to leave her bedroom, and she owned to " a good deal of fever at times." Nevertheless, she wrote part of a new novel (which was published in 1925,

[1] See *Personal Aspects of Jane Austen* by Mary Augusta Austen-Leigh (Murray, 1920).

under the title of *Sanditon*), between January and March, 1817.
Jane Austen's illness came to be regarded in the family as
" a decline."   In May, 1817, she and Cassandra moved into
Winchester in order to have more expert medical advice.
The sisters settled in rooms in College Street, and in the
remaining two months of Jane's life neither her own " sweet
reasonableness "—in accepting the inevitable and doing all
she could to make it easier for her sorrowing family—nor
Cassandra's brave devotion failed them for an hour.   On
July 18th, 1817, Jane Austen died, at the age of forty-one.
She was buried in Winchester Cathedral.   After death her
fame grew steadily, for she left behind her, living and
breathing in her books, the greatest of her gifts, which was
well described by Thackeray's daughter (Lady Ritchie) as
" a natural genius for life."

IV

JANE AUSTEN'S NOVELS

Juvenilia.

Volume the First. (*Oxford University Press*) 1933. A collection of juvenilia hitherto unpublished, short satirical pieces.

Love and Freindship[1] and Other Early Works. Said to have been written when Jane Austen was seventeen. The *Other Early Works* are *Lesley Castle* (a tale in letters), *The History of England from the Reign of Henry IV to the Death of Charles I*, a *Collection of Letters*, and *Scraps*, (letters, a tale and fragment of a play). First published, with introduction by G. K. Chesterton (*Chatto and Windus*) 1922.

The Mystery, an Unfinished Comedy. Published with the 2nd edition of the *Memoir* by J. E. Austen-Leigh in 1871.

The Novels.

Sense and Sensibility. The first draft was written about the year 1792 in the form of letters, under the title of *Elinor and Marianne*. Revised in 1797 and given the present title. Finally polished and published in 1811.

Pride and Prejudice. First written in 1796–'97 under the title *First Impressions*. Revised in 1811 and published under the present title in 1813.

Northanger Abbey. First written about the year 1798. Revised in 1803 and sold to a bookseller in Bath, who did not publish it. After the appearance of the first novels Henry Austen bought it back for the same price. Published after Jane Austen's death, with *Persuasion*, in 1818.

Mansfield Park. Written during 1812–'14. Published in 1814.

Emma. Written 1814–'15. Published late in 1815, although the date of publication on the title-page is 1816.

Persuasion. Begun after *Emma* was finished, completed in August, 1816. Published with *Northanger Abbey* in 1818.

Other Works.

Lady Susan. A short story in letters, probably of much the same date as *Elinor and Marianne*. First published with the second edition of the *Memoir*, 1871.

An edition by Oxford University Press was published in 1925. An edition with introduction by Brimley Johnson, 1931.

[1] Jane Austen's spelling.

The Watsons. Fragment of a novel. The date of writing is not known, but the water-marks on the paper used were 1803 and 1804. First published with the 2nd edition of the *Memoir* in 1871.
Published with a conclusion by L. Oulton in 1923.
Oxford University Press Edition, 1927.
Edition with a conclusion by E. and F. Brown (Rescue Series), 1928.
Sanditon. A fragment of a novel. Written in 1817. First published, edited by R. W. Chapman (Oxford University Press), 1925.
Two *Discarded Chapters* for *Persuasion.* First published with the 2nd edition of the *Memoir*, 1871.
Oxford University Press edition in 1926.

The Letters.

The Letters of Jane Austen. Edited from MSS. inherited by his mother Fanny Knight, Lady Knatchbull, by Edward Knatchbull Hugessen, first Lord Brabourne, and published in 1884.
The Life and Letters of Jane Austen, by W. Austen-Leigh and R. A Austen-Leigh, published in 1913 ; out of print in 1932. Of this book R. W. Chapman says that it contains quotations from " almost every extant letter, but relatively few are given entire." It is an excellent background for the study of Jane Austen.
Jane Austen's Letters. 2 vols. Edited by R. W. Chapman, published by the Oxford University Press in 1932. These two volumes contain all the known letters up to date, and helpful notes.
The Letters of Jane Austen. A selection. This selection is edited by Brimley Johnson (Bodley Head). Useful to those who do not wish to read the full edition, or cannot easily get it.
Five Letters to Fanny Knight. Printed in facsimile (Oxford University Press), 1924.

The true lover of Jane Austen—one of those to whom Kipling has given the name of *the Janeites*—will not wish one word of her novels altered. These six books are, in fact, all but perfect in their *genre*, and those who rejoice in that *genre* will not cavil at Jane Austen for not going outside it. They would not exchange the least of her parlours or dining-rooms, one ball or " shade of a departed ball," a single barouche or curricle, lime-walk, wilderness or ha-ha, for any more varied or striking scenes that can be suggested, or even for " the wind on the heath " ; that impalpable " consequence " which is the native air of most of her characters is more to them than all the glory and storm of the Romantics at their best. In short, to Janeites it is impossible to criticise the novels for what is in them, the only concession that can be made to the critical spirit is to indicate some things that are not to be found in Jane Austen, and let those deplore it who must.

G. K. Chesterton classes Jane Austen and William Cobbett together as having " the four sharpest eyes that God had given to the England of that time," adding " but two of them were turned inward into the home and two were looking out of the window." Jane Austen's scenes are certainly chiefly indoors, and in the drawing-room (there are no excursions into kitchen or cottage), and where her characters do go out it is generally, in the words of Charlotte Brontë, into " a carefully-fenced, highly-cultivated garden with neat borders and delicate flowers." The one deliberate " exploring party "—to Box Hill—became, under Mrs. Elton's direction, a bustling affair, based on pigeon pies and cold lamb, and we are left in doubt as to how Emma would have managed it in " the quiet, unpretending, elegant way " which she would have preferred. Marianne Dashwood certainly exercised her " potent " sensibility in admiration of scenery, but even in this Jane Austen brings her to earth as quickly as possible :—

" ' Now, Edward,' said she, calling his attention to the prospect, ' here is Barton Valley. Look up it, and be tranquil if you can. Look at those hills. Did you ever see their equals ? . . . And there, beneath that farthest hill, which rises with such grandeur, is our cottage.'
' It is a beautiful country,' he replied ; ' but these bottoms must be dirty in winter.'
' How can you think of dirt, with such objects before you ? '
' Because,' replied he, smiling, ' among the rest of the objects before me I see a very dirty lane.'
' How strange ! ' said Marianne to herself, as she walked on.

Elizabeth Bennet enjoyed the Derbyshire views which " gave the eye power to wander," but her attention was soon distracted by the appearance of the owner of Pemberley. So Charlotte Brontë, closing *Pride and Prejudice*, was overcome by a surge of nostalgia for her beloved moors, and wrote of the book to G. H. Lewes, " no open country, no fresh air, no blue hill, no bonny beck ! "

There will always be some readers who will, like Charlotte Brontë, feel stifled in Jane Austen's atmosphere, but many others will like her the better for her frank disclaimer of any attempt to introduce romantic scenery—" it is not the object of this work[1] to give a description of Derbyshire." Why, indeed, should it have been ? Jane Austen's dramas of character in action do not depend on a romantic setting ; she is chiefly concerned with mind interpreted through behaviour and manners. There are writers to whom their scene is as much as their characters, or who make the two derive from one another : Exmoor in *Lorna Doone*, the Haworth moors in *Wuthering Heights*, and Egdon Heath in *The Return of the Native*, are almost personalities taking part in the tale to be told. This is excellence of one order ; Jane Austen's excellence is of another. Professor Courthope, a fine literary critic, claimed for her work that " under a commonplace surface a great artist has revealed a most dramatic conflict of universal human emotions." As the greater part of humanity works out its emotional conflicts under a commonplace surface, most people can find something of themselves or their own experience in Jane Austen's themes and characters, despite the lapse of more than a century since she wrote. In *Sense and Sensibility* we have the old, eternal triumph of a Cordelia ; the very title of *Pride and Prejudice* implies another conflict which will be re-enacted in infinite variety as long as there is no radical change in human nature. *Pride and Prejudice*, too, represents a familiar minor conflict, that of a clever man who, like Mr. Palmer in *Sense and Sensibility*, finds himself " the husband of a very silly woman," and who, in this case, consoles himself with irony. *Mansfield Park* has the Cinderella motive which has been a constant delight since the early days of story-telling ; in *Emma* we have an example of the confident young woman who believes in her power to play Providence to her friends and has to learn by disillusionment. *Emma* also adds two immortal types to Jane Austen's gallery of satirical portraits, the valetudinarian and the garrulous elderly lady—Mr. Woodhouse is in the tradition of *le malade imaginaire*, Miss Bates is of the same sisterhood as Mrs. Nickleby. *Northanger Abbey* presents the constantly repeated drama of " a young lady's entrance into the world," combined with a picture of romantic credulity fed upon the novel of mystery-mongering and melodrama. In *Persuasion* Anne Elliot suffers grievously for an over-pliable nature, owing to which she allows herself

[1] *Pride and Prejudice*.

D

to be persuaded out of the faith and courage which belong to young love into a prudence more befitting middle-age.

These are themes and characters as universal and as dateless as Shakespeare's, but in her treatment of them Jane Austen cannot altogether transcend the influence of period. This impregnation with period is a stumbling block to some, but a delight to others, who love the flavour of a bye-gone society, and find a piquancy which the modern, familiar style cannot give in such phrases as " his indifference to a confusion of rank bordered on inelegance of mind," " Isabella had connected herself unexceptionably," and "engaging the general good opinion of the surrounding acquaintance" (stigmatised by Alice Meynell as a "mouthful of thick words"). A period sense is, in fact, essential to the full appreciation of Jane Austen, and much of the criticism of her work comes from those who judge her by the standards of to-day, and write her down a woman of the limited and narrow interests of one class, and a very perfect snob. Certainly she did limit her field to the class she knew intimately—the country gentry of her day—at a time when well-disposed people on the comfortable side of life had sympathy and helpfulness enough for individuals amongst their poorer neighbours but had not begun to concern themselves with their position and barely dawning aspirations *as a class.* Jane Austen and her sister made clothes for needy neighbours at Chawton and taught some of the village boys and girls to read, and her letters provide many instances of her interest in the welfare of their servants and their families. She would be familiar with the acts of charity and kindliness which were part of the routine of every decently conducted " Great House," but these would scarcely occur to her as material to be worked into her novels ; they could be taken for granted. When she has a natural occasion to introduce the relations between master or mistress and servant, they are generally particularly happy, as in the case of Mr. Knightley and William Larkins, Miss Bates and Patty, and Mr. Woodhouse's consideration for his coachman ; but she was not in advance of her time in social ideals, if she had been, her novels would not give such a true picture of the normal life of the country gentry. Nor is it surprising that she does not take her heroines into the kitchen ; in those days of cheap and plentiful domestic labour—the Dashwoods set up at Barton Cottage with two maids and a man on £500 a year !—the daughters of a comfortable house would not do much more than give orders, if they happened to be responsible for the house-keeping. Jane Austen herself no doubt made a visit to an old servant an object for a walk, as Emma did, but she was not brought up in close contact with the kitchen as the Brontës were, nor could she know the farmhouse and the mill from the inside as George Eliot did, nor was she brought into natural intimacy with " the poor " as Mrs. Gaskell was in the course of her thirty-two years as a minister's wife in Manchester, years which included " the hungry forties." It was part of Jane Austen's genius to recognise, or to choose, her limitations ; she wrote of her material as " the little bit of ivory (two inches wide) on which I work with so fine a brush as produces little effect after much labour," and her results remind us that a miniature can be a masterpiece, just as well as the crowded canvas of a Hogarth.

As regards the accusation of snobbery, democracy was still a more or less slumbering force in England until the educative campaign which led up to the Reform Bill of 1832 : in the quarter of a century preceding that campaign all progressive movements in this country were suffering from a severe check due to the excesses of the Reign of Terror in France. In Jane Austen's world the inequality of opportunity in education, and in experience which went beyond the narrowly local, fixed wide gulfs between classes and individuals, and snobbery was partly founded on a distressing difference in outlook, tastes and manners. When Emma reflects on Frank Churchill's reprehensible " indifference to a confusion of rank," which she attributes to lively spirits and ignorance of " the evil he was holding cheap," she should not be judged by modern standards. Reading *Emma*, we feel that snobbery might be more readily excused if it saved one from enforced intimacy with such a neighbour as Mrs. Elton ! Emma is certainly the worst offender amongst Jane Austen's characters in this respect, but even in her own circle she was teased for the importance she attached to social observances. For instance, when she tries to encourage Mr. Knightley to use his carriage as often as she thought " became the owner of Donwell Abbey " :—

" ' This is coming as you should do,' said she, ' like a gentleman. I am quite glad to see you.'

He thanked her, observing, ' How lucky that we should arrive at the same moment ; for if we had first met in the drawing-room I doubt whether you would have discerned me to be more of the gentleman than usual. You might not have distinguished how I came by my look and manner.'

' Yes, I should ; I am sure I should. There is always a look of consciousness or bustle when people come in a way which they know to be beneath them. . . . I always observe it whenever I meet you under those circumstances. *Now* you have nothing to try for. You are not afraid of being supposed ashamed. You are not striving to look taller than anybody else. *Now* I shall really be very happy to walk into the same room with you.'

' Nonsensical girl ! ' was his reply, but not at all in anger."

No doubt Jane Austen regarded " inferiority of situation " or " connections " as a serious evil which even love could not quite surmount, but she had a keen eye for the absurdities of snobbery. In *The Watsons* she exposes these in Tom Musgrave with gusto. He is shown waiting about in a draughty passage in order to make his entry into the ball-room at the tail end of the Osborne Castle party, and ruefully withdrawing to solitude when they leave. He is contrasted to his disadvantage with Elizabeth Watson when he deliberately takes Lord Osborne to call just at the Watsons' un-fashionably early dinner hour. The two men shut their eyes and ears to the obvious signs of the approaching meal until the maid announces at the door with anxious urgency, " Please, ma'am, Master wants to know why he be'nt to have his dinner ? " Whereupon Elizabeth calls briskly after her to take up the fowls, and turns to the smart visitors, who have at last risen apologetically :—

" ' I am sorry it happens so,' she added, turning good-humouredly to Musgrave, ' but you know what early hours we keep.' Tom had nothing to say for himself, he knew it very well, and such honest simplicity, such shameless truth, rather bewildered him."

In addition to these examples, how refreshing it is when Elizabeth Bennet trounces Lady Catherine de Bourgh ! In fact, the whole of *Pride and Prejudice* is an argument against the extremes of snobbery. Extremes of all kinds had short shrift from Jane Austen.

Another subject on which it is not fair to expect a modern outlook from her is the importance attached to the " fortunes " of marriageable girls. The opening of *Mansfield Park*, so much relished by a period enthusiast like Birrell, presents the prevailing attitude, perhaps with just a hint of sarcasm : Miss Maria Ward of Huntingdon, with only seven thousand pounds, is thought uncommonly lucky to have captured a baronet and acquired " all the comforts and consequences of a handsome house and a large income," and even her uncle the lawyer allows that she was " at least three thousand pounds short of any equitable claim to it." All the novels of the day are full of this necessity for regulating the feelings according to the prospect of a " respectable " or an " elegant " establishment in this or that marriage ; it was one of the duties of the " well-regulated mind " which Jane Austen's contemporaries, including Maria Edgeworth and Susan Ferrier, also exalt in their heroines. No doubt this, and the equally prevalent waiting for dead men's shoes, were part of the price which society paid for its many leisured and landed gentlemen, with their " consequence " and their large families. The frequency of families of ten and more, accepted as gifts of God, should be remembered when Jane Austen is accused of allowing prudence to encroach too much upon love. As in all else, Jane Austen represents the moderate, rational view, and she does not underrate feeling because she is clear-sighted enough to see reason. At the age of seventeen her characteristic attitude is already developed as a passage in *Love and Freindship* testifies, in which his sister ventures to suggest to the Noble Youth that he may have to apply to his father for support for his bride :—

" ' Never, never, Augusta, will I so demean myself ' (said Edward). ' Support ! What support will Laura want which she can receive from him ? '
' Only those very insignificant ones of Victuals and Drink ' (answered she).
' Victuals and Drink ! ' (replied my husband in a most nobly contemptuous manner) ' and dost thou then imagine that there is no other support for ar. exalted mind (such as is my Laura's) than the mean and indelicate employment of eating and drinking ? '
' None that I know of, so efficacious ' (returned Augusta).
' And did you then never feel the pleasing Pangs of Love, Augusta ? ' (replied my Edward). ' Does it appear impossible to your vile and corrupted palate to exist on Love ? Can you not conceive the luxury of living in every distress that Poverty can inflict, with the object of your tenderest affection ? ' "

A dialogue between the Watson sisters is particularly interesting as showing the attitude of women of the period who had no " provision " from father or brother to save them from the limited and unpleasant alternatives to marriage. Emma Watson, whose opinion no doubt represents Jane Austen's own, has had a superior up-bringing compared to that of her sisters, and expresses herself accordingly :—

> " ' To be so bent on marriage—to pursue a man merely for the sake of situation, is a sort of thing that shocks me ; I cannot understand it. Poverty is a great evil ; but to a woman of education and feeling it ought not, it cannot be the greatest. I would rather be a teacher in a school (and I can think of nothing worse) than marry a man I did not like.'
> ' I would rather do anything than be a teacher in a school,' said her sister, ' *I* have been at school, Emma, and know what a life they lead ; *you* never have. I should not like marrying a disagreeable man any more than yourself ; but I do not think there are very many disagreeable men ; I think I could like any good-humoured man with a comfortable income. I suppose my aunt brought you up to be rather refined.' "

All Jane Austen's heroines are refined in this sense, and they all clearly regarded love and character as the foundations of a happy marriage ; but even romantic Marianne Dashwood admitted that there might be extreme cases requiring extreme measures, to the extent of considering marriage with a man of thirty-five who wore flannel waistcoats to ward off rheumatism :—

> " ' A woman of seven-and-twenty,' said Marianne, after pausing a moment, ' can never hope to feel or inspire affection again, and if her home be uncomfortable, or her fortune small, I can suppose that she might bring herself to submit to the offices of a nurse, for the sake of the provision and security of a wife.' "

None of Jane Austen's heroines were tempted to marry outside their own world of country houses and estates ; but this is the normal way of life, and their feelings were none the less genuine ; even the extreme suitability of a match between Emma and Mr. Knightley did not serve them as a substitute for love. Elizabeth Bennet's friendship for Charlotte Lucas was never so warm and unforced after the shock of her acceptance of Mr. Collins, a man to whom she could not look up with respect, for the sake of an establishment. In Elizabeth's own case, her father took her part in rejecting Mr. Collins, although he was the heir to the Bennet's estate. Anne Elliot's whole story is a bitter expiation of her mistake in listening too obediently to the dictates of prudence in the mouth of Lady Russell ; and yet Lady Russell is not unreasonable in her fear that Anne, with " all her claims of birth, beauty and mind," might be " sunk by him " (Mr. Wentworth) " into a state of most wearing, anxious, youth-killing dependence." So it happens that Anne's youth is wasted quite as effectually in vain regrets. Sir Thomas Bertram is brought by his troubles with his own daughters to welcome penniless Fanny Price as a most desirable daughter-in-law. Even Mrs. Price's imprudent marriage is represented as deplorable, not from poverty alone, but because she had not the stamina to cope with " such a super-fluity of children and such a want of almost everything else," and also her husband drank more than was good for him. Mrs. Norris, we are told, would have managed to be a more respectable mother of nine children under the same circumstances. Comparative poverty had no terrors for the Harvilles, whose busy, happy household made such a pleasant impression on Anne Elliot at Lyme.

Jane Austen, then, accepted the standards of her day (in this case well exemplified by Catherine Morland's parents) but did not carry them to excess. Her heart is evidently with the sensible Elinor Dashwood when she forces from her sister Marianne the admission that " a competence " is desirable, even to romantic lovers.

There is a stronger charge against Jane Austen in her treatment of love than mere over-attention to prudence ; she has been accused of incapacity to understand deep or passionate feeling. Charlotte Brontë went so far as to say that " the passions are perfectly unknown to her," and that " even to the feelings she vouchsafes no more than an occasional, graceful but distant recognition." Alice Meynell was still more scathing :—

" With Miss Austen love, vengeance, devotion, duty, maternity, sacrifice are infinitely trivial."

And :—

" There is, in almost every second page of Miss Austen, a detest-able thing called ' consequence,' and to the heroine's love of it is promptly sacrificed all that might have seemed the beginnings or suggestions of spirituality."

Jane Austen was, indeed, a Cordelia in the expression of feeling, and since her time the tide has set steadily the other way. Taking the standards of her world for granted, whether religious or social, she is often content to indicate the finer feelings by inference only ; but when she is explicit what she says rings true, and true to common experience, rather than to that of the exceptional character. Marianne Dash-wood's strong susceptibility to the joys and sorrows of romantic love is intentionally exaggerated, but only the fevered imagination of a Marianne could fail to find genuine feeling in the scene in *Persuasion* in which Captain Wentworth listens to Anne and Captain Harville discussing constancy in love, and seizes a pen to write the convincing love-letter which wins Anne to him a second time. There is a still, deep radiance from their happiness when they come together again which loses nothing because the scene is in the gravel walk of a public garden in Bath ; many such commonplace surroundings have acquired for lovers " all the immortality which the happiest recollections of their own future lives could bestow." Anne Elliot and her story are, in fact, the best refutation of all Alice Meynell's strictures : it is impossible to believe she would be merely " trivial " in any relation of life.

Emma, too, had her ordeal and her blissful hour of re-assurance. Ordinary life could hold nothing more dreary than the long wet evening during which Mr. Woodhouse could " only be kept tolerably comfortable by ceaseless attentions on his daughter's side, and by exertions which had never cost her half so much before," while she faced the prospect of a lifetime of such interminable evenings, with Mr. Knightley, whom she now realised that she loved, driven away through her own blindness and folly. He was lost to her—even as a friend who would drop in and relieve their monotony from time to time—and lost for Harriet's sake, a wife who would be so far his inferior in every respect, and whom she herself had practically thrust upon him ! No wonder that " when it came to such a pitch as this, she was not able to refrain from a start, a heavy sigh, or even from walking about the room for a few seconds." Emma's joy when she is undeceived, and knows Mr. Knightley is hers, is equally convincing :—

" She wanted to be alone. Her mind was in a state of flutter and wonder which made it impossible for her to be collected. She was in dancing, singing spirits ; and till she had moved about and talked to herself, and laughed and reflected, she could be fit for nothing rational."

Again, there is no more poignant picture of the bitter humiliation and unrelieved despair to which youth and inexperience is subject than the misery of Catherine Morland when Henry Tilney has shown her the enormity of her suspicions about his father :—

" Most grievously was she humbled. Most bitterly did she cry. It was not only with herself that she was sunk, but with Henry. Her folly, which now seemed even criminal, was all exposed to him, and he must despise her for ever. The liberty which her imagination had dared to take with the character of his father, could he ever forgive it ? The absurdity of her curiosity and her fears, could they ever be forgotten ? She hated herself more than she could express."

There remains another accusation of omission ; that Jane Austen ignores idealism, not one of her young people is carried away by enthusiasm for a cause. Moreover, neither she nor her heroines seem to be aware of the crises the nation was passing through during the long struggle with Napoleon, although all her novels were published within a few years of Waterloo. No doubt in this, again, she reflects the temper of country society as she knew it, and we must bear in mind that only a small proportion of the population was actually engaged in the war (which was carried on intermittently for more than twenty years) as armies were still on a small scale compared with those of modern times. She does show that she understands the love and loyalty of a sailor for his calling ; but the Romantics had not yet made enthusiasm generally fashionable in England, and Jane had nurtured herself on the rational and satiric vein of the eighteenth century. However, she is not without ideals, of a practical nature ; in Edmund Bertram she exalts an earnest determination to take a stricter view of his duties as a priest than was common in those days of non-resident vicars and rectors. He can never be content to " be the clergyman of Thornton Lacy every seventh day for three or four hours," and even the insinuations of fascinating Mary Crawford cannot shake him as to this, although his heart is wrung. Mary had to realise that she was no longer able, in the picture she had been forming of a future Thornton, "to shut out the Church, sink the clergyman, and see only the respectable, elegant, modernised and *occasional* residence of a man of independent fortune." Mr. Knightley, Mr. Darcy and Sir Thomas Bertram set themselves high standards in personal conduct, and in their responsibilities as landlords. In fact, although Jane Austen is little concerned with religious or theoretic idealism, character—and the fruit it bears—is always of supreme importance in her novels. Almost all her heroines are schooled by trials and mistakes into a finer flowering of character, which is always the bedrock of the story, the determining factor in the fate of her men and women.

All Jane Austen's novels are wonderfully even in quality ; each one contains its gallery of comedy figures (although these are not drawn from so wide a social range as those of Fanny Burney) and "there is scarcely a chapter which is not adroitly opened or artistically ended."[1] The characters from *Sense and Sensibility* are, perhaps, less well-known and quoted than the others : *Pride and Prejudice, Persuasion* and *Emma* are each of them first favourite with many, and J. E. Austen-Leigh, author of the *Memoir*, relates a story of a house-party of literary people who each wrote down the name of their favourite novel and found that *Mansfield Park* had been chosen by seven of their number. Amongst these conflicting claims there is little doubt that Elizabeth Bennet is one of the heroines of fiction who has most often excited in men the feeling that Jane Austen herself professed to have when she read Crabbe—that she "thought she could fancy marrying Mr. Crabbe." In sending Elizabeth into the world her author confessed to thinking her as delightful a creature as ever appeared in print, and that she did not know how she should tolerate those who did not like her ; but in the case of Emma she thought she was taking a heroine whom no one would like but herself.

Sense and Sensibility was the first of her novels to be published, in 1811, after a period of lying fallow in an earlier

[1] Austin Dobson.

form (began about 1792) as a series of letters under the title of *Elinor and Marianne*. At the time of its publication *Pride and Prejudice* and *Northanger Abbey* were already written, the first having been refused by a publisher and the second lying in a drawer in the shop of the Bath book-seller to whom it had been sold in 1803.

Although the heroines of *Sense and Sensibility* are over-shadowed by Elizabeth, Emma and Anne, and there are no comedy characters in it to compete with Mr. Collins, Mrs. Norris, Miss Bates, and Mr. Woodhouse, Jane Austen's quality, especially her gift for satire, is fully apparent. There is an excellent scene early in the book, in which Mrs. John Dashwood whittles down her husband's intention to settle £1,000 each upon his sisters to a mere offer to help them in their removal from their old home, in which good intention he is eventually frustrated by the fact that it proves more convenient to send the furniture by water than by road. Sir John and Lady Middleton are well drawn—Sir John was a sportsman, Lady Middleton a mother ; as these were their only resources, she had the advantage of him because she could spoil her children all the year round. There is, too, Charlotte Palmer, with her unfailing good-humour, always " highly diverted " when her husband is rude or cross to her, exclaiming with admiration—" Mr. Palmer is so droll ! He is always out of humour." Mr. Palmer may be regarded as an understudy for Mr. Bennet of *Pride and Prejudice*, but his refuge from the irritation of having a foolish wife is in bearishness instead of in irony. There is a typical bit of dialogue between the Palmers about Willoughby's house :—

" ' I never was at his house ; but they say it is a sweet, pretty place.'
' As vile a spot as ever I saw in my life,' said Mr. Palmer.
. . . ' Is it very ugly ?' continued Mrs. Palmer ;—' then it must be some other place that is so pretty, I suppose.' "

The theme of *Sense and Sensibility* affords a good oppor-tunity for a further study of the cult of sensibility, still fashionable enough to be an excellent subject for satire. Marianne Dashwood practises it very thoroughly :—

" Marianne would have thought herself very inexcusable had she been able to sleep at all the first night after parting from Willoughby.

She would have been ashamed to look her family in the face the next morning, had she not risen from her bed in more need of repose than when she lay down on it. . . . She was awake the whole night, and she wept the greatest part of it. She got up with a headache, was unable to talk, and unwilling to take any nourishment ; giving pain every moment to her Mother and sisters, and forbidding all attempt at consolation from either. Her sensibility was potent enough ! ''

This sensibility was extended to a romantic love of scenery (including a *tendresse* for dead leaves which her sister regarded as an originality), music and poetry, and a horror of second marriages. Elinor Dashwood personifies good sense and reasonable consideration for others, but even she has her moment of " sensibility " ; when Miss Lucy Steele has made her amazing confidence that she is interested in Edward Ferrars, Elinor's own lover, she is thankful that " though her complexion varied, she stood firm in incredulity, and felt in no danger of an hysterical fit, or a swoon." This does not seem so very much more strong-minded than the practice of Fanny Burney's day, when a similar revelation completely unnerved Cecilia and Henrietta Belfield :— " the deepest blushes overspread the cheeks of both as their eyes met each other, and while Miss Belfield trembled in every limb, Cecilia herself was hardly able to stand."

In another respect Jane Austen's women have made a definite advance on Fanny Burney's : we learn from *Sense and Sensibility* that it was now possible for girls to take walks alone, even in the country. The Dashwood sisters walked on the downs together, and Marianne was also teased for her rambles in the direction of the village where Willoughby had stayed. Nevertheless, when Elizabeth Bennet walked three miles to see her sister Jane when she was ill at the Bingleys' house Miss Bingley tried to make capital out of the incident to discredit Elizabeth with Mr. Darcy. She drew attention to the fact that her petticoat was six inches deep in mud, and she looked " almost wild," to which Mrs. Hurst added distastefully—" Why must *she* be scampering about the country because her sister has a cold ? " After more reflections on Elizabeth's " conceited independence " and " country-town indifference to decorum," Miss Bingley appeals openly to Darcy : " I am afraid, Mr. Darcy, that this adventure has rather affected your admiration for her fine eyes ? " But she got no satisfaction, as he only replied that the exercise had brightened them. Emma would perhaps have agreed with Miss Bingley, as she found it unpleasant to walk to Randalls alone, and did not repeat the experiment.

Northanger Abbey does its work of ridiculing the fashionable novel of mystery-mongering and horror extremely well, it was a vein in which Jane had exercised herself already in her youthful farce *Love and Freindship*. The portrait of Catherine Morland has a touching charm, but she is a little less interesting than Jane's later heroines because she is—intentionally—so very young and " artless." Henry Tilney is, on the other hand, one of Jane's successful heroes ; he is clever and lively, with her favourite brother in mind Jane could not draw a dull Henry.

Students of manners can draw an interesting comparison between the balls of Evelina's London and those in the Assembly Rooms of Bath in Catherine Morland's day—the one novel giving a picture of " a young lady's entrance into the world " in 1778, and the other of a similar event about twenty years later. Sir Clement Willoughby and Henry Tilney are equally voluble as dance partners, but Henry's cheerful and amusing raillery about how Catherine will describe him in her journal, and the quality of her muslin, is a great advance on the insolent insinuations and extravagant compliments with which Sir Clement reduces the wretched Evelina to tears. The study of ballroom manners can be pursued all though Jane Austen's novels. It shows that the fops and beaux are passing off the stage, and with the " my dear Madam," which supersedes the " my dear creature " of Evelina's day, manners have fined down. The term beau, even, has gone down in the social scale : Jane Austen relegates it to the vulgar Miss Steele, to whom all admirers are " beaux." Perhaps the nearest in succession to Sir Clement amongst Jane Austen's men is Henry Crawford, but he is subtle and insidious where Sir Clement was bold and insolent, and Maria Rushworth would have been safe enough with him if she had wished to be. He has, also, a saving grace of humour, and it is difficult to be too wroth with him when he pleads with his sister that he must " make a small hole in Fanny Price's heart," excusing himself because " it can only be for a fortnight, and if a fortnight can kill her, she must have a constitution which nothing can save."

In Mr. Darcy's behaviour at the Meryton Assembly we see that the insolent quizzing of the ladies seated by the wall was not quite a thing of the past, although Darcy had not the cold-blooded effrontery of the eighteenth century beau who made his comments on purpose to embarrass. However, when his friend Bingley urges him to dance he replies with fastidious haughtiness :—

" I certainly shall not. You know how I detest it, unless I am particularly acquainted with my partner. At such an Assembly as this, it would be insupportable. Your sisters are engaged, and there is not another woman in the room whom it would not be a punishment to me to stand up with."

Bingley urges the charms of the younger sister of his own delightful partner, Jane Bennet, but without success :—

" ' Which do you mean ? ' and turning round, he looked for a moment at Elizabeth, till, catching her eye, he withdrew his own, and coldly said, ' she is tolerable ; but not handsome enough to tempt *me* ; and I am in no humour at present to give consequence to young ladies who are slighted by other men. You had better return to your partner and enjoy her smiles, for you are wasting your time with me.' "

Pride and Prejudice " needs no bush," it is probably the best known of the six novels. It is delicious from the opening sentence :—

" It is a truth universally acknowledged that a single man in possession of a good fortune must be in want of a wife."

Mr. Bingley, with his four or five thousand a year, had settled at Netherfield Park ; Mrs. Bennet has five daughters ; Mr. Bennet perversely refuses to call on the eligible neighbour. Mr. Bennet's bark however, is worse than his bite, and when he has called, unbeknown to his family, he breaks the good news characteristically :—

" Observing his second daughter trimming a hat, he suddenly addressed her with—' I hope Mr. Bingley will like it, Lizzie.'
' We are not in a way to know *what* Mr. Bingley likes,' said her Mother, resentfully, ' since we are not to visit.' "

Mr. Bennet tantalises them a little longer—indulging his

satirical humour with such scenes is his chief compensation for having married a woman so much his intellectual inferior. At last the overwrought Mrs. Bennet is stung to retort :—

" ' I am sick of Mr. Bingley ! ' cried his wife.

' I am sorry to hear *that* ; but why did you not tell me so before ? If I had known as much this morning, I certainly would not have called on him. It is very unlucky ; but as I have actually paid the visit, we cannot escape the acquaintance now."

And so the whole delightful drama is launched, with Darcy, Lady Catherine de Bourgh and Mr. Collins to supply romance and comedy, and one of the most attractive heroines in fiction—sweet but " arch "—dominating them all.

Between the writing of these three novels and Jane Austen's second group there was, as we have seen, a gap of about ten years. *Mansfield Park*, the first of the more mature group, is pitched in a rather more serious key. None of the novels are wholly " polite comedy," but as a rule Jane Austen kept, with light but sure touch, within the range of faults and foibles such as can be laughed at or easily forgiven. In *Mansfield Park* lack of genuine religion and principle bear very bitter fruit and cause lasting suffering. In the case of Mary Crawford it is made clear enough that her up-bringing prevented her from rising to the highest in her nature ; in regard to the daughters of Sir Thomas Bertram, the visitation of the faults of their training upon them and their father seems rather extreme. There had been over-attention to manners and accomplishments, in fact to appearances in general, in their education—we are told that their vanity was in such good order that they seemed to be quite free from it—and their Aunt Norris had lavished injudicious praise on them ; but in their father's house there was no lack of principle and personal dignity, and it is not very convincing that Maria should first marry Mr. Rushworth, who had only his wealth to recommend him, and then run away with Henry Crawford. Nor does either moral or poetic justice seem to require that Julia should immediately elope with the empty-headed Yates. Mary and Henry Crawford, too, for whom we should have liked a better fate, are ruthlessly sacrificed to enhance the priggish virtue of Edmund Bertram and the triumph of dear but inflexible little Fanny Price.

Nevertheless, *Mansfield Park*, with the appeal of its Cinderella motive, is a good story. The episode of the private theatricals is extremely good in bringing out the various characters : Sir Thomas Bertram's sudden return to a scene so repugnant to his principles and his taste is an excellent piece of domestic drama : with Tom Bertram we cannot but appreciate its humours even while, with Jane Austen's period spell upon us, we take it very seriously.

Mansfield Park has its share of comedy in Mrs. Norris and Lady Bertram, and in the Price household at Portsmouth Jane Austen took a new field with signal success. No uncomfortable detail of a thoroughly ill-managed house is wanting, from the moment of Fanny's arrival, when her mother, explaining that she could not tell whether she would be for some meat or only a dish of tea after her journey, finds that there is no meat in the house, no kettle on, only a sad fire, and the bell out of order, to the moment of her departure, when the breakfast is just assembled on the table by the time the carriage is driving away with her.

Emma, again, is one of the best known of Jane Austen's novels, and in no other is the " comedy of manners " better done, or the humour more sparkling and mordant. The immortal Miss Bates, with her incessant spate of talk, cannot be illustrated by short quotation ! The Eltons are a triumph of conceit and vulgarity just not burlesqued ; beside Mrs. Elton's snobbery Emma's seems almost estimable in its refinement. When Mrs. Elton is astonished to find Mrs. Weston, Emma's ex-governess " really quite the gentle-woman," Emma replies haughtily that " Mrs. Weston's manners were always particularly good . . . their propriety, simplicity and elegance would make them the safest model for any young woman," and we feel that these are qualities which Emma would always value sincerely wherever she found them. Mrs. Elton's frequent references to her brother-in-law's house and grounds at Maple Grove and his wife's barouche-landau are only matched by the fatuous pride of Mr. Collins in the size and shape of the rooms at Rosings, where it is the crowning glory of his life to be entertained by his patroness, Lady Catherine de Bourgh.

Mr. Woodhouse is the valetudinarian to perfection ; Emma has to be a diplomatist indeed to ensure that their

guests are allowed to eat the good things she has provided,
and not relegated to "a nice basin of gruel" like his own ;
when his son-in-law has been ill-humoured he reinstates
himself in the old gentleman's (Mr. Woodhouse cannot be
called "the old man ! ") opinion by seeming—" if not quite
ready to join him in a basin of gruel, perfectly sensible of
its being exceedingly wholesome." There is a pleasing
dialogue when Emma shows him her portrait of Harriet :—

" ' It is very pretty,' said Mr. Woodhouse. ' So prettily done !
Just as your drawings always are, my dear. I do not know anybody
who draws as well as you do. The only thing I do not thoroughly
like is, that she seems to be sitting out-of-doors, with only a little
shawl over her shoulders ; it makes me think she must catch cold.'
    ' But, my dear Papa, it is supposed to be summer ; a warm day
in summer. Look at the trees.'
    ' But it is never safe to sit out-of-doors, my dear.' "

Mr. Knightley is decried by some critics as a stick of a
hero ; but when we are momentarily irritated by some
conceit or folly, he often brings in just that breath of common-
sense or irony that is wanting. He makes for us the very
comments we feel are needed. When Mrs. Elton, who
called him " Knightley " with arch sprightliness after their
first meeting, wants to manage his strawberry party at Donwell
Abbey for him, he takes just the right line with her :—

" No,' he calmly replied, ' there is but one married woman in
the world whom I can ever allow to invite what guests she pleases to
Donwell, and that one is—— '
    ' Mrs. Weston, I suppose,' interrupted Mrs. Elton, rather
mortified.
    ' No,—Mrs. Knightley ; and till she is in being, I will manage
such matters for myself.' "

It is seldom that Jane Austen makes two men talk to each
other ; but what can be more satisfactory than the reticence
of the two Mr. Knightleys when they meet after a separation ?

" ' How d'ye do, George ? ' and ' John, how are you ? ' succeeded
in the true English style, burying under a calmness that seemed
all but indifference the real attachment which would have led either
of them if requisite, to do everything for the good of the other."

Later in the evening the brothers discussed their own concerns,
chiefly the state of affairs at Donwell Abbey, where " the
plan of a drain, the change of a fence, the felling of a tree,

E

and the destination of every acre for wheat, turnips or spring
corn " were almost equally interesting to both.   Jane Austen
knew her English country gentleman, and Mr. Knightley
is a most satisfactory sample.

Emma is a self-confident young woman who does not
enlist our affections so readily as Elizabeth Bennet or Anne
Elliot, but her conceit is sweetened by a lively sense of
humour, and in the long-run she has the good sense and good
feeling to be ashamed when she has been in the wrong :
Mr. Knightley is the very man for her to marry, and if we
could have had a sequel in which she played her part as
Mrs. Knightley she might well have become a first favourite.

In *Persuasion*, her last completed novel, none of Jane
Austen's powers are lost.   There are no farcical characters,
such as Miss Bates or Mr. Collins, but they are scarcely
missed as the charm of the story grows on the reader.   The
whole tone of the book is the most mellow she achieved,
Anne Elliot is drawn with a tenderness which the spirited
Elizabeth and the confident Emma did not call for, and
which we scarcely realised that Jane Austen possessed.
It is in *Persuasion*, too, that we have her two happiest examples
of marriage—in the Harvilles and the Crofts—and we feel
that Anne and Captain Wentworth will be happier still.
Humour, of course, is not wanting, and Charles and Mary
Musgrove are excellent character drawing ; but here Jane's
high spirits do not run riot in satire, and the charm of the
book is chiefly vested in Anne and her story.   It is a gentle
charm, and grows upon the reader almost imperceptibly
until he is apt to find, probably with a sense of surprise,
that this is, after all, his favourite Jane Austen !   Yet, had
all her novels been in the key of *Persuasion* her genius might
not have been so readily recognised.   G. K. Chesterton
claimed for her that " her power came, as all power comes,
from the control and direction of exuberance . . . there
is the presence and pressure of that vitality behind her
thousand trivialities."   In *Persuasion* the exuberance is
rather farther below the surface than in her other novels,
but it has a grace that is all its own.   Anne Elliot's charming
ghost and those of her friends have certainly haunted Bath
and Lyme for over a hundred years.   When Tennyson
first went to Lyme the place where the Duke of Monmouth

landed was pointed out to him, but he turned away impatiently—" Don't talk to me of Monmouth! Show me the spot where Louisa Musgrove fell."

Of the work which Jane Austen left unpublished the only finished stories are *Lady Susan* and *Love and Freindship*,[1] the latter said to have been written at the age of seventeen, except for short pieces amongst her *Juvenilia*, of which a selection is included in the 1922 edition of *Love and Freindship*, and a further collection has appeared under the title of *Volume the First* (1933). There could be no greater contrast than that between these delicious juvenile burlesques of Jane Austen's and the romantic and heroic tales of Charlotte Brontë's adolescence. A typical example of the quality of *Volume the First* is the story of Sir William Mountague, whose lady named September 1st for their wedding day, whereupon he explained that he could not lose the shooting on such a day, even for such a cause. The lady was enraged and took her departure, and " Sir William was sorry to lose her, but as he knew that he should have been much more grieved by the loss of the 1st of September, his sorrow was not without a mixture of happiness, and his affliction was considerably lessened by his joy." Another characteristic theme is the dispute between Sir Godfrey and Lady Marlow as to whose fault it is that they are in " such deplorable lodgings . . . in a paltry market-town," when they ·have three good houses of their own, " situated in some of the finest parts of England, and perfectly ready to receive us."

Love and Freindship is a supreme example of Jane's glorious exuberance ; it is an extravagant youthful farce, written as a skit on the sensational novel of the day. The Noble Youth who wanders into the humble cottage in the Vale of Usk in the course of his haphazard journey from his father's house in Bedfordshire to his aunt's in Middlesex, and there finds a heroine waiting for him, explains his flight :—

" ' My Father, seduced by the false glare of Fortune and the Deluding Pomp of Title, insisted on my giving my hand to Lady Dorothea. No never exclaimed I. Lady Dorothea is lovely and Engaging ; I prefer no woman to her ; but know, sir, that I scorn to marry in compliance with your wishes. No! Never shall it be said that I obliged my Father.' We all admired the noble Manliness of his reply."

[1] Jane Austen's spelling.

This admiration does its work so quickly that as soon as this recital is finished the Noble Youth and the lovely Laura, the heroine of the cottage, are united by her father, " who tho' he had never taken orders had been bred to the Church." The happy pair join their fortunes to those of another Noble Youth, the friend of Edward, and his bride. The meeting between the two bridegrooms is so highly fraught with touching sensibility that the brides, Laura and Sophia, are soon reduced to fainting alternately on the sofa. Unfortunately their " exalted " indifference to finance—they would " have blushed to pay their debts "—did not meet with the consideration which such " disinterested behaviour " deserved, and Augustus was thrown into prison. Everything seen or said feeds Sophia's sensibility on the subject :—

" ' What a beautiful sky ! ' said I. ' How charmingly is the azure varied by those delicate streaks of white ! '
' Oh ! my Laura,' (replied she hastily withdrawing her eyes from a momentary glance at the sky) ' do not thus distress me by calling my attention to an object which so cruelly reminds me of my Augustus's blue satin waistcoat striped with white ! In pity to your unhappy friend avoid a subject so distressing.' "

Eventually the two husbands are thrown from a phaeton and lie dying on the road while Laura and Sophia out-rival each other in fainting fits and " running mad," until Sophia points out that it is growing late, and the evening damps are beginning to fall, upon which they retire to a conveniently handy and sufficiently picturesque white cottage.

Lady Susan is thought to be a more mature production, but it has none of the uproarious fun of some of the juvenilia, and little of Jane's usual delicious irony. It is a cynical story of the intrigues of a beautiful and heartless woman to secure a wealthy second husband, and also to dispose advantageously of her daughter of seventeen. It is thought that it may have been founded on a manuscript in the possession of the Austen family containing the private history of an actual family, represented as " well-connected," in which there were five daughters who were treated with extraordinary harshness by their mother, who was herself a beautiful woman and very successful in society. Such a manuscript may well have afforded the young Jane Austen a preliminary exercise of her imagination before she realised

that she had no need of " sources " outside her own experience
and fancy. Lady Susan Vernon has no redeeming feature,
no touch of that blend of sweetness and alloy which makes
the charm of Jane's heroines, but her machinations are
subtly drawn, as when she intends to bring indirect coercion
to bear on her daughter :—

" . . . I could not reconcile it to myself to force Frederica into
a marriage from which her heart revolted, and instead of adopting
so harsh a measure merely propose to make it her choice, by render-
ing her thoroughly uncomfortable until she does accept him—but
enough of this tiresome girl."

The Watsons, of which only enough was written to introduce
the family and their environment, and take Emma Watson
to one ball, was deliberately given up by Jane Austen, as
she probably wrote *Persuasion*, and certainly began *Sanditon*
(written in January—March, 1817, after which she was never
well enough to continue it), after this fragment. The only
clue to its date is that the watermarks on the paper are 1803
and 1804, during which years Jane was in Bath and the
apparent break in her writing—between *Northanger Abbey*
(sold in 1803) and *Mansfield Park* (published on completion
in 1814)—had begun.

One theory is that Jane Austen gave up *The Watsons*
because she had pitched it in too vulgar a key, although
Emma Watson, the heroine, had been brought up by an
aunt in a home which had " many of the elegancies of life."
The family as a whole is certainly on a lower social plane
than the Dashwoods, Bennets and Woodhouses ; the
characters nearest to Emma's sisters in that respect are the
Miss Steeles of *Sense and Sensibility*. Some features of the
Watson family even remind us of Fanny Burney's Branghtons :
they had the same fault of sparring with one another, so that the
presence of strangers in their evening circle was welcome to
Emma as securing their " complaisance " and the good
manners which might otherwise have broken down in " a
party of such very near relations." Elizabeth Watson is
redeemed by some good feeling, and a downright simplicity
of manner ; as Fanny Burney pointed out in the case of the
Branghtons, it is " pretensions " which are objectionable.
Emma Watson shines superior both to pretensions and to
the other fault of allowing smart young men to patronise

her with too easy a familiarity. The description of her personal appearance suggests the author's own in several respects, especially the " air of healthy vigour," the skin which was " clear, smooth and glowing," the " lively eyes, sweet smile and open countenance which gave beauty to attract, and expression to make that beauty improve on acquaintance."

The Watsons adds one more ballroom to Jane Austen's gallery of such scenes, and one nice boy to her group of child characters.

The last fragment of a novel which Jane wrote, first published in 1925 under the title of *Sanditon*, has a promising theme, and characters which might have developed very satisfactorily. Mr. Parker is an enthusiast, engrossed in the project of turning the small sea-side village in which he had been born into a fashionable bathing-place, with an active imagination which could convert all checks into hopes. There were checks in plenty, such as the rumour of two new residents, heard of from different quarters, resolving itself into one small party, contained in two hack-chaises.

Miss Diana Parker almost out-ran her brother in enthusiasm, and the other brother was a hearty young man whose principal interest was to oblige his sisters by cosseting his health, even to the point of being absorbed in making himself cocoa and toast at his first meeting with the heroine. There are several of Jane Austen's promising chapter openings, such as " Every neighbourhood should have a great lady," " ' Whose very snug-looking place is this ? ' said Charlotte " (out of the carriage window).

There is no waning in Jane Austen's powers in her last work comparable to that we see in Charlotte Brontë's unfinished fragment *Emma*.

In Jane Austen's style there lingers still some of the formality and elaboration of the age of elegance : to-day it would be thought " precious " to balance phrases or round off sentiments so neatly. Yet her choice of words is always fitted to express her exact meaning, and a comparison with the deliberately unartificial style of the twentieth century suggests that too many good words may be neglected from fear of pedantry. Although none of Jane Austen's characters talk in the exalted style of Lord Orville and

Mortimer Delvile, there is still a flavour of the well-bound book in some of the speeches of her most dignified men and women. Mr. Darcy, for instance, in a discussion on the merit of yielding readily to the persuasion of a friend, pronounces weightily :—"Will not it be advisable before we proceed on this subject, to arrange with rather more precision the degree of importance which is to appertain to this request, as well as the degree of intimacy subsisting between the parties ? "

Jane, however, always writes in character, and when Bingley joins in this discussion a lighter note is struck :—

" ' By all means,' cried Bingley, ' let us hear all the particulars, not forgetting their comparative height and size, for that will have more weight in the argument, Miss Bennet, than you may be aware of. I assure you that if Darcy were not such a great tall fellow in comparison with myself, I should not pay him half so much deference. I declare I do not know a more awful object than Darcy on particular occasions, and in particular places ; at his own house especially, and of a Sunday evening, when he has nothing to do '."

Character, therefore, is the supreme consideration in Jane Austen's style, as in her presentment of her plots, and upon character and irony her fame rests, and rests as surely as that of any novelist who has stood the test of over a hundred years, and been accepted as a " classic."

BOOKS ABOUT JANE AUSTEN

Biographical Notice by *Henry Austen* prefaced to the first edition of *Northanger Abbey and Persuasion*. This has been reprinted as an introduction to later editions.

**Memoir of Jane Austen*. *J. E. Austen-Leigh*, 1870. The first life of Jane Austen to be published, written by her nephew, Edward, the eldest son of James Austen-Leigh. An expanded edition was published in 1871, including *Lady Susan*, *The Watsons*, the alternative chapters of *Persuasion* and *The Mystery*, an early unfinished comedy. Oxford University Press edition, 1926.

Jane Austen : her Homes and her Friends. Constance Hill (Lane), 1902. Constance Hill had access to the Lefroy and other family papers. The sketches by Ellen Hill give corners of rooms, staircases, etc. from Jane Austen's homes.

Jane Austen and her Times. G. E. Mitton (Methuen), 1905. Quite a good period background.

Chawton Manor and its Owners. W. Austen-Leigh and *M. G. Knight*, 1911. Beautiful reproductions of Austen and Knight family portraits. Costly.

Jane Austen. Warre Cornish (English Men of Letters), 1914. Not so good as this series usually is.

Personal Aspects of Jane Austen. M. A. Austen-Leigh. (Murray), 1920. Some interesting side-lights on the Austen family life.

Jane Austen : a French Appreciation. Léonie Villard. Translated, 1924. Scholarly, but contains some misconceptions about English life.

The Plan of a Novel. Oxford University Press, 1926. A collection of opinions of *Mansfield Park* and *Emma*, preserved in Jane Austen's writing.

Jane Austen : a Bibliography. Geoffrey Langdon Keynes (Nonesuch Press), 1929. A complete and scholarly bibliography. Costly.

**Jane Austen : a Survey. Clara Thomson*, 1929. Reliable and readable.

Jane Austen : her Life and her Critics. Brimley Johnson, 1930.

Introductions to Jane Austen. J. C. Bailey (Oxford University Press), 1931.

Jane Austen : her Life and her Art. David Rhydderch (Cap.), 1932. Vivacious and unconventional: should not be read without one of the recommended lives in addition.

***The Life and Letters of Jane Austen* (already listed under *Letters*) by *W. and R. A. Austen-Leigh* should be read if possible, although some further particulars about Jane Austen have been established since its publication in 1913.

The *Introductions* to various good editions of the novels (notably those of the Oxford University Press) contain much valuable criticism.

Jane Austen : Guy Rawlence (Duckworth's Great Lives Series), 1934.

V

MARIA EDGEWORTH AND HER NOVELS
(1767–1849)

The following is a list of Maria Edgeworth's novels and " tales," as grouped in the Longford Edition, 1893 :—

1. *Moral Tales.*
2. *Popular Tales.*
3. *Belinda.*
4. *Castle Rackrent ; Essay on Irish Bulls ; The Science of Self-justification ; Ennui ; The Dun.*
5. *Manœuvring ; Almeria ; Vivien.*
6. *The Absentee ; Madame de Fleury ; Émilie de Coulanges ; The Modern Griselda.*
7. *Patronage.*
8. *Patronage* (concluded); *Comic Dramas ; Leonora ; Letters.*
9. *Harrington ; Thoughts on Bores ; Ormond.*
10. *Helen.*

Maria Edgeworth was one of the educative influences of her generation, and her name became a household word in many families. The second of Richard Lovell Edgeworth's nineteen children (by four marriages) she forms a link between the old order of the eighteenth century and the Victorian era. Her eldest brother was brought up on the principles of Rousseau's *Émile* and presented to Rousseau himself for inspection ; one of her father's cousins, the Abbé Edgeworth, attended Louis XVI to the guillotine at the risk of his own life ; her first step-mother was the lovely Honora Sneyd (Romney's model for " Serena Reading "), who rejected Thomas Day, the eccentric author of *Sandford and Merton*, and was ardently loved by the gallant and ill-fated Major André, who was shot as a spy in the American War of Independence. Maria's second step-mother was Honora's sister Elizabeth, and her father owed his acquaintance with the Sneyd sisters to Anna Seward, the " Swan of Lichfield," who presided over one of the most celebrated of provincial literary circles, of which Dr. Darwin, the grandfather of Charles Darwin, was an intimate. As a girl

Maria stayed in the house of Thomas Day, who stood over her bed every morning in his dressing-gown, an alarming figure with unruly black hair, while she drank the large glass of tar water which he prescribed for her weak eyes. She was also put through a severe course of training in deportment at a fashionable school, including being swung by the neck every day in the hope of making her grow a little taller ! In later life she met various distinguished people of the day, sampled the society of London and Paris, received a proposal of marriage from the King of Sweden's scientific secretary, and became a friend of Sir Walter Scott, who was her guest in Ireland, and her host at Abbotsford.

In the summer of 1782, when Maria was fifteen, Mr. Edgeworth decided to settle on his Irish estate with his already numerous family. It was a patriarchal cavalcade which set out on the journey to Edgeworthstown, including Mr. Edgeworth and the children of his first two wives, the third Mrs. Edgeworth and two of her unmarried sisters, and a generous complement of horses, carriages, menservants and maid servants and luggage. On one of the family migrations the landlady at the inn where they were unloading for the night at last exclaimed, " Haven't yez brought the kitchen grates with you too ? "

Edgeworthstown was to be Maria's home for the rest of her life, and it was no poor lot. Here the two main streams of interest in her life (and sources of inspiration in her writing) were happily developed and combined. Her father was an enthusiastic educationist and had plenty of material for experiment in his own family ; Maria became his devoted assistant, and helped him to create the perpetual atmosphere of " practical education " in which the young Edgeworths were brought up. All the work and repairs on the estate were so much grist to the educational mill : the children learned the secrets of locks and pumps, made bricks and dyes and were rewarded for intelligent questions by scientific experiments and demonstrations even at the breakfast table. They took part in their father's inventions and ingenious contrivances, amongst which was a new spire for the Church, with an iron framework surmounted by gilt ball and arrow : it must have been a proud day for William Edgeworth, one of the youngest of the family, as he stood on the Church tower blowing a paean on a bugle while the spire gradually rose to its full height in twelve and a half minutes ! The children learned reading without tears in lessons of five minutes at a time ; in fact, Mr. Edgeworth claimed that the tear-fall in his house was not more than one a month. For recreation they had a home theatre, and Maria wrote her first children's stories on a slate day by day for her brothers and sisters. Children to whom Harry and Lucy, Rosamond, Simple Susan and Lazy Lawrence, and even the over-pious Frank, were daily companions must have found their doses of moral precepts and useful information very happily tempered. Maria, on her side, learned to keep the children of her imagination (especially the naughty ones), delightfully human and real, however relentless and stunning the morals they had to illustrate or however scientific and improving the instruction they were designed to pass on to young readers.

The second fruitful aspect of Maria's life at Edgeworthstown was her association with her father in the management of the estate : almost every day she rode out with him on her pony Dapple to inspect land, farms and cottages and supervise improvements and repairs, and under his eye she kept the business accounts. In this way she grew familiar with the Irish countryside, and with the cabins and the characters of the peasants, and with this inspiration she became the first novelist of genuine Irish life.

Maria Edgeworth's first literary work was undertaken in collaboration with her father or under his close supervision : between them two volumes called *Practical Education* were launched upon the world in 1798, and Maria dutifully set forth the parental views on the education of women in her *Letters to Literary Ladies*. These were followed by the more spontaneous children's stories, collected under the titles of *The Parent's Assistant* and *Early Lessons*. Children loved these stories in a way in which it was impossible to love the *Fairchild Family*, and when Sir Walter Scott had read *Simple Susan*, he wrote : " When the boy brings back the lamb to the little girl there is nothing for it but to put down the book and cry."

The years did not all roll smoothly by in Edgeworthstown : consumption took a tragic toll of the handsome children of the two Sneyd sisters ; Honora Edgeworth herself had died of it, and in 1797 Elizabeth, Maria's second step-mother, fell a victim. In 1798 the daughter of a rector in a neighbouring county undertook to illustrate *The Parent's Assistant*, under Mr. Edgeworth's supervision, and she shortly became the fourth, and last, Mrs. Edgeworth. She was younger than Maria, but their relationship was a particularly happy one. The year 1798 also brought Edgeworthstown into the zone of the rebellion which was then seething in Ireland, fostered by the encouragement of Napoleon. The Edgeworths were obliged to leave their home for the greater safety of an inn at Longford. Mr. Edgeworth undertook the defence of Longford goal, and narrowly escaped a mauling by a mob because he had lighted candles to read a newspaper, and a report spread that he was signalling to the French !

In 1800 Maria's first purely Irish tale—*Castle Rackrent*—was published, and thenceforth a stream of novels and stories, including " moral tales," " popular tales," and " tales of fashionable life," poured from her pen.

In 1817 Mr. Edgeworth died, and his surviving wife recorded that for his family " the rest of that year was a blank." Henceforth Maria was the estate manager, business woman and gardener in chief of the establishment. She continued to write and compiled a memoir of her father. Her friendship with Sir Walter Scott was a joy of these later years. At eighty-one she was still able to be active in work for the relief of distress in the Irish famine of 1848. In May, 1849, she had a sudden seizure and died in a few hours, to the great grief of her devoted stepmother, who found some consolation in writing a memoir of her.

Apart from her children's stories, Maria Edgeworth's chief claim to fame is as the first author of novels of Irish life, and in this respect she has scarcely had the praise her work deserves. How well she knew her Irish background is illustrated by a letter she wrote in 1808 :—

" My father and mother have gone to the Hills to settle a whole clan of tenants whose leases are out, and who expect that because they all lived under his Honour, they and theirs these hundred years, that his Honour shall and will contrive to divide the land that supported ten people amongst their sons and sons' sons, to the number of a hundred. And there is Cormac with the reverend locks, and Bryan with the flaxen wig, and Brady with the long brogue, and Paddy with the short, and Terry with the butcher's-blue coat, and Dennis with no coat at all, and Eneas Hosey's widow, and all the Devines pleading, and quarrelling about boundaries and bits of bog."[1]

In *Castle Rackrent* Maria Edgeworth escaped completely from the obsession of which her Father proudly boasts in his Preface to *Ennui* : " It has therefore been my daughter's aim to promote, by all her writings, the progress of education from the cradle to the grave."

Castle Rackrent is not so much a story as a sketch, and represents " old Ireland " as it was before Maria's own day ; the characterisation, conversation and humour are excellent, as Old Thady, the faithful servant of more than one generation of the Rackrent family, tells his " plain round tale " of its Sir Patrick, Sir Murtagh, Sir Kit and Sir Conolly, familiarly known as Sir Condy. It is a sad story of decline in prosperity and high spirit misapplied, but it is graphic, and Sir Condy, at least, endears himself to readers.

The story of a real Lady Cathcart supplied an original for that of Lady Rackrent, wife of Sir Kit, whom her husband kept locked up in her room for seven years, proposing her health whenever he had company and sending up a servant to know if there was anything he might offer her from the dinner-table. There is also precedent for Sir Condy's election tactics. The freeholders entitled to vote were tested by lawyers, who enquired whether they had ever set foot on their freeholds : as many nominal freeholders had " never had a freehold they could safely swear to," Sir Condy set their consciences at ease by having a load of sods fetched from his farm at Gulteeshinnagh and making each man stand upon his sod before appearing before the lawyers. Poor Sir Condy's marriage was typical of him : he tossed up as to whether he should marry old Thady's pretty niece Judy or Miss Isabella Moneygawl and her fortune. Old Thady, who was drawn from life, is in character from beginning to end : the incident of his wiping the window-seat with his wig and then clapping it on his head is founded on truth—Maria Edgeworth had seen an Irish servant sweep a flight of stairs with his wig and then put it on again !

The Absentee is another mainly Irish story with a good

---

[1] *The Black Book of Edgeworthstown.*

theme : Lord Clonbrony, like many another Irish landlora,
is induced by his wife to leave Ireland and squander his
money in London, but his son, Lord Colambre, returns to
Clonbrony in disguise, and sees for himself the oppressions
of the rascally agent, and the results of his father's frequent
demands for money from the estate, in the dilapidation of
the town, farms and cabins and the degradation of the half-
famished people. It is a readable story with some good
scenes, although Lord Colambre is a little too consciously
virtuous to be entirely pleasing. The scene in which he
throws off his disguise and confronts the agent was compared
by Macaulay to the return of Ulysses in the *Odyssey* !

In *Ormond* there are some graphic pictures of Irish life,
especially of the almost mediæval state kept up by Sir Cornelius
O'Shane, known as " King Corny," on his estate in the Black
Islands. Young Harry Ormond comes to him when his
adopted father, Sir Ulick O'Shane, wants to be rid of him,
and he is given the welcome of an hereditary prince, with a
horse decked with ribbons, and a ragged escort headed by a
boy with a horn proclaiming " Prince Harry." Dinner was
served with " a strange mixture of profusion and carelessness,"
the ragged crowd being admitted to watch, as courtiers were
to the French King's supper at Versailles. As each dish was
removed the remaining contents were given to these watching
subjects of King Corny, until they at last departed, calling
for a blessing on him and " Prince Harry," and praying that
they might long reign over them. The door was then locked
and King Corny, his chaplain and Harry were left to drink
the night out. The next night Harry determined to leave
the table before he was drunk : King Corny was outraged,
but when Harry protested vehemently against the accusation
of ingratitude which had been flung at him, his host's apology
was equally warm. Nevertheless King Corny claimed for
himself that he could " never go to bed without a proper
quantity of liquor under his belt, but he defied the universe
to say he was ever known to be drunk." The only justification for this rash assertion was the opinion held in the Black
Islands that " no man could be called drunk so long as he
could lie upon the ground without holding it."

Of course King Corny proves to be a rough diamond, and
Harry Ormond to have a heart of gold : but the characterisa-

tion is not quite so good as that of *Castle Rackrent*, nor the story so satisfactory as that of *The Absentee*. *Ormond* provides some interesting glimpses of Parisian society before the Revolution, and of the court at Versailles, where Harry watched the King at supper.

Ennui is another Irish tale, which opens well with a wealthy and bored young English lord visiting his large estate in the extreme wilds of Ireland for the first time since babyhood. Unfortunately the end is hackneyed melodrama, as it is discovered that the young lord had been exchanged at birth by his Irish foster-mother and he has to surrender the estate. There is in *Ennui* a memorable account of the difficulties and dangers of a journey in the wilds of Ireland. The description of the chaise provided for Lord Glenthorn's superior "gentleman's gentlemen" is grim indeed : the horses were "wretched little dog-tired creatures," the wheels had their iron half loose, there were wooden pegs for linch-pins, ropes for harness, and various parts of the high, spring-less carriage were tied together. The postillion looked like a mad beggar, with his tattered coat tied round his waist by a hay-rope, showing "his bare legs marbled of many colours, while something like stockings hung loose about his ankles."

The innkeeper assures them that there is "sorrow better chaise in the county," but as the frightened English valet and French chef are still too dismayed to get into it, Paddy suggests they shall travel in state with four horses instead of a pair :—

" And straight he put the knuckle of his forefinger in his mouth, and whistled shrill and strong ; and in a moment, a whistle some-where out in the fields answered him. I protested against these proceedings, but in vain ; before the first pair of horses were fastened to the chaise up came a little boy with the others *fresh* from the plough. They were quick enough in putting these to ; yet how they managed it with their tackle, I know not.

' Now we're fixed handsomely,' said Paddy.

' But this chaise will break down the first mile.'

' Is it this chaise, plase your honour ? I'll engage it will go to the world's end. The universe wouldn't break it down now ; sure it was mended but last night.'

" Then seizing his whip and reins in one hand, he clawed up his stockings with the other : so with one easy step he got into his place, and seated himself, coachman-like, upon a well-worn bar of wood, that served as a coach-box."

Then he called for his postillion :—

" Where are you, Hosey ? ' cried he.

' Sure, I'm only rowling a wisp of straw on my leg,' replied Hosey.
' Throw me up,' added this paragon of postillions, turning to one
of the crowd of by-standers. ' Arrah, push me up, can't ye ? '

A man took hold of his knee, and threw him upon the horse :
he was in his seat in a trice ; then clinging by the mane of his horse,
he scrambled for the bridle, which was under the other horse's
feet."

At last Lord Glenthorn's protesting servants were coaxed
and manœuvred into the chaise, where they were " instantly
shut up in straw and darkness," and the adventurous drive
began, and very good reading it makes. When some of the
harness breaks after a fearsome and rattling descent of a
steep hill, and Lord Glenthorn remonstrates from his own
carriage, telling Paddy that it would have been all over with
him if it had happened on the hill, Paddy replies airily :—

" That's true, plase your honour: but it never happened me
going down hill—nor never will, by the blessing of God, if I've any
luck."

Maria Edgeworth's Irish drivers are always good ; Larry
of *The Absentee* is another excellent specimen.

Amongst the " tales from fashionable life " the most
considerable are *Belinda* (highly praised by Jane Austen),
Patronage and *Helen*. In these three novels students of
manners will find material which follows very aptly on Fanny
Burney's social panorama. There is a masquerade in
Belinda reminiscent of that in *Cecilia*, and *Helen* provides, in
Lord Beltravers, a bored beau in a slightly later style than
Mr. Meadows and Sir Sedley Clarendel : his obvious bore-
dom is in striking contrast with the studied elegance of his
dress, but when he is asked if he considers himself an *ennuyé*
he refuses to accept so old-fashioned a label, but graciously
permits the ladies to call him *blasé*. There are allusions to
" blue " coteries of ladies with literary tastes, and many
references to sensibility, of which there is a very good
exponent in Lady Millicent, of *Ormond*. The military
flirt in *Patronage* tries to enliven his dance partner with
allusions to " darts, flames, wounds and anguish," and
proceeds to " bright eyes, bewitching smiles and heavenly
grace," but the heroine remains unshaken in modest and
virtuous calm. All the heroines have wise heads on young
shoulders, their " well-regulated minds " make them models

of discretion as well as virtue, and yet the bloom of innocent modesty is still fresh upon them. *Patronage* is the least worth reading of the group ; in it the moral purpose almost swamps the human quality, which Maria Edgeworth can impart when she chooses, as she does in drawing Lady Cecilia of *Helen*, one of her erring (but not irredeemable) characters, with a genuine charm, reminiscent of that of Rosamond in her children's stories.

All her full-length novels (except *The Absentee*) suffer from the vogue for the long novel, if they could be judiciously pruned their quality would be more apparent, for Maria Edgeworth's best is genuinely good, combining much knowledge of the world (and particularly of Ireland), trenchant characterisation and humour.

BOOKS ABOUT MARIA EDGEWORTH

The Life and Letters of Maria Edgeworth (2 vols.). *Augustus Hare*, 1894.

Maria Edgeworth. Emily Lawless. (English Men of Letters). 1904.

Maria Edgeworth and her Circle in the Days of Bonaparte and Bourbon. Constance Hill. 1910. This book has the intimate charm of C. Hill's work and E. Hill's illustrations.

The Edgeworths. Paterson. (University Tutorial Press), 1914. A very good study of R. L. Edgeworth and his daughter as educationists.

**The Black Book of Edgeworthstown and Other Edgeworth Memoirs* (1585–1817). *Harriet J. and H. Edgeworth Butler* (*Faber and Gwyer*), 1927. Compiled by a niece and great-nephew of Maria Edgeworth, this book contains most interesting family records, including the Abbé Edgeworth's account of the last hours of Louis XVI, whom he attended as Confessor. There is also an excellent Memoir of Richard Lovell Edgeworth, and a chapter on his relations with his daughter.

Maria Edgeworth. Helen Zimmern (Eminent Women Series)

F

VI

SUSAN FERRIER AND HER NOVELS
(1782–1854)

Marriage, begun 1797, published 1818. Obtainable in *Everyman*
  edition.
The Inheritance, 1824.
Destiny, 1831.

Susan Ferrier's three novels provide pictures of Scottish
life and character between 1797 and 1831 which were drawn
by one who knew the Scottish castle and its laird as intimately
as Maria Edgeworth knew their Irish counterparts, or as
Jane Austen knew the English country gentry of her day.
Probably if Susan Ferrier's work had not been so far out-
shone by that of " the wizard of the North " her novels
would still be cherished faithfully by all lovers of Scotland
as inimitable chronicles of by-gone days.   No one was more
generous in her praise than Sir Walter Scott himself ; he
even took pleasure in the fact that *Marriage*, published
anonymously, was attributed to him, and at the end of
Tales of My Landlord he wrote that in retiring himself from
the field of Scottish fiction he left behind " not only a large
harvest, but labourers capable of gathering it in," amongst
whom he " would mention in particular the author of the very
lively work entitled *Marriage*."

" Christopher North " pointed out the distinguishing
historical quality of her work with insight :—

" They are the works of a very clever woman, sir, and they have
one feature of true and melancholy interest quite peculiar to themselves.   It is in them alone that the ultimate breaking down and
debasement of the Highland character has been depicted.   Sir
Walter Scott had fixed the enamel of genius over the last fitful
gleams of their half-savage chivalry, but a humbler and sadder
scene—the age of lucre—banished clans—of chieftains dwindled
into imitation squires, and of chiefs content to barter the recollections of a thousand years for a few gaudy seasons of Almacks
and Crockfords, the euthanasia of kilted aldermen and steamboat
pibrochs was reserved for Miss Ferrier."

Susan Ferrier was born in Edinburgh in 1782, the fourth daughter of James Ferrier, a Writer to the Signet, who succeeded a Campbell relative in the management of the great Argyll estates ; her grandfather was the last laird of Kirklands, County Renfrew. When Susan was fifteen she lost her mother, and soon afterwards her father took her with him on a visit to Inverary Castle, where she formed a lifelong friendship with Charlotte Clavering, a niece of the Duke of Argyll, who inspired her to try her hand at writing, at first collaborated with her, and was always a helpful critic. It was largely owing to her close connection with the Duke of Argyll's family that Susan Ferrier was able to feel on sure ground in representing aristocratic Scottish life and character.

The glory of Susan Ferrier's books is the character-drawing, in which lively satire is just sufficiently mitigated by touches of tenderness : she knew a variety of Scottish types, and a great number of individuals whose idiosyncrasies, fostered by the comparative remoteness of the Highlands and the proud faith of the Chief's family in their own tradition and standing as part of the immutable order of things, made them tempting and delightful material for a novelist. Unfortunately these gems of character are set in plots which abound in the paralysing tendencies of the minor novelists of the period : they are written to illustrate inexorable moral purposes, and there is frequent recourse in them to premature deaths, mysteries of birth and unexpected inheritances, in order to provide trials of virtue and apportion rewards and punishments with a lavish and confident hand. In *Marriage* the heroine, Mary Douglas, is too good to be altogether lovable, and she is rewarded by the totally unforeseen accession of her lover to the very Highland castle in the shadow of which she has been brought up by her dear adopted mother, and which is her *beau ideal* of a home. In *The Inheritance* Edward Lyndsay out-rivals even Mary Douglas in conscious perfection of character, and no less than three Earls of Rossville die unexpectedly or prematurely in order that the hearts of the chief characters may be thoroughly searched out and the moral inexorably pointed. In *Destiny* an early death and a supposed loss in a ship-wreck serve the same moral and dramatic ends, and there are tedious conversations on such subjects as Sabbath keeping and the superiority of reading John Howard's Journal to amusing oneself with Pepys. Another trying habit of Susan Ferrier's is to make her characters burst into long quotations of verse, which only do credit to their remarkable memories, prefaced by some remark about " these pretty and well-known lines," of which the following is a fair sample :—

> " To feel that we adore
> With such refined excess,
> That though the heart would break with more,
> We could not love with less—
> This is love—faithful love—
> Such as saints might feel above."

Discounting these faults as chiefly due to the influence of period, which only genius can over-ride, we can still agree with the verdict of "Timothy Tickler," whose criticism was influential in his own day, that, in spite of defects, these novels are " all thick-set " with " sagacity, happy traits of nature, flashes of genuine satire, humour, sterling good sense and mature knowledge of the world."

Marriage opens with a very promising theme : the handsome but impecunious Harry Douglas has persuaded the superfine and spoiled young Lady Juliana, an Earl's daughter, to elope with him instead of marrying the Duke for whom her father intended her. Harry has resigned from the army and has no means of support for his bride, so he is obliged to take her as soon as possible to the Douglas ancestral castle of Glenfern, which he himself has not visited for many years. There his father ekes out a livelihood for his large household of unmarried sisters and daughters by farming the estate. The arrival is most graphic. They are ushered into a long, narrow, low-roofed drawing-room, reeking with the smoke of a newly lighted fire, scantily and shabbily furnished, with small windows which are more effectual in letting in the driving rain and wind than in clearing off the smoke. The family is waiting to greet them :—

" At the entrance of the strangers a flock of females rushed forward to meet them. Douglas good-humouredly submitted to be hugged by three long-chinned spinsters whom he recognised as his aunts ; and warmly saluted the five awkward, purple girls he guessed to be his sisters ; while Lady Juliana " (already quite unnerved by the terrors of Highland scenery) " stood the image of despair, and, scarcely conscious, admitted in silence the civilities of her new relations. . . . The Laird, who had been hastily summoned from his farming operations, now entered. He was a good-looking old man, with something the air of a gentleman, in spite of the inelegance of his dress, his rough manner and provincial accent. After warmly welcoming his son, he advanced to his beautiful daughter-in-law, and, taking her in his arms, bestowed a loud and hearty kiss on each cheek ; then, observing the paleness of her complexion, and the tears that swam in her eyes, ' What ! Not frightened by our Hieland hills, my leddy ? Come, cheer up—trust me, ye'll find as warm hearts among them as any ye ha'e left in your fine English *policies* '—shaking her delicate fingers in his hard muscular gripe as he spoke."

On escaping to her own room Lady Juliana is confronted by her outraged lady's-maid, who, having inspected the servants' quarters at Glenfern Castle, insists on returning to England in the chaise which brought the party. Lady Juliana has never handled her own clothes or dressed herself, and her sisters-in-law are almost as helpless with the profusion of lovely frocks : we are told that they themselves wore good solid dark stays, which were apt to show between skirt and bodice when they rushed in from their tom-boyish outdoor amusements only just in time to scramble into their clothes for dinner. Harry, fortunately, proves more *au fait* at lady's maiding than his sisters. Dinner passes off well— the Laird's mutton and grouse are fit for even a dainty appetite—but Lady Juliana becomes hysterical when the piper is called and the bag-pipes break into a dance tune, while the Laird calls genially to his five hoyden daughters— " Whar's the girlies ? Ho ! Belle, Becky, Betty, Baby, Beeny—to your posts ! " The breakfast-table the next morning, redolent of old cheese and herrings, with piled up plates of barley-meal scones and pease bannocks, is a terrible ordeal : a faint request for chocolate and muffins, or even toast, is met with the reply that the Castle is " out of loaf bread."

The only entertainment proposed is a walk, for which the aunts make awesome preparations, and press upon Lady Juliana a tartan cloak and hood, old bonnets, fur tippets, hair soles, clogs and pattens ; but she insists on taking her chance in a lace cap, lilac satin pelisse and silk slippers, to the dismay of the aunts, who feel that such imprudence threatens " ruin to the whole race of Glenfern, present and future."

A minor character in Susan Ferrier's best vein is Lady Maclaughlan, evidently drawn from life—in fact the author almost expunged her in fear of identification—with the elderly husband whom she insists on keeping an invalid and a cipher, whilst spending much of her time concocting physic for him in her " laboratory." She is not bad at heart, but had dictatorial manners, extraordinarily voluminous and complicated clothes, and a sharp and clever tongue : a good instance of the last is her comment on a local elopement— " Miss M'Kraken has bounced off with her father's footman, I hope he will clean his knives on her." Another good minor character is Dr. Redgill, the gourmet doctor who has taken up his quarters in the Earl of Courtland's establishment and tries to ensure that the young ladies of the family shall appraise their suitors by the extent of their grouse-moors or the quality of their fishing. Young Lady Emily Lindore's satirical wit is a refreshing antidote to her cousin Mary Douglas's insipid virtue. Lady Juliana develops consistently into a mother with a horror of love-matches : when she has accepted a lover for Mary on the strength of " the excessive good establishment " he can offer her, and Mary ventures to call his character and principles in question, she breaks out—" Character and principles ! One would suppose you were talking of your footman ! "

The student of manners will find in *Marriage* the fullest account in fiction of a blue-stocking *conversazione*, under the auspices of Mrs. Bluemits of Bath. She boasted that " nothing but conversation was spoke in her house," and received her guests with " that air of condescension which great souls practice towards ordinary mortals." The two Scottish ladies (Mary and her great-aunt Grizzy from Glenfern) are welcomed as hailing from " the land of poetry and romance," and soon verse is being freely bandied, and the opinion of " the sensitive poet of Olney " clinches an argument. Aunt Grizzy sees no opportunity to shine until she catches the name Campbell in the poetic maelstrom, whereat she eagerly seizes the chance of asserting herself with *éclat* :—

" 'Oh, I know plenty of Campbells; there's the Campbells of Mireside, relations of ours ; and there's the Campbells of Blackbrae, married into our family ; and there's the Campbells of Windlestrae Glen, are not very distant by my Mother's side.' "

At last the " blue " ladies take their leave with appropriate parting shots :—

" Another now advanced—' Wilt thou be gone ? It is not yet near day.'
' I have less will to go than care to stay,' was the reply.
' *Parto ti lascio adio,*' warbled Miss Parkins.
' I vanish,' said Mrs. Aspley, snatching up her tippet, reticule, etc., ' and, like the baseless fabric of a vision, leave not a wreck behind.' "

The Inheritance is not so definitely Scotch, as the Earl of Rossville's household is more closely in touch with the fashionable life of London than Glenfern Castle or the Glenroy of *Destiny*. The plot hinges on melodramatic circumstances, and the morality is obtrusive, but the character-drawing is excellent. The old Earl and his sister are convincing from the outset. Miss Pratt is a perfect example of the perennial visitor who contrives to spend the greater part of her life in other people's houses. She has established cousinship of some degree with most families in Scotland which own a comfortable ancestral home, and always makes much of the pains she has been at to look them up. On one occasion drifts of snow almost defeat her, but she commandeers a hearse with eight horses, on its way back from a funeral, and emerges triumphant at Rossville Castle, exclaiming to the outraged Earl :—

" ' I may well say I've come through thick and thin to get to you. At one time, I assure you I thought you would never have seen me but in my coffin, and a great mercy it is it's only in a hearse. I fancy I'm the first that ever thought themselves in luck to get into one ; but, however, I think I'm still luckier in having got well out of it ! ' "

Miss Pratt basks in the reflected glory of a wealthy nephew called Anthony Whyte, whose name crops up in her talk as often as King Charles' head in Mr. Dick's, but he never appears.

Almost as good is Miss Becky Duguid, the victim of what Susan Ferrier calls *Auntimony*. As a single woman Miss Becky " had vainly expected to escape the cares and anxieties of the married state," but she finds that these are thrust upon her by her married relations and friends, while they reserve the blessings of married life for themselves. They supposed that a single woman " could have nothing to do but oblige her friends," so Miss Becky is overwhelmed with commissions and sent for to bear the brunt of innumerable family crises :—

> " Whenever a gay husband was leaving home, Miss Becky was in requisition to keep his dull, sickly wife company in his absence—or, *vice versa*, when a young wife wished to amuse herself abroad,' that good creature, Becky Duguid,' was sent for to play backgammon with her old, ill-natured husband ; and when both man and wife were leaving home, then Becky Duguid was called upon to nurse the children and manage the servants in their absence. . . . She was expected to attend all accouchements, christenings, deaths, chestings and burials ; but she was seldom asked to a marriage, and never to any party of pleasure."

The Inheritance contains one good cottage scene, where the wife of a sick man refuses all suggested gifts—" no but what we might put up wi' "—this or that—" if he had ither things that are a hantel more needfu'." The " ither things " turn out to be " dead claise," and she appeals to her husband for support :—

> " ' An' sic a comfort as, nae doot, it wad be to him to see awthing ready and wise-like afore he gae'd out o' the world. A suit o' gude bein' comfortable dead claise, Tammas,' appealing to her husband, ' wad set ye better than aw the braw chyres an' carpets i' the toon.' "

Destiny has less lively satire than the two earlier novels, but it is impregnated with Scottish scenery and Scottish air from start to finish : the brief episodes in England only serve to make the Highlands even more present to the mind. It opens with an incomparable picture of the Chief of Glenroy, living on his vast estate in " a rude magnificence of feudal state " which recalls Maria Edgeworth's " King Corny " of the Black Islands, although there is more refinement and comfort at Glenroy. Glenroy's boon companion was the bachelor Laird of Benbowie, who took up his quarters with his friend, although he had a good estate of his own, and maddened the Chief's lady by his stupidities and slovenly habits : but to Glenroy " Benbowie was the very apple of his eye, because he was devoted to *him*." He never contradicted him, he fell in with his inclination whatever the direction it took, and " when there was no-one else, did well enough to be beaten at billiards." Benbowie is consistent to the end, and equally sparing of his own money and his Chief's.

Mrs. Molly Macauley, who looked after the welfare of the children when the Chief's lady had left him, and became the kindly and familiar presiding spirit of the household, could not easily be surpassed as a faithful and touching portrait of a dear, simple soul.

It is a great pity that so much tedious matter is combined with the satirical humour, good feeling and insight which Susan Ferrier certainly possessed : but those who have acquired the judicious art of " skipping " will reap a pleasant harvest in these three novels, and lovers of Scotland should find more to be grateful for than to excuse.

BOOK ABOUT SUSAN FERRIER

Memoir and Correspondence of Susan Ferrier. Edited by *J. A. Doyle,* (*Murray*), 1898.

VII

EMILY EDEN AND HER NOVELS
(1797-1869)

The Semi-Attached Couple. Written about 1834, published 1860.
Republished in the *Rescue Series*, 1928.
The Semi-Detached House. Published in 1860. Republished in
the *Rescue Series*, 1928.

Lovers of Jane Austen, who lay down *Persuasion* or
Sanditon with a sigh, because there is no more for them to
re-read until a lapse of time has made it possible to begin
once more with *Sense and Sensibility*, may find a welcome
balm in two novels by Emily Eden, which are in the same
tradition and yet have their own individuality and period
bouquet. It is not claimed that these two novels are works
of genius, but they amply fulfil the promise of their titles—
The Semi-Attached Couple and *The Semi-Detached House*—
with an attractive blend of satire and scenes of particularly
pleasing family life, and they were written by a woman of
the world about the society which she knew as intimately as
Jane Austen knew that of the country gentry of her day.

The Hon. Emily Eden was the seventh daughter of the
first Lord Auckland, who, as William Eden, had been English
Ambassador in Spain and Holland, and her mother was
sister of the Earl of Minto ; her eldest sister was William
Pitt's only love, but she married the Earl of Buckinghamshire.
Emily Eden was born in 1797, the year that Jane Austen
completed the first draft of *Pride and Prejudice* and revised
Sense and Sensibility, but her first novel was not written until
after 1830, and not published until her second had achieved a
success in 1860. Writing was not the chief pre-occupation
of her life : she was keenly and actively interested in the
political, diplomatic and social incident of her day, and
particularly in the part played by her brother George, who
was appointed Governor-General of India and became Earl
of Auckland. The second Lord Auckland never married, and
Emily Eden lived with him in England, and she and her sister

Fanny accompanied him to India, which in those days was no light adventure, and a complete exile from the kind of life she relished so much at home. When her brother died in 1849 Charles Greville (there is more than one allusion to Emily Eden in the Greville Memoirs) wrote :—

" His loss to the Government is irreparable, and to his family it is unspeakably great. To his sisters he was as a husband, a brother, and a friend in one, and to them it is a bereavement full of sadness, almost amounting to despair."

Here we have a clue to the happy and charmingly drawn relations between Helen Eskdale, the endearing young heroine of *The Semi-Attached Couple*, and her family, and between the sisters and brother in *The Semi-Detached House*.

A woman of distinctive personality and decided views, Emily Eden is, nevertheless, a faithful mirror of her class and period, and these had the strongly-marked features of the last phase of ascendant aristocracy and privilege, before industrialism and democracy had completed the transformation between mid-eighteenth and mid-nineteenth century England. Her background is excellently sketched by Mr. Anthony Eden in his *Introduction* to the re-issue of *The Semi-Detached House* in 1928 :—

" Miss Eden wrote of those among whom she had been born, and with whom she was to spend all but a few years of her life. She was Emily Eden, with all the gifts and prejudices of her birth and up-bringing, the daughter of ' Haughty Nell,' a Whig in the days of government by Whig oligarchy. All her life was spent in that small circle which to her was England, and which indeed did represent England abroad and govern England at home. She knew that world and loved it ; what more natural than that she should write about it with ease and charm, and with a rare gift of humour ?
We may complain that the world which Miss Eden portrays for us is small, but for her it was complete ; and how well she knew it ! We shall not regret the experience if we follow her into it."

After her brother's death Emily Eden spent the greater part of the remaining twenty years of her life at Eden Lodge, Kensington Gore. In 1860 she was induced to publish *The Semi-Detached House*, anonymously, and its success led her to disinter the novel she had written nearly thirty years earlier. She found it already old-fashioned, but decided it was worth publishing, and fortunately refrained from tempering its vivacity or grafting any maturer sentiments on to it. To modern readers, to whom both books are necessarily *period pieces*, *The Semi-Attached Couple* is the more attractive of the two, even if the other is a better constructed story : when it was re-published in 1928, J. C. Squire gave it a panegyric in the *Observer* as " a rescued jewel."

The main theme of *The Semi-Attached Couple* is the marriage of a young girl who has been idolised in a particularly charming family circle, and who has repaid generously all the affection she has received, to an equally young and attractive lord, regarded as the great *parti* of the season, but whose love develops a passionate and exacting quality which frightens and distresses his bride. Lord Teviot becomes jealous of her family, and jealousy breeds suspicion, both of which are absolutely foreign to Helen's nature and experience : the story of her loyal but bewildered efforts to respond to him and lay his suspicions to rest is delicately and touchingly told, and of course ends happily. The incidentals of the story include some good minor characters and pictures of castle life (there is no character below manorial rank) and a vein of satirical humour. The Douglas family, who live in a manor near Eskdale Castle, supply the secondary interest. The following dialogue between Mr. and Mrs. Douglas is reminiscent of Mr. and Mrs. Bennet in *Pride and Prejudice*, and Mrs. Douglas's remarks are further witness of the importance of "fortunes" and "expectations." She is belittling the eligible marriage of Lady Eskdale's elder daughter :—

" ' Then Amelia is married, *I* think, though nobody will agree with me, to a man who looks like a fool, and moreover his father is alive, and may live for ages, or marry again and have heaps of children ; so in a worldly point of view that is a deplorable marriage.'

' My dear, how you do run on imagining grievances ! The Trevors are very well off.'

' How can you know, Mr. Douglas ? Nobody who has a father alive is ever well off.' "

There is a good account of the flutter in Church when Lord Teviot is expected to appear in the Castle pew for the first time. Eyes stray constantly to the stranger, and some think him too attentive to his prayers for a man in love, others too attentive to Lady Helen for a man in Church. The congregation is considerably dashed when it is learned afterwards that the stranger was not Lord Teviot, but merely a visiting architect.

One of the most pleasing chapters in *The Semi-Attached Couple* is that in which Lord and Lady Eskdale face their solitude *à deux* when the last daughter is married.   They had not lost their affection for each other, and had always enjoyed a comfortable half-hour's talk every day in Lord Eskdale's library uninterrupted by their children, but when they sat down to dinner *tête à tête* for the first time for ten years they were dismayed.   Lady Eskdale wondered if she could " rub up enough music " to entertain her husband after dinner, but by the time he joined her in the drawing-room she was almost asleep on the sofa, after the unaccustomed effort of riding with him in the morning and of attending to her own business and charities without a daughter's help. When a note was brought in requiring an answer she almost cried :—

" ' I don't think I can ever exist in this way, Lord Eskdale,' she said.   ' What is to be done ?   Here is this note to be answered.'
    ' Give it to me, Jane ;   I will be your secretary.'
    ' Thank you, that is very good of you.   It is a great relief for this once ;   but how am I to get on when you are out ? ' "

Scarcely is the note disposed of when the groom of the chambers comes in to announce

" ' The schoolmistress, my lady, is waiting for directions about the children's stuff books.'
    ' There again, now !   What am I to do ?   I have mislaid the patterns.   Very well, tell her I will send to her.   Now, Lord Eskdale, you know you cannot settle about the school-children's frocks ; that was poor Helen's business.' "

Her reflections end in the inspiration of inviting Eliza Douglas to stay, after wishing that one of her daughters had married a poor man :—

" ' If any one of them had married a younger son without a shilling they must have lived with us, but my girls had no time allowed them to look about them and choose for themselves ;   and so they have all married men with country-houses of their own, and I have lost them all.'
    And roused by this overpowering calamity of wealthy sons-in-law, Lady Eskdale sat up to write her note to Mrs. Douglas."

She perseveres in being Lord Eskdale's riding companion and incurs Mrs. Douglas's strictures for " doing the youthful, galloping about the country flirting with her husband."

The Semi-Detached House is not, as the title suggests, a story of comparatively humble life : Pleasance, the house in question, is quite a large one, with a garden running down to the Thames, and the new tenant is young Lady Chester, who is unable to travel with her husband on his diplomatic mission to Berlin.   Blanche Chester, and her sister Aileen are only a little less charming than Helen, and their neighbours, the Hopkinsons, prove an unexpected source of interest.   The minor characters are well developed, with play for Emily Eden's satirical vein.   There is " poor Willis," Mrs. Hopkinson's widower son-in-law, who had " a passion for being a victim," and the *nouveau riche* Baron Sampson and wife : she suffers much chagrin on finding the Miss Hopkinsons intimate at Pleasance, but ascribes it to a school feast and explains, " I believe, in these days, a little attention to the poor is not a bad speculation."   The Baroness is rather too much exaggerated to be convincing, but the Hopkinson circle is very real.

These two novels are slight and short, but they leave a pleasant taste on the mental palate, and their blend of irony and good feeling saves them from insipidity : they are also free from tedious padding and over-strained morality.   Once again, they are to be recommended to lovers of Jane Austen to bridge at least one of the recurring gaps between re-readings of her novels.

BOOK ABOUT EMILY EDEN

Miss Eden's Letters.   Edited by *Violet Dickinson* (*Macmillan*), 1919.

VIII

THE LIVES OF THE BRONTË SISTERS

From Brunty to Brontë : such was the romantic progress of the father of the Brontës, born in Drumballyroney, County Down, on St. Patrick's Day, 1777, one of the ten children of Hugh Brunty, an Irish peasant-farmer. It was after Patrick had passed through the callings of weaver, school-teacher and tutor, and achieved the triumph of entering St. John's College, Cambridge, that he began to tamper with the surname which had so far served him adequately. He had excuse enough, for in the parish registers of County Down his relations are entered impartially as Brunty, Bruntie and Brontee. Patrick's first extant signature—that of his matriculation—is Bronte ; later he tried Bronté and Brontĕ, and finally Brontë. Possibly both the Greek $\beta\rho\acute{o}\nu\tau\eta$ (thunder) and the fact that Nelson had been created Duke of Brontë in 1799, influenced him, but, be that as it may, the change from commonplace Brunty to romantic Brontë seems aptly symbolic of his daughters' supreme faculty for transmuting common life into the stuff of vivid and passionate dreams.

Here is the ultimate secret of the spell which the Brontës have laid upon lovers of literature for nearly a century : with meagre experience of life's greater occasions—they were closely acquainted only with death—more practised in patience and renunciation than in satisfaction and fulfilment, yet the creations of their minds have held the imagination of readers with an enduring appeal which even far-reaching changes in life and manners have not been able to weaken. In fact, the limiting conditions of their lives have been the Brontës' great enablement : not only was such experience as came their way more keenly savoured, even when the savour was bitter, and their presentation of it more intense, but, in being driven in upon themselves, they tapped sources of inspiration too often over-laid by a multiplicity of events and preoccupations. The very contrast between their circumstances and their achievement is part of the fascination which clings persistently about them, a fascination more finely founded than at first appears. M. Maeterlinck revealed the essential quality of it in his beautiful passages on Emily Brontë in *Wisdom & Destiny*, where he makes great claims for her :—

" Not a single event ever paused as it passed by her threshold ; yet did every event she could claim take place in her heart, with incomparable force and beauty, with matchless precision and detail . . . Not in the soul of the best of those whose happiness has lasted longest, been the most active, diversified, perfect, could more imperishable harvest be found, than in the soul Emily Brontë lays bare. If to her there came nothing of all that passes in love, sorrow, passion or anguish, still did she possess all that abides when emotion has faded away."

The evidence that the spell of the Brontës is still potent is indisputable : the names of those who have written books on them, or introductions to their works, or read papers about them and their novels may be accounted legion, and amongst them are many men and women who have themselves won literary distinction. The long list opens with Mrs. Gaskell and includes Swinburne, Wemys Reid, Mrs. Oliphant, Mary Robinson (Madame Duclaux), Mrs. Humphrey Ward, Augustine Birrell, Theodore Watts Dunton, Alice Meynell, M. Maeterlinck, Ernest Dimnet, Edmund Gosse, G. K. Chesterton, May Sinclair, Romer Wilson, Virginia Woolf, Robert Bridges, A. C. Benson, Lascelles Abercrombie, E. F. Benson, Charles Morgan, Alfred Sangster and Clemence Dane. In addition to these and less notable writers on the Brontës, we have the solid compilations of Brontë letters and papers which we owe to Clement Shorter, the volumes of printed Transactions of the Brontë Society (and their Museum collection at Haworth) and the four volumes of *The Brontës : their Lives, Friendships and Correspondence* (Shakespeare Head Edition, Blackwell, 1932), in which T. J. Wise, a leading collector of Brontëana, and J. A. Symington, ex-Biblio-graphical Secretary and Librarian to the Brontë Society, have brought together every document and scrap of evidence bearing on the sisters' lives. Close upon this publication came the production of two Brontë plays in London— *The Brontës*, by Alfred Sangster and *Wild Decembers* by Clemence Dane. Last and least, but irresistibly presenting itself for allusion, is Stella Gibbons' delicious bit of satire in her novel *Cold Comfort Farm* (1932), in which she represents a literary crank as engaged upon a book which is to prove incontrovertibly not only that Branwell Brontë wrote all the novels, allowing his sisters, whom he worshipped, to take credit of them, but that he visited the Black Bull and ingratiated himself with the landlord for the sole purpose of obtaining supplies of gin for Anne, who was a secret drinker !

Amongst all the welter of literature and conjecture about the Brontës, it becomes increasingly difficult to extract a plain tale of their lives. For long Mrs. Gaskell's *Life of Charlotte Brontë* (first edition, 1857), held the field, and in the opinion of many it is still the supreme introduction to the Brontës ; even those who cavil at it often do not realise what all Brontë lovers owe to Mrs. Gaskell. As a piece of literature her book ranks in the first half-dozen of English biographies, and if she had not set the stage with so fine a sense of the romantic and spiritual appeal of the three sisters and their environment, it is doubtful whether the great Brontë cult would have arisen, although it owes its endurance partly to the pungent vitality of Charlotte's letters. Later interpreters may have revealed more of Charlotte's passionate and Emily's mystic quality, but these are implicit in Mrs. Gaskell's narrative, even if unacknowledged, and none can take from her the supreme advantage of writing as a contemporary, who had actually been Charlotte Brontë's guest at Haworth Parsonage.

Accepting that Mrs. Gaskell's biography is still the best approach to the Brontës, it is essential to read a modern commentary with it, as she was at once convicted of inaccuracies and unjustifiable statements, and even threatened with two libel actions, and to these accusations later critics have added that of the presentation of half-truths. The most offending passages were withdrawn, and do not appear in any of the numerous editions after the first two, and Mrs. Gaskell was so bitterly disillusioned about the whole art and practice of biography that she stipulated that her own life should not be written. Nevertheless we have valuable contemporary evidence that her book was true *in spirit* from the pen of Mary Taylor, Charlotte Brontë's intimate friend from their schooldays together at Roe Head, a woman whose correspondence bears the stamp of a strong character and vigorous intelligence. On receiving a copy of the biography in 1857, she wrote to Mrs. Gaskell :—

G

" The book is a perfect success, in giving a true picture of a melancholy life, and you have practically answered my puzzle as to how you would give an account of her not being at liberty to give a true description of those around. Though not so gloomy as the truth, it is perhaps as much so as people will accept without calling it exaggerated, and feeling the desire to doubt and contradict it."

It was Mary Taylor who had compared the Brontë girls to " potatoes growing in a cellar." When, in 1858, an account of Mrs. Gaskell's arraignment for false statements and conclusions reached her in New Zealand, she wrote to Charlotte's other faithful school-friend, Ellen Nussey, that whether the book was libellous or not, she regarded it as true in essentials and regretted " the mutilated edition " which was to replace the first, concluding in a characteristically caustic phrase—" you know one dare not always say the world moves."

Many writers have set themselves to describe Haworth, the Yorkshire village forever associated with the Brontës, and which, even in modern times, makes an extraordinarily strong and distinctive impression on literary pilgrims, with its steep cobbled Main Street, the houses and the walls which separate field from field of a grim stone which weathers black, the inordinate number of tomb-stones round the Church and Parsonage, and the moors as an ultimate background. As a contemporary description of the place and its folk, Mrs. Gaskell's two opening chapters remain unsurpassed. Yorkshire people did complain at once that the Lancashire lady represented them as too uncouth and savage, but the isolation which she pictures must have been familiar to Mr. Brontë and to Tabby, the servant whose Yorkshire tales were one of the sources of the Brontë children's knowledge of life. Roads were few and far between, and one woollen manufacturer told Mrs. Gaskell, in 1855 how, " not five-and-twenty years ago," he used to set out before dawn with a waggon-load of goods for Bradford, examining the horses' feet by lantern-light, and sending someone ahead to grope on hands and knees and sound with a staff down the slippery " brow " to find where the horses could safely tread.

Coming to Mrs. Gaskell's description of Haworth itself, she begins with the approach from Keighley, four miles of road which " never quite melts into country " :—

" Right before the traveller on this road rises Haworth village ; he can see it for two miles before he arrives, for it is situated on the side of a pretty steep hill, with a background of dun and purple moors, rising and sweeping away yet higher than the Church, which is built at the very summit of the long, narrow street. All round the horizon there is this same line of sinuous wavelike hills ; the scoops into which they fall only revealing other hills beyond of similar colour and shape, crowned with wild bleak moors—grand, from the ideas of solitude and loneliness which they suggest, or oppressive from the feeling which they give of being pent-up by some monotonous and illimitable barrier, according to the mood of mind in which the spectator may be."

This passage paints the back-cloth for the drama which is to come, conveying the immanence of " the dun and purple moors." In the front of the stage Mrs. Gaskell sets the main street of the village, and then the Parsonage itself :—

" The flag-stones with which it is paved are placed endways, in order to give a better hold to the horses' feet ; and, even with this help, they seem to be in constant danger of slipping backwards. The old stone houses are high compared with the width of the street, which makes an abrupt turn before reaching the more level ground at the head of the village, so that the steep aspect of the place, in one part, is almost like that of a wall . . . the parsonage stands at right angles to the road, facing down upon the Church."

The principal features of Mrs. Gaskell's description of the Parsonage are the heavy flags with which the two-storied stone house is roofed " in order to resist the winds that might strip off a lighter covering," the crowded churchyard, which only seems restrained from overflowing the modest oblong of the Parsonage garden by stone walls, and the carefully tended flower borders beneath the windows, although " only the most hardy plants could be made to grow there."

Nevertheless, it is a mistake to become too much obsessed by the gloomy aspect of Haworth Parsonage. To the Brontë sisters it became a beloved home, and they would surely have resented a description of it as " joyless and girdled with sepulchres " with " the dank air of its empty rooms tempered by no bursts of song," from the pens of biographers who " pressed pitying faces against the bars of their sepulchre."[1] Mrs. Gaskell's picture ends on quite another note :—

" Everything about the place tells of the most dainty order, the most exquisite cleanliness. The door-steps are spotless, the small,

[1] Emilie and Georges Romieu in The Brontë Sisters (Skeffington, 1931).

old-fashioned window-panes glitter like looking-glass. Inside and outside of that house cleanliness grows up into its essence, purity."

This impression has the support of Ellen Nussey, who, in describing the interior of Haworth Parsonage as she was familiar with it twenty-four years before Mrs. Gaskell's book was published, wrote of " the hall and stairs done with sandstone, always beautifully clean, as everything was about the house," of plain walls stained a pleasing dove-colour, hairseated chairs, mahogany tables and a few book-shelves, concluding :—

" Scant and bare indeed, many will say, yet it was not a scantness that made itself felt. Mind and thought, I had almost said elegance, but certainly refinement, diffused themselves over all, and made nothing really wanting."

Although Haworth Parsonage is more closely associated with tragedy than with joy, there were some happy interludes and some exhilarating moments : the dining-room echoed to Martha Taylor's impudent fun, William Weightman's sallies and Ellen Nussey's pleasant banter, and within the walls of this " sepulchre " four proposals of marriage reached Charlotte.

Nevertheless, frail Mrs. Brontë, born and bred in the soft climate of Cornwall, and her six slight, highly-strung, potentially delicate children, were not sufficiently " hardy flowers " to take kindly to their transplantation to Haworth, with its bleak air, questionable drainage and water supply, and frequent visitations of " low fever " : the flesh was bound to suffer, sooner or later, although the spirit of one child, at least, throve and exulted to be " a nursling of the moors."

Haworth was not the birth-place of the Brontës. On leaving Cambridge, Patrick Brontë held successive curacies in Essex, Shropshire and Yorkshire. At Hartshead, near Huddersfield, he met his future wife, Maria Branwell, of Penzance, on a visit to her uncle, Mr. John Fennell, Governor of Woodhouse Grove Wesleyan Academy. Nine of Maria Branwell's letters to her lover remain to paint, in her own words, a shadowy picture of the mother of the Brontës. She wrote with facility, with *niceness* of thought and phrase ; we sense through the letters the unpretentious " elegance " and " refinement " which her daughters—under the direction of her sister—set as their seal upon Haworth Parsonage, and which doubtless had a rare charm for her " dear saucy Pat," the robust and impetuous Irishman, né Brunty. The letters also show deep religious feeling, inherited by her daughter Anne, and an early claim to independence of character. Maria Branwell explains—with modest circumlocution—that her elder sister, and even her mother, " used to consult me in every case of importance, and scarcely ever doubted the propriety of my opinions and actions." This quality of natural leadership was passed on to Charlotte, who was certainly didactic to her friends and wrought herself and her sisters up to all their achievements.

At Hartshead, the two eldest of the Brontë family, Maria and Elizabeth were born, in 1813 and 1815. Before the end of 1815, Mr. Brontë moved to another Yorkshire parish, Thornton, which was the birth-place of Charlotte (April 21st, 1816), Patrick Branwell (June 26th, 1817), Emily Jane (July 30th, 1818), and Anne (January 17th, 1820). During this period Patrick Brontë and his wife both put forth literary efforts : he had already published two books of verse (*Cottage Poems* and *The Rural Minstrel*), and now he produced a prose romance called *The Maid of Killarney*, containing a vivid warning against indulgence in dancing. Mrs. Brontë wrote an article intended for a periodical (but not published) with the title *The Advantage of Poverty in Religious Concerns*. These efforts are not noteworthy in themselves, but they show how natural it was for the Brontë children, who had to devise their own amusements, to take to their pens.

On February 25th, 1820, the move to Haworth was made, seven carts crawling up the steep Main Street, laden with the Brontë's household goods. Here, almost at once, tragedy set in. Fragile Mrs. Brontë had been ailing ever since Anne's birth, and it was soon found that she was suffering from cancer. The material direction of the household fell on the two Yorkshire servants, Nancy and Sarah Garrs, and a Haworth woman was engaged to nurse Mrs. Brontë.

It was Mrs. Brontë's sick-nurse who—in her old age—was the source of various stories which Mrs. Gaskell rashly incorporated in her first edition of Charlotte's biography. According to her picture, while the servants indulged in unchecked waste and extravagance in the kitchen, the six children, ranging in age from eight years to eighteen months, wandered unshepherded on the Moors and returned to dinners of potatoes.   Their father was represented by the nurse as a grim, almost savage figure, who crammed into the fire the little coloured boots she had rummaged out of a cupboard and set to air for the children, cut his wife's one silk gown to shreds, and relieved his fits of rage by firing pistols from the back-door, sawing off chair-backs and stuffing the hearth-rug up the chimney.

It is worth while to sift the evidence as to the truth of these stories, because they have persisted most obstinately, and after being withdrawn by Mrs. Gaskell, have reappeared in more than one twentieth-century book on the Brontës.

Mr. Brontë declared himself bitterly hurt by these assertions and he found it necessary to give Nancy and Sarah Garrs a signed statement certifying that, far from being wasteful and extravagant, they were honest, careful and trusted servants. Nancy Garrs, in her turn, gave testimony as to Mr. Brontë's kindness as a master, and that the dinner always consisted of a joint of beef or mutton, followed by a milk pudding.   Ellen Nussey gives the same account of the dinners when she stayed at the Parsonage, in 1833 ; but the children apparently did not like meat, Mary Taylor records that Charlotte had to be coaxed to eat it at school, and Ellen Nussey found that Emily and Anne preferred to live chiefly on porridge, rice and milk.

The story of Mr. Brontë firing pistols from the back-door apparently arose from the fact that after the Luddite riots he slept with a loaded pistol by his bed, and used to discharge it in the morning.   Nancy Garr's version of his cutting up his wife's silk dress is that it was a *print* gown, with new-fangled sleeves, which Mr. Brontë considered ridiculous.   He cut off the offending sleeves, but made amendment by walking into Keighley the next day to buy a length of silk for her, which was made up with due reference to his taste.   This version is the more probable because Ellen Nussey has recorded that Mr. Brontë's intense dread of fire " caused him to prohibit all but silk or woollen dresses for his daughters ; indeed, for anyone to wear any other kind of fabric was almost to forfeit his respect."   Miss Branwell, his sister-in-law, always wore silk.

These instances are sufficient to show that Mrs. Gaskell's

first edition contained unsubstantiated stories which represented both the household and its master in too lurid a light.
Mr. Brontë was evidently both hot-tempered and eccentric,
but not a maniac. He helped to nurse his wife in her last
illness, and she was able to say, " Ought I not to be thankful
that he never gave me an angry word ? " His children
probably felt that he was not to be approached lightly—he
took his dinner alone in the study and did not sit with them
in the evenings—but Ellen Nussey describes how Miss
Branwell would " tilt arguments against Mr. Brontë without
fear." It was certainly possible for his sister-in-law and his
servants to live comfortably under his roof, and he was
always ready to show old-world courtesy to his daughters'
guests.

After Mrs. Brontë's death (September, 1821), Mr. Brontë
made two attempts to secure a step-mother for his family, but
eventually, Miss Branwell, his wife's elder sister, settled down
to preside over the household. She made a plucky renunciation of Penzance, with its soft air and congenial socialities,
and came with her complement of work-boxes, snuff-box,
unusually large cap and " front " of auburn curls, to immure
herself for the rest of her life in Haworth Parsonage, where
she spent most of her time in her bedroom and protected
herself with pattens when she had to brave the chill of the
stone floors downstairs. Her traditions were of the same
neatness, order and propriety as Mrs. Brontë's ; she taught
her nieces to sew uncommonly well, and to be industrious
and competent in house-work, and she read aloud to Mr.
Brontë and carried on " lively and intelligent discussions "[1]
with him on the subjects of their reading.

At this period the children spent much of their time in the
tiny room upstairs, sandwiched between the two best front
bedrooms, and with no fireplace, which was known as " the
children's study." Here Maria read the newspapers aloud
to her sisters and brother, who early became eager little
politicians. Mr. Brontë, who recognised his family's intellectual precosity, said he would as soon discuss politics with
Maria at the age of eleven as with any grown-up person.
Maria was more of a mother to the little flock than " Aunt " ;
Charlotte, who was only nine when she died, described her

[1] Ellen Nussey.

to her school-friend as " a little mother among the rest, superhuman in goodness and cleverness."

In July, 1824, Mr. Brontë, zealous for the education of his clever children, took Maria and Elizabeth to the newly opened Clergy Daughters' School at Cowan Bridge, the original of the famous Lowood of *Jane Eyre*. For long after the appearance of Mrs. Gaskell's first edition controversy raged over the identification of the school with Lowood, many witnesses sprang to the defence of Mr. Carus Wilson, a founder and moving spirit in the direction of the school, and Mrs. Gaskell was threatened with a law-suit.[1] The case is much the same as that of the stories of Mr. Brontë's violence, but there was probably less exaggeration in the account of conditions at Cowan Bridge in 1824–1825. One of the strongest points in the defence is that the unpalatable food was due to one bad cook, who was soon dismissed, although she appears to have been kept rather longer that she should have been, because she was a trusted dependent of the Carus Wilson family.

Charlotte Brontë's own evidence is unfaltering, but she was only eight years old when she was at Cowan Bridge. In 1849, writing to W. S. Williams (her publisher's reader), in answer to a criticism of the first chapter of *Shirley*, she said : " I feel reluctant to withdraw it, because, as I formerly said of the Lowood part of *Jane Eyre*, *it is true*." This cannot be taken literally, as, for instance, Mr. Carus Wilson had no daughters then of the ages of the Misses Brocklehurst in *Jane Eyre*, and in another letter (also referring to *Shirley*) Charlotte warns Ellen Nussey against taking her characters as literal portraits, adding " it would not suit the rules of art nor of my own feelings to write in that style. We only suffer reality to *suggest*, never to *dictate*." In this latter sense, Mr. Carus Wilson certainly supplied an original for Mr. Brocklehurst, and the books he wrote for children, which were no doubt to be found in many evangelical homes of his day, supply evidence that Charlotte's childhood impression was founded on truth.

One tale, of a child of three whose naughty temper caused

---

[1] Pros and cons can be read in appendices iii and viii to Shorter, Vol. ii, and in *A Vindication of the Clergy Daughters' School and the Rev. W. Carus Wilson from the Remarks in " The Life of Charlotte Brontë*," by Rev. H. Shepheard (Sealey, Jackson & Halliday, 1857).

God to strike her dead, concludes with monosyllabic bluntness, intended for the reading of infants : " Where is she now ? We know that bad girls go to Hell.   She is in a rage with herself now."

Years after the publication of *Jane Eyre*, Mr. Carus Wilson wrote *Thoughts Suggested to the Superintendent and Ladies of the Clergy Daughters' School*, in which he urges that the girls must be " made useful and kept humble," and every symptom of vanity firmly checked at once, and that such embellishments as crochet and worsted work must only be allowed to those who can cut out and make their own garments.

In one figure of these Lowood scenes, Charlotte claims that she did allow reality to dictate.   " You are right in having faith in Helen Burns' character," she wrote to W. S. Williams, " she was real enough.   I exaggerated nothing there.   I refrained from recording much that I remember respecting her, lest the narrative should sound incredible.   I could not but smile at the quiet, self-complacent dogmatism with which one of the journals lays it down that ' such creations as Helen Burns are very beautiful but very untrue.' "

There is a pitiful little bit of corroboration that Helen Burns was drawn from Maria Brontë in the entry under Maria's name in the school register, where one item in her record is " Works badly."   Maria had not had the benefit of Aunt's instruction in needlework long enough to be up to school standard, and suffered accordingly at the hands of " Miss Scatcherd."

Charlotte may, perhaps, have felt a poignant satisfaction that, as Helen Burns, her idolised Maria had her part in the literary fame of the Brontë sisters.

Maria and Elizabeth had been taken to Cowan Bridge when barely convalescent after measles and whooping cough in succession : Charlotte followed them there in August, 1824, and Emily in November.   In February, 1825, Maria was taken home in an advanced stage of consumption, to die on May 6th.   On May 31st, Elizabeth also was sent home, and also died of consumption on June 25th.   The mid-summer holiday was due in June, and in the school register, Charlotte and Emily are recorded as having left school on June 1st.

There followed five and a half years of unbroken home life at Haworth Parsonage.   There were regular lessons in Aunt's bedroom, and for Branwell in his father's study ; but the chief intellectual stimulus came from Mr. Brontë's habit of discussing the political news of the day with his family, and from the eagerness with which both elders and children read and marked the few good periodicals at their command, especially *Blackwood's Magazine*, described by Charlotte, at thirteen, as " the most able periodical there is." The children, largely dependent on their imagination for amusement, developed a world of their own peopled at first with heroes of history. Charlotte for years appropriated the Duke of Wellington in this way, and identified herself with one of his sons, for whom she invented adventures and in whose name she wrote many stories. Later on, a long series of imaginary characters and dynasties was invented. Many of Charlotte's childish manuscripts have survived, in such minute handwriting that a magnifying glass is necessary to read much of it. The stories and miniature magazines are made up into tiny books, and at first it was supposed this was due to shortage of paper, but a more probable reason is that the booklets were intended to be on the scale of the wooden soldiers who represented to the Brontë children the heroes of their dramas, and also the authors of some of the tales.

Charlotte wrote at the time a description of the foundation of one of their imaginary plays :—

" The play of the *Islanders* was formed in December, 1827, in the following manner. One night, about the time when the cold sleet and stormy fogs of November are succeeded by the snow-storms, and high piercing night winds of confirmed winter, we were all sitting round the warm blazing kitchen fire, having just concluded a quarrel with Tabby concerning the propriety of lighting a candle, from which she came off victorious, no candle having been produced. A long pause succeeded which was at last broken by Branwell saying, in a lazy manner, ' I don't know what to do.' This was echoed by Emily and Anne.

Tabby : ' Whe ya may go t'bed.'
Branwell : 'I'd rather do anything than that.'
Charlotte : ' Why are you so glum to-night, Tabþy ? Oh ! suppose we each had an island of our own.' "

Charlotte's suggestion was enough to fire quick imaginations : each child became the owner of the island of its fancy peopled by characters from history and the literary world, as they knew it. The " play " was " established " and endured, and eventually two kingdoms were evolved—that of Angria (capital Verdopolis), located in Africa, the invention and property of Charlotte and Branwell, and the land of the Gondals, shared by Emily and Anne. There is a great mass of juvenile Angrian literature[1], and evidently there must have been a similar output concerning Gondal-land, but the latter has not been preserved, although Emily and Anne were writing Gondal Chronicles as late as 1845. Many of Emily's poems belong to a Gondal cycle, including the beautiful, passionate lament

Cold in the earth and the deep snow piled above thee

which (whatever other interpretations have been put upon it), appears to have been written as the heart-broken meditation of Queen Rosina—fifteen years after the event—on the death of King Julius, a notable figure in the Gondal saga.

The kitchen at Haworth Parsonage was a great feature in the Brontës' childhood, and some of the best vignettes of kitchens and servants to be found in fiction belong to their novels. In *Wuthering Heights* the kitchen in the early chapters has a glow which accentuates the savageness of dogs and master, while Nelly Dean is a solid, wholesome presence flitting in and out of the maelstrom of emotions. In *Jane Eyre* the relief is intense when, after her blind flight from the forbidden wedding, the exhausted, famished Jane has struggled across the moor to the beam of light thrown by a candle in the Rivers' kitchen, and peeps into that bright and cosy interior, with its presiding genius—sanity and safety personified—an elderly woman, rough but clean, knitting a stocking. *Shirley* has a charming little kitchen idyll in which Caroline Helstone undertakes to cut out a dress for the maid on the kitchen table, with one ear on the stormy bluster outside to catch the footsteps of the home-coming Robert Moore.

Nevertheless the Brontës knew better than to sentimentalise in their portraits of servants ; the calm and sometimes crusty common-sense of the elderly ones, so welcome at some junctures, was an aggravating phlegm and stolidity at others.

---

[1] For Charlotte's *Juvenilea* see Shorter, Appendix V, Vol. ii, and *The Brontës ; their Lives, Friendships and Correspondence* by Wise and Symington. Also *Legends of Angria*, compiled by Fannie Ratchford (Milford, 1933).

The limitation of imagination in Nelly Dean and Bessie[1]
are so well brought out that we feel the Brontë children knew
by experience the checks which such a limitation can impose
on sensitive, eager young spirits under its control.   Their
own servants stood for much in their lives, especially Tabby
(Tabitha Ackroyd) who came to them about the year 1825,
and died, a very old woman, at the Parsonage, in 1855, just
before Charlotte's death.

This intensively imaginative life was broken for Charlotte
in 1831, when, at the age of nearly fifteen, she was sent to
Miss Wooler's school at Roe Head, where, despite home-
sickness at first, she showed an eager hunger for knowledge,
a gift for telling dramatic stories, and a further gift for making
friends.   She never lost touch with Miss Wooler, and she also
made at Roe Head two life-long friends, whose personalities
are henceforth an indispensable part of her background.   The
best beloved and most intimate was Ellen Nussey (from
whom she drew Caroline Helstone), whose correspondence
with Charlotte is the principal source of our detailed knowledge
of the Brontës' lives.   Ellen was with her when Anne died,
and at her wedding, and received from her a last pencilled
note written just before her death.   Charlotte herself sketched
Ellen's portrait in terms which show she was not really the
naturally congenial spirit one would have expected Charlotte
to cherish in friendship.   Writing to W. S. Williams in 1849,
she said :—

" My friend Ellen is with us.   I find her presence a solace.   She
is a calm, steady girl—not brilliant, but good and true.   She suits
and always has suited me well.   I like her, with her phlegm, repose,
sense and sincerity, better than I should like the most talented
without these qualifications."

In another letter Charlotte complains that Ellen is without
romance, and that she cannot bear to hear her read poetry
or poetic prose.   Not for years, however, until in fact, fame
had brought clever and original men and women within her
circle, did Charlotte realise to this extent Ellen's inadequacy in
romantic and intellectual response.   After Roe Head there
was a period of passionate adolescent friendship, in which
Ellen's religious bias at one time helped to make havoc of

[1] See Rebecca West's essay on Charlotte Brontë in *Great Victorians*
(Nicholson and Watson, 1932).

Charlotte's peace of mind. Mrs. Gaskell suppresses the warmest expression in Charlotte's early letters to her friend. In later life, Ellen, with her unfailing love and loyalty, was a presence of comfort and peace in Charlotte's life for which every reader of the Brontë letters is grateful.

Mary Taylor, Charlotte's other school-friend, was of a different calibre, and more nearly Charlotte's intellectual equal. She was quick enough to note Charlotte's inspired use of an unusual word when, amongst a group of school-girls discussing great writers, she said : " Sheridan might be clever ; yes, Sheridan was clever—scamps often are—but Johnson hadn't a spark of *cleverality* in him."

Charlotte drew portraits of Mary Taylor and her sister Martha as Rose and Jessy Yorke in *Shirley*, and of the rest of the family. Mary's comment was " you make us all talk as I think we should have done if we'd ventured to speak at all."

In the volumes of Brontë correspondence, a letter from Mary Taylor is always refreshing in its gallant outlook and trenchant style.[1] She went out to New Zealand in 1845, hoping to establish an independence for herself with some initial help from her brothers. She wrote characteristically of the venture to Ellen Nussey : " There are no means for a woman to live in England but by teaching, sewing or washing. The last is the best. The best paid, the least unhealthy and the most free."

Charlotte left Roe Head in July, 1832, and supplemented Aunt's efforts in the education of her sisters. There is a charming picture of the family in 1833 from the pen of Ellen Nussey,[2] who paid her first visit to Haworth Parsonage in that year. The chief impressions are of a tall, lithe Emily, aged 15, with beautiful eyes (" kind, kindling, liquid eyes "), but a poor complexion, silent, boyish—qualifying already for the nickname of " the Major "—and of her inseparable companion Anne (" dear, gentle Anne "), Aunt's favourite, with her pretty brown curls, violet eyes and transparent complexion. Branwell is represented as the bright, particular star in the family's eyes, already painting in the intervals of

---

[1] See also her description of Charlotte's arrival at Roe Head : Shorter, Vol. I.

[2] Shorter, Vol. I.

his classical studies with his father, and expected to distinguish himself. · Ellen gives a vivid picture of walks on the moors, when " every moss, every flower, every tint and form were noticed and enjoyed," and Emily's " reserve " vanished for the time, as she helped Branwell to set stepping-stones for the others and played Providence to the tadpoles in the pools.

Some commentators on Emily's work have adopted the theory that she suffered from a brooding sense of injustice or frustration because there seemed to be no fitting rôle for her in the family : Branwell was its acclaimed genius, Charlotte its leading spirit, Anne, Aunt's favourite. It is suggested that she found compensation in the dream-drama of an outcast or doomed child, which haunts the Gondal poems and finds its final form in Heathcliff. An elaborate, psychological theory has been built up round the bare facts and the few suppositions for which there is any ground in the meagre accounts of Emily's youth.[1] Ellen Nussey's picture does not favour this view, but Emily was certainly capable of leading one life of the body and quite another of the spirit.

This oasis between school-days and responsibility could not last long. Charlotte, the leader, was always forward-looking, and she soon arrived at the same conclusion as Mary Taylor— " there are no means for a woman to live in England but by teaching, sewing and washing." Mr. Brontë's health was not considered very stable, and if they lost their home at the Parsonage, the girls would have nothing to depend on. So, in 1835, Charlotte returned to Roe Head as a teacher, taking Emily with her to complete her education.

Emily soon drooped and pined away from home and the moors, as she always did : probably home life with its domestic routine, and the dear, familiar way of escape up

A little and a lone green lane, that opened on a common wide

already represented for her " the activity in the midst of which she had learned how to feed upon the spirit within her."[2] The experiment proved too drastic and Emily was allowed to return home after three months, the more pliable Anne taking her place at Roe Head.

[1] See *All Alone*, by Romer Wilson (Chatto & Windus, 1928).
[2] *Emily Brontë*, by Charles Morgan in *Great Victorians*.

Charlotte's health was also sorely tried by the long hours
and unremitting routine of a school-teacher's life, although
Miss Wooler allowed her respites of leisure and recreation in
excess of the usual teacher's portion at that period.   She
moved with the school to Dewsbury Moor, but left finally in
1838, a short time after securing Anne's removal on account
of a long-continued cough.   Emily, meanwhile, had made a
brave attempt at teaching and spent six months in a school at
Law Hill, near Halifax, where, according to Charlotte's report
to Ellen, her duties began at 6 a.m. and were not over and
done with until 11 p.m.   It is not to be wondered at that
six months saw Emily at the limit of her endurance.   Charlotte
seems to have overlooked this episode in writing later of
Emily's life.

Practically nothing is known of what Law Hill added to
Emily's experience of life, but some interesting parallels have
been drawn between landscapes and country houses round
Halifax and details of description in *Wuthering Heights*.[1]

The years 1836-1842 cannot contribute much to a short
study of the major events and influences in the Brontë's
lives, but there are some vivid glimpses of this period in Mrs.
Gaskell's biography : for instance, of the evening's liberty
when sewing was folded away at 9 p.m. and Aunt went to
bed, while the girls blew out the candles, for economy's sake,
and paced the room backwards and forwards in happy or
anxious talk—" their figures glancing into the fire-light, and
out into the shadow, perpetually." (In later days they
discussed the plots of their novels so.)   There was Charlotte's
venturesome letter to the Poet Laureate, Southey, pleading
for a verdict on some poems, and his kindly-meant reply,
in which he allows that it is good to " write poetry for its
own sake," but warns her that " literature cannot be the
business of a woman's life, and it ought not to be."   Branwell,
too, wrote in a similar strain to Wordsworth.   To these years,
also, belong two of Charlotte's proposals of marriage—the
first from Ellen's brother, the Reverend Henry Nussey, who
required a wife to look after his pupils—and the gay badinage
of a new curate, William Weightman, who sent the sisters
their first valentines, walking ten miles to post them.
Charlotte had a momentary temptation to accept Henry

[1] See *Emily Brontë* by Charles Simpson (Country Life Ltd., 1929).

Nussey in order, as she frankly expressed it to Ellen, that "his sister could live with me!" However, she chose the wiser part. Henry, she said, knew so little of her that he could scarcely be conscious to whom he was writing : if she married she must be free to laugh and satirise and say whatever came into her head, and " if he were a clever man, and loved me, the whole world weighed in the balance against his smallest wish should be light as air. Could I, knowing my mind to be such as that, conscientiously say that I would take a grave, quiet, young man like Henry?" Nevertheless, it was pleasant to correspond with him for a time in the tone of a wise aunt (she herself writes " you will see my letters are all didactic ") and finally to sanction his forthcoming marriage in these terms : " from what you say of your future partner I doubt not she will be one who will help you to get cheerfully through the difficulties of this world and to obtain a permanent rest in the next."

Charlotte's second suitor was as impetuous and precipitate as Henry Nussey was cool and deliberate. He was also a clergyman, a curate who came with his vicar to spend a day at Haworth, found Charlotte in her best vein (she explained to Ellen, " at home, you know, I talk with ease, and am never shy "), and a few days later proposed by letter !

This must have been a period of good health and high spirits, the latter certainly enlivened by William Weightman, a pleasant rattle, whom the girls called Celia Amelia, on account of his pretty complexion : he was also clever, or Charlotte, at least, would have had no patience with him. Her letters sparkle with fun centred round him and his innocently wandering affections : he is accused at one time of endangering Ellen's peace of mind, and Emily—" the Major " on this occasion—chaperoned them on a walk. At another time, it was reported that he sat sighing and gazing at Anne in Church. Mrs. Gaskell omits much of this banter, and suppresses the nickname.

It was their first contact with an attractive young man who was their intellectual match, and it has been argued that they could scarcely have come out of the ordeal unscathed. It is reported that he was the only one of her father's curates whom Emily tolerated, and on this foundation—and argument from probability—a theory has been put forward that Emily in reality lost her heart to William Weightman, and knew all the bitterness of loss, when he died in 1842, during her absence in Brussels.[1] One argument for this theory is that she could not have written her more passionate and poignant poems, or certain passages of *Wuthering Heights*, unless she had had personal experience of love and loss. The poem *Remembrance* is said to have been written of William Weightman, with the " fifteen wild Decembers " as camouflage, prompted by Emily's reserve. There is no proof whatever, and the testimony of those writers who themselves know something of the mystic's nature (such as M. Maeterlinck and Charles Morgan) is that actual, personal experience is not essential to the apprehension of the heights and depths of emotion.

To this period also belong various experiments in teaching. Anne, in fact, settled down into the rut, spending eight months of 1839 as governess with the Ingham family of Blake Hall and then four years with the Robinsons at Thorp Green. She had to surmount her excessive shyness, on account of which even the partial Charlotte feared that " Mrs. Ingham will sometimes conclude that she has a natural impediment of speech " ; and in 1841 Charlotte wrote, " I have one aching feeling at my heart . . . It is about Anne . . . when my thoughts turn to her, they always see her as a patient, persecuted stranger." Anne has incorporated much of her own experience as a governess in *Agnes Grey :* she was certainly not naturally fitted for the part, but she was valued in the Robinson family, and her pupils visited her at Haworth shortly before her death.

Charlotte's experience was more episodic. In 1839 she spent three months as governess to the children of Mr. and Mrs. John Sidgwick at Stonegappe, near Shipton, a sojourn which gave rise to incidents since widely quoted as evidence of the trials of the early Victorian governess. It appears that when one of the children exclaimed at table, " I love 'ou, Miss Brontë ! " Mrs. Sidgwick reproved him with " Love the *governess*, my dear ! " that Charlotte's pleasantest afternoon there was when she had orders to follow a little way behind, in case her services should be needed, while Mr. Sidgwick took his children for a walk : that Mrs.

[1] See *Haworth Parsonage* by Isabel Clarke (Hutchinson, 1927).

H

Sidgwick, finding that her ineffectual and morbidly shy
governess had at least one talent, overwhelmed her with
sewing. On behalf of the Sidgwicks it is recorded that if
they asked her to walk to Church with them she thought she
was being treated as a slave, but if they did not she felt
aggrieved at being excluded from the family circle.

Charlotte stands self-confessed as " having no knack for
my vocation," and two sentences from her letters bear this
out. The first is " I find it so hard to repel the rude familiarity
of children " ; the second, referring to Mr. Sidgwick's
remarks to her, " he never asks me to wipe the children's
smutty noses or tie their shoes or fetch their pinafores or
set them a chair." Nevertheless, the children in her novels
(especially little Polly and the baby Georgette in *Villette*),
and, in real life, the mutual attraction between her and Mrs.
Gaskell's youngest child, Julia, make Swinburne's statement
that she " had not the little golden key which unlocks the
heart of childhood " seem extreme. The *constant* care of
children is always burdensome to women with an intellectual
bias, who are conscious of the need which Charles Lamb
expressed as a yearning for " an hour for my head to work
quietly its own workings." It is those who depend on stimuli
outside themselves for their mental life and the direction
of their activities who can happily spend the whole day in
what, to them, is the cheerful busy-ness of a nursery or schoolroom, with the children's continual calls on their attention
and authority.

Charlotte Brontë approached children as she did adults,
appraising them as individuals, in whom she must see something to respect before she could love, rather than as a class,
on a different plane from her own. Thus her affection for
" that dear but dangerous little person," Julia Gaskell, was
founded on respect for her character—" I think hers a fine
little nature, frank and of genuine promise . . . I believe
in Julia's future ; I like what speaks in her movements,
and what is written on her face." Such an individual
approach led Charlotte to feel that children might have
reserves of their own, and to be shy even with those she liked
most.

Charlotte's second experience as a governess was with
Mr. and Mrs. White of Upperwood House, Rawdon, where

she was not happy, but admitted that " my place is a favourable one, for a governess." She makes a characteristic and original complaint of " the estrangement from one's real character," necessitated by living as a dependent in other people's houses.[1]

The disadvantages of being governesses led the sisters to form a bolder project, that of starting a school of their own, less on account of the attraction of school-keeping than because it would mean maintaining themselves together and at home. Charlotte, as usual the leading spirit, realised that their educational equipment was poor, and that the chance of success would be greater if they could offer expert teaching in languages. Aunt was approached, and generously agreed to advance money out of her own small capital to enable two of the girls to study abroad. So it came about that, in February, 1842, Charlotte and Emily took up their residence in the Pensionnat Heger at Brussels, partly influenced by the fact that Mary and Martha Taylor were at a similar (but more expensive) establishment there.

It would be waste of time to describe the Pensionnat Heger,[2] so vividly pictured in all essentials in *Villette*. M. Heger, the original (in Charlotte's sense of allowing reality to suggest but not to dictate) of M. Paul Emanuel, became one of the strongest and most disturbing influences in Charlotte Brontë's life. At first his temperamental vagaries only roused her amusement, possibly a touch of contempt, when, for instance, she first described him to Ellen :—

" He is professor of rhetoric, a man of power as to mind, but very choleric and irritable in temperament ; a little, black being, with a face which varies in expression. Sometimes he borrows the lineaments of an insane tom-cat, sometimes those of a delirious hyena ; occasionally, but very seldom, he discards these perilous attractions and assumes an air not above 100 degrees removed from mild and gentlemanlike."

" A man of power as to mind . . ." Here was his potential attraction for Charlotte : to work—to write—for a judicious and vigorous critic with a fine sense of style, this was a new

[1] For Charlotte's views on governessing see also Mrs. Pryor's talk in *Shirley*.
[2] The Heger family have dropped the accent which used to be placed on the first e. The modern usage is more correct.

and heady joy.   Mrs. Gaskell gives an example of the literary
advice which Charlotte so earnestly imbibed from him :
" When you are writing, place your argument first in cool,
prosaic language ; but when you have thrown the reins on
the neck of your imagination, do not pull her up to reason."
We cannot judge now much Charlotte owed to him in literary
progress, but the schooling was evidently most exhilarating.

M. Heger showed his quality in his discernment of Emily's
peculiar strength : his testimony is one of the most convincing
corroborations that Charlotte did not exaggerate in claiming
that her sister was in nature " stronger than a man and
simpler than a child." M. Heger, impressed by Emily's
forceful, intrepid, original mind, declared, " She should have
been a man—a great navigator. Her powerful reason would
have deduced new spheres of discovery from the knowledge of
the old ; and her strong, imperious will would never have
been daunted by opposition or difficulty ; never have given
way, but with life."

Nevertheless Emily and M. Heger, on the whole, " did not
draw well together." Emily was at her most *farouche* in
Brussels, proudly unabashed in her unbecoming, old-fashioned
clothes, so silent and unapproachable when the sisters visited
English friends that invitations ceased. She may have found
some solace in music, as her playing was considerably above
the average, and before she left Brussels she was earning
part of her fees by giving music lessons to the younger pupils.

The girls were recalled home by Aunt's illness in October
1842, too late to see her again alive. Very shortly after their
return a letter arrived from M. Heger, urging with what he
himself described as an *affection presque paternelle* that at
least one of them should go back as a student-teacher. The
terms offered meant a further opportunity to acquire languages
at practically no cost, and Charlotte decided to take it and
devote herself to the study of German. It is not possible
to know how far M. Heger was the magnet which drew her
back, but, since the publication in 1913 of four letters from
her to her " Master," the long controversy between her
biographers and apologists—as to whether she eventually had
for him a more passionate feeling than intellectual discipleship
—is decided, in the affirmative.

Charlotte suffered bitterly during her second sojourn in

Brussels, especially in the long summer vacation, which she spent almost alone in the Pensionnat, and when she was driven, like Lucy Snowe in *Villette*, to seek a transient relief by making a confession in a Roman Catholic Church.   At first she gave English lessons to M. Heger and his brother-in-law, but these came to an end ; Madame Heger grew cold and distant, and Monsieur's kindly interest in her studies was fitful.   If she had mingled more freely in the life of the school he might, perhaps, have been kinder to her without particularity, but the school, as she saw it, has been aptly described as " the Belgian hubbub in which Charlotte took no interest—indeed it desolated her."[1]   When she proposed to leave in October, 1843, M. Heger protested warmly, but by the following New Year's Day she could no longer bear to stay and wrenched herself away.

No biographer or commentator has ever suggested that either Charlotte or M. Heger harboured a thought or a fear of any guilty relation : there would be no excuse for any aspersion of the kind.   What Charlotte visualised as a possibility was a bond of intellectual sympathy, which, in her eyes, would not trench on Madame Heger's influence in any way. This side of emotion—the affinity of mind and spirit—is the one that is always stressed in the Brontë novels : even Heathcliff and Catherine, who stand for untamed intensity of feeling, are more concerned with the fact that, as she expressed it, " whatever our souls are made of, his and mine are the same," than with erotic desire.   Charlotte Brontë, already inured to curbing her aspirations within the limits of a meagre possibility, believed that she was capable of sustaining an intellectual—but yet heart-warming—friendship on " the crumbs that fall from the rich man's table," for which she pleads in one of her letters to M. Heger.

She tried to keep her secret, but some pitiful *cris de coeur* escaped her when she grew heart-sick with hope deferred, watching for the arrival of the post day by day in vain. Schooling herself, as ever, in a personal philosophy which would not allow her hopes to outrun a low estimate of possibility, she wrote :—

" I do not need much affection from those I love.   I should not know what to do with a friendship entire and complete—I am not

[1] See *The Brontës* by Irene Cooper Willis (Duckworth, 1933).

used to it. But you showed me of yore a *little* interest, when I was your pupil in Brussels, and I hold on to the maintenance of that *little* interest—I hold on to it as I would hold on to life."

Some Brontë commentators think this was the supreme experience of Charlotte's life, without which she could not have drawn Jane Eyre or Lucy Snowe : others feel that far too much had been made of it, especially since the dramatic and belated publication of the four Brontë-Heger letters in 1913. In regard to the latter view, it seems too casual to dismiss Charlotte's emotion, which cost her (on her own admission) the " total withdrawal for more than two years of happiness and peace of mind," as " a case of super-heated *schwärmerei*, the inflammation of which might have been reduced easily enough by a few kindly and humorous replies."[1] There is no doubt that Charlotte knew the bitter suffering that is comprehended in unfulfilled and unrequited love, although her principles would not allow her to recognise it as such ; how far it enriched her mind is an open question.

Mrs. Gaskell has been blamed, since 1913, for suppressing such an important clue to Charlotte's sources of experiences as her letters to her " Master." The four letters which M. Heger's son handed to Mr. Spielmann in 1913, and afterwards presented to the British Museum, were said to have been thrown away by M. Heger—on one he had noted the address of a boot-maker—and taken up and preserved by Madame.[2] Twenty-one years later her daughter, Mdlle. Louise Heger (the original of Georgette Beck !), attended a public lecture on Charlotte Brontë and was shocked to hear severe aspersions of unkindness made upon her parents. Her mother then showed her Charlotte's letters, which she, in her turn, rescued from M. Heger's destroying hand on Madame's death. Mrs. Gaskell actually quotes phrases from three of them. She had been to Brussels and had a personal interview with M. Heger, but Madame had refused to see her. Doubts have been expressed as to whether she saw the originals of the letters or was furnished with the extracts by the Hegers, but a passage in a letter which she wrote to her friend Mrs. Shaen in Septem-

---

ber, 1856,[1] obviously implies that she had seen them. She
wrote just after Sir James Kay Shuttleworth had persuaded
Mr. Nicholls to allow him and Mrs. Gaskell to see the manuscript of *The Professor*, which he hoped would be published.
Mrs. Gaskell awaited the manuscript with some anxiety :—

> "I dreaded lest *The Professor* should involve anything with
> M. Heger—I had heard her say that it related to her Brussels life,
> and I thought if he were again brought before the public what
> would he think of me ? I believed him too good to publish those
> letters, but I felt that his friends might really with some justice
> urge him to do so."

Mrs. Gaskell was in a very different position from that of
the modern biographer. It was not then universally accepted
that the first duty of a biographer is to present the naked truth
about his subject ; facts were often modified for the sake of
edification, of loyalty in friendship or convention. Moreover,
Charlotte's husband was still living, and was extremely
sensitive to the publicity about his wife, which had always
been distasteful to him. He had certainly suffered enough for
his brief spell of happiness in marriage. The Brontë-Heger
letters would have shocked the susceptibilities of the period,
when a woman was scarcely supposed to allow herself any
warmth of expression to a man until he had proposed marriage,
and a correspondence with a married man was very
reprehensible.

When Charlotte returned from her second year in Brussels
life seemed a maimed and broken thing. She could have no
inkling that fame and death were soon to fold brooding wings
over Haworth Parsonage, making it holy ground to generations
of pilgrims. Meanwhile there was sufficient trouble ; her
father's eye-sight was failing, he had to be strengthened
against a temptation to drink ; the idea of opening a school
in a more favourable place had to be given up, and an attempt
to secure some pupils at Haworth failed. Charlotte wrote
desperately to Ellen :—

> "I can hardly tell you how time gets on at Haworth. There is
> no event to mark its progress. One day resembles another ; and
> all have heavy, lifeless, physiognomies. . . . I shall soon be thirty,
> and I have done nothing."

[1] See *Mrs. Gaskell and her Friends* by Elizabeth Haldane (Hodder
and Stoughton, 1930).

A worse state than stagnation was to come.   In the summer
of 1845, Branwell was dismissed from his tutorship in the
family of the Reverend Edmund Robinson of Thorp Green
(where Anne was governess) and returned, embittered and
reckless, to become an addict of drink and opium, and to waste
out his life for three more wretched years, which took a
heavy toll of his sisters' peace and vitality.   The darling
pride of his family from childhood, he had basked in their
bright dreams of his future without being stimulated thereby
to effort and application.   He had early learned to mitigate
the quiet life of the Parsonage, where only imagination could
be active and virile, by long visits to the Black Bull, where the
landlord showed off the brilliant, lively boy for the entertainment of his guests.   Patrick Brontë, the father, was, after all,
lacking in experience of the world ; when he had taught his son
the classics he had little idea what more to do for him, or—
still more important—how to do it.   Branwell was given his
opportunity to go to London, where he failed to establish
himself at the Royal Academy School, and later a studio was
taken for him in Bradford and art lessons paid for.   After the
failure of these two efforts the family seems to have been
baffled, and the best he could do was to secure a post as railway
clerk at a lonely station where the staff consisted of himself
and one porter.   He was dismissed for absenting himself
and allowing the porter the opportunity of stealing the Company's money.   The only remaining resource was to become a
tutor, and finally he was engaged at Thorp Green, disastrously
for himself, and poor sensitive Anne.   He fell in love with
Mrs. Robinson, the wife of his invalid employer, and sixteen
years older than himself.   He claimed that she returned his
passion, and declared that he was only living until the death
of her husband should set her free to marry him.   Mr.
Robinson died, but there was no prospect of the marriage.
Branwell told his family that a clause in her husband's will
expressly forbade Mrs. Robinson to marry him on pain of
losing her life interest in his fortune.   Actually, there is no
mention of Branwell Brontë in Mr. Robinson's will, and Mrs.
Gaskell's original version of the story, implying guilt on
Mrs. Robinson's part, was hotly contested by her relations,
who seemed to have a good case for a libel action.   Finally
Mrs. Gaskell's book had to be withdrawn for alteration, and

a public recantation made by her in the *Times*. It is, therefore, probable that Branwell's was a case of erotic delusion
such as are not uncommon in opium addicts.   His vehement,
clamorous despair and abandonment to the consolations of
drink and drugs, when he could not be prevented from getting
them, made further havoc with his constitution, and he was
soon in no state to seek the one obvious remedy—work in a
new scene.

The next three years were a nightmare in Haworth Parsonage, when the girls never knew what they might awake to after
the frequent nights of struggle and raving which Branwell
spent in his ageing father's bedroom.   Charlotte, who had
herself wrestled with and crushed down a hopeless longing for
M. Heger's friendship, was probably the least sympathetic of
the sisters ; the sight of her brother's degradation killed first
her love and then her pity.   Emily did not shrink from doing
all she could for him : how deeply the tragedy branded Anne's
gentle nature may be gauged from *The Tenant of Wildfell Hall*,
which she wrote as an attempt at expiation by warning—a
book which must have cost her an agony.

It has been suggested that Charlotte's incapacity to pity
Branwell hurt Emily deeply and led to a cold reserve on her
part towards her sister : the days when Charlotte could
write to Emily as " Mine own bonnie Love " were gone for
ever.   Certainly these two do not seem to have been so close to
one another during the last few years of Emily's life ; it was
Emily and Anne who were inseparables.

In the midst of this ordeal the indomitable Charlotte
launched the sisters' first literary venture.   Opening Emily's
desk one day she found some poems, of which the force and
originality impressed her deeply.   Emily resented this rifling
of her secret manuscripts ; probably her poems embodied the
dearest and the most dread experiences of her mystic, inner
life.   It took, as Charlotte relates, " hours to reconcile her to
the discovery."   However, she was at last reconciled : Anne
then produced poems of her own, chiefly plaintive religious
musings, and Charlotte confessed that she also was a poet.   The
girls had now each a small capital from Aunt, and they were
able to pay the expenses of publishing a little volume of *Poems
by Currer, Ellis and Acton Bell*.[1]   Exactly two copies were sold.

[1]Aylott & Jones, 1846.

Still undaunted, probably seeking relief from the tragedy within their walls, each of the sisters began a novel. Charlotte's —*The Professor*, a foreshadowing of *Villette*—was destined not to be published until after her death, but Emily and Anne succeeded in placing their joint venture—*Wuthering Heights and Agnes Grey*, incongruously yoked together—with a publisher named Newby. Publication was delayed, and meanwhile Charlotte completed *Jane Eyre*. She had taken her father to Manchester to undergo an operation for cataract (fortunately successful), and on the very day of the operation *The Professor* was returned from one publisher and sent off to another, and in these Manchester rooms *Jane Eyre* was begun.

Jane Eyre was despatched to Messrs. Smith and Elder, who had returned *The Professor* with some helpful advice and an encouraging intimation that a longer book, of more varied interest, might be acceptable. *Jane Eyre* proved so, and was published in October, 1847, and *Wuthering Heights and Agnes Grey* followed it into the world in December.

The success of *Jane Eyre* was immediate, and Charlotte had the sympathy of her sisters in her first triumph. Mr. Brontë, presented with the accomplished fact in print, emerged from his study at tea-time to announce to his younger daughters. " Girls, do you know Charlotte has been writing a book, and it is much better than likely ? "

Wuthering Heights, eventually acclaimed as the greatest and most original of the Brontë novels, was too crudely forcible, and too unconventional, for the taste of the day. Compared with *Jane Eyre* it was a failure, and in place of the glow of fame Emily had to savour, as gaily as she could, such comments as those Charlotte read out to her in her last illness, stigmatising Ellis Bell as a " man of uncommon talents, but dogged, brutal and morose."[1]

Trouble arose through Newby's unscrupulous attempt to draw the mantle of Currer Bell's fame over the productions of Ellis and Acton, especially on the eve of the publication of *The Tenant of Wildfell Hall*, and Charlotte and Anne actually went to London and presented themselves before the astonished and almost incredulous eyes of the partners of Smith and Elder to prove that they really were two and not

[1] For the theory that Branwell wrote all or part of *Wuthering Heights*, see page 149.

one. Mr. George Smith and his mother did their best to do
them honour, and insisted on taking them to the Opera in the
day dresses which were their best wear in the chill and
unmodish Haworth.

In September, 1848, came Branwell's death—according to
tradition he insisted upon standing up to die. From that day
Emily's health declined rapidly ; it is said that she took cold
at her brother's funeral.

Charlotte's letters now become heartrending reading. Her
regular correspondents had been increased by W. S. Williams,
Smith and Elder's reader, whose intellectual and personal
sympathy never failed her, and drew forth her great qualities
as a letter-writer more completely than Ellen Nussey
could.

The tragic story of Emily's death has been told many times.
Always indomitable—as when she went away by herself and
seared her arm with a hot iron after a bite from a dog she
believed to be mad—she now refused all concessions to her
fast failing body, in the grip of rapid consumption. She
refused to see a doctor. Again and again her sisters listened
in agony to her slow progress up the stone staircase, pausing
to cough and to draw her painful breath. On the very day of
her death she dressed herself and came downstairs, although
she could give no sign that she recognised the sprig of heather
which Charlotte had so anxiously sought for her on the wintry
moors. She died on December 19th, 1848, in the dining-
room where the sisters had spent so large a part of their lives
and written their books.

Scarcely was Emily buried, followed, amongst the mourners,
by her great dog Keeper, which only she had dared to control
and punish, when Charlotte was writing : " When we lost
Emily I thought we had drained the very dregs of our cup of
trial, but now when I hear Anne cough as Emily coughed,
I tremble lest there should be exquisite bitterness yet to
taste." That bitterness came. Anne's death was gentler,
she was upheld by her faith that " soon all will be well, by
the merits of our Redeemer," and her release came more
easily. She died on May 28th, 1849, at Scarborough, where
Charlotte had taken her, at her own desire, in a last desperate
attempt to re-establish her health. Ellen Nussey was with
them, and she received Anne's dying charge—" Be a sister in

my stead. Give Charlotte as much of your company as you can "—a charge which she fulfilled faithfully.

Gentleness seems to have been Anne Brontë's predominant quality, but it was not the gentleness of weakness ; there was a tough fibre of courage and sense of duty running through her quiet, clinging, melancholy nature.

After Anne had been buried at Scarborough, Charlotte stayed on there a little while with Ellen, preparing herself for the return to Haworth, which she insisted upon making alone. Her courage in rallying her forces to face her lonely life was the finest effort of an heroic spirit. She wrote to Ellen :—

" I got here a little before eight o'clock. All was clean and bright, waiting for me. Papa and the servants were well ; and all received me with an affection which should have consoled. The dogs seemed in a strange ecstasy. I am certain they regarded me as the harbinger of others . . . I left Papa soon, and went into the dining-room : I shut the door—I tried to be glad I was come home I have always been glad before—except once—" (that is, after the second return from Brussels)—" and then I was cheered . . . . But this time joy was not to be the sensation . . . The agony that *was to be undergone*, and *was not* to be avoided, came on . . . . To-day I am better."

A few days later she wrote :—

" My life is what I expected it to be . . . Sometimes, Nell, I have a heavy heart of it. But crushed, I am not yet ; nor robbed of elasticity, nor of hope, nor quite of endeavour. I have some strength to fight the battle of life. I am aware, and can acknowledge, I have many comforts, many mercies. Still I can *get on*."

Not quite robbed of endeavour, indeed, Charlotte turned to her half-finished novel *Shirley*, which was published in October, 1849.

The story of Charlotte's few years of fame is haunted by the memory of the sisters who could not share it—happiness unshared, she wrote, " has no taste." Nervousness and poor health made every excursion into the greater world an anxious ordeal : but yet this " tiny, delicate, anxious little lady, pale, with fair hair and steady eyes," dressed in " a little barège dress with a pattern of faint green moss," entering " in mittens, in silence, in seriousness,"[1] to a distinguished company whose hearts were " beating with wild excitement " on

[1] Description by Lady Ritchie, Thackeray's daughter.

seeing the authoress of *Jane Eyre*, enjoyed giving Thackeray a piece of her mind about his dealings with his characters, and corresponded briskly (and not seldom brusquely) with other notable authors and literary critics.

Messrs. Smith and Elder delighted in their proprietorship of the demure, nervous little literary lion whom fortune had sent them, and boxes of new books, carefully selected by members of the firm, brought frequent breaths of cultured London to Haworth Parsonage. Charlotte paid visits to the house of Mr. George Smith (who " suggested " Dr. John of *Villette*), presided over by his mother, and under their kindly wing met many celebrities and saw the Great Exhibition of 1851, and other " sights," congenial and uncongenial. When she attended one of Thackeray's popular lectures the audience formed an aisle down which she had to pass, trembling, out of the hall, and at the door Thackeray himself was waiting for her with a naïve query as to her opinion of his performance (an incident transferred to Paul Emanuel in *Villette*).

Charlotte stayed also with Harriet Martineau at Ambleside, with Sir James and Lady Kay-Shuttleworth, and with Mrs. Gaskell in Manchester ; but still Haworth was the scene of her daily life and of at least three-quarters of her year, and at Haworth there soon came to her a third opportunity to change her state, in an offer of marriage from a member of Smith and Elder's firm, Mr. James Taylor. He had a position in life, Mr. Brontë favoured him, he was clever. Charlotte herself, described him to Ellen as " horribly intelligent, quick, searching, sagacious, and with a memory of relentless tenacity. To turn to Williams after him, or to Smith himself, is to turn from granite to easy down or warm fur." In spite of her own liking for a flavour of acerbity, this was too much for her—his determined nose, she said, cut into her soul like iron. So Mr. Taylor said good-bye to her at Haworth and pursued the firm's business to Bombay.

In 1852 *Villette* was published and established Charlotte's reputation more firmly still, although in conventional quarters there clung about her name a suggestion of unfeminine warmth and openness, and a lack of religious motive, in the treatment of love and life. The *Quarterly Review* went so far as to say that the authoress of *Jane Eyre* must have been " a woman who had long forfeited the society of her sex," and one

authoress shocked her by exclaiming, "You and I, Miss
Brontë, have both written naughty books!" The Bishop
of Ripon, having to stay at Haworth Parsonage for a confirmation, was not a little nervous, and afterwards recorded grate-
fully that he found Miss Brontë quite a "gentle and un-
assuming hostess," and was favourably impressed by "the
perfect propriety and consistency of the arrangements of the
modest household."[1] Domestic duties, indeed, still claimed
much of Charlotte's attention. She had an invaluable and
trusted servant in Martha Brown, but Tabby was growing
feeble, and Charlotte used surreptitiously to complete the
potato peeling which the half-blind old woman thought she
had done satisfactorily.

Charlotte's fame did not bring riches, although the income
from her books was a substantial help. In 1851 when she
went to Leeds to do some preparatory shopping for a visit
to London, then in *gala* trim for the Great Exhibition, she
reluctantly turned away from some "beautiful silks in sweet,
pale colours" because she dare not "launch out at the rate
of five shillings a yard," and chose a more economical black ;
a prudence which she regretted when, on her return, Papa
said that he would have lent her a sovereign. She wished
Ellen had been there to urge her to extravagance. So do we.

The last phase of Charlotte's life is dominated by Arthur
Bell Nicholls, who had been her father's curate for some
years (described in *Shirley* as Mr. Macarthey). He was not
an intellectual, Charlotte had once complained to Ellen of his
"narrowness of mind," and he loved her in spite of her
books : but he was capable of a *grande passion*, which gave
him a power and a tenderness which she could not long with-
stand. It has been well said that "Charlotte idealised love.
She loved the passion itself."[2] Naturally she was much
moved when Mr. Nicholls first showed the quality of his
feeling for her. Ellen was taken into her confidence :—

"His manner you can hardly realise, nor can I forget it. He made
me, for the first time, realise what it costs a man to declare affection
when he doubts response . . . The spectacle of one, ordinarily so
statue-like, thus trembling, stirred and overcome, gave me a strange
shock. I could only entreat him to leave me then, and promise

[1] Mrs. Gaskell's phrases.
[2] Irene Cooper Willis in *The Brontës*.

a reply on the morrow. I asked if he had spoken to Papa. He said he dared not. I think I half-led, half-put him out of the room."

A new scene for the familiar Parsonage dining-room! Papa was outraged : a marriage with his curate would be too banal for his last, his famous, daughter. For a time Mr. Nicholls left Haworth, but the parting was too moving to allow Charlotte to put him out of her mind : she had three times turned away from the second-best in love, but here was a passion which compelled her deepest sympathy, although there had been no simultaneous growth of love in her own heart. Eventually she and Mr. Nicholls came together again and bore down her father's opposition, and on June 29th, 1854, they were married in Haworth Church. Mr. Brontë contrived to be unwell and did not attend the service : Miss Wooler, her old head-mistress, gave the bride away, and of course Ellen was with her.

Now Haworth Parsonage took on itself a new life ; the " peat-room," behind the dining room, was converted into a study for Mr. Nicholls ; Charlotte took a more active part in parish life than ever before. She wrote : " I have not so much time for thinking : I am obliged to be more practical, for my dear Arthur is a very practical, as well as a very punctual and methodical man."

Charlotte gloried in these qualities, and practised them herself with the zest of an intellectual awakened from the isolation of thought to plunge into a more human daily round of incidents and duties. Her husband's tenderness won upon her more and more.

The opening of a new novel was written—*Emma*—but it bears no marks of distinction, and Mr. Nicholls justly observed when it was read to him " the critics will accuse you of repetition." It seems extremely doubtful whether Charlotte happy and companioned would ever again have reached the literary power of Charlotte chafing at fate and unappeased.

Early in 1855 she knew that life had established yet another claim upon her, she expected to become a mother. She was too frail to stay the course of normal happiness and fulfil-ment now set for her. She suffered from perpetual, violent sickness and grew weaker and weaker. She scribbled to Ellen from her bed, " I find in my husband the tenderest nurse, the kindest support, the best earthly comfort that ever woman had. His patience never fails, and it is tried by sad days and broken nights."

Realisation of her danger came, and Charlotte whispered to her stricken husband, " Oh ! I am not going to die, am I ? He will not separate us, we have been so happy."

On March 31st, 1855, within a month of her thirty-ninth birthday, Charlotte Brontë died.

Mr. Nicholls remained at Haworth in faithful guardianship of Mr. Brontë until the old man died, six years later. With his consent, Mr. Brontë asked Mrs. Gaskell to write Charlotte's biography, and she undertook the task with a high sense of her mission, of which she wrote :—

" I weighed every line with my whole power and heart, so that every line should go to its great purpose of making *her* known and valued, as one who had gone through such a terrible life with a brave and faithful heart."

That life has been a force of inspiration ever since, and not least to those whom Charlotte Brontë would most have cared to help and fortify—those to whom both experience and hope have come meagrely, and who have faced a poor or a sad life more bravely because of the courageous spirit which was nurtured in Haworth Parsonage.

IX

CHARLOTTE BRONTË'S NOVELS

The Professor, written 1846, first published, 1857.
Jane Eyre, 1847.
Shirley, 1849.
Villette, 1853 (January).
Emma, a fragment only, published in the *Cornhill*, see Vol. I, 1860.
The Twelve Adventurers and Other Stories (Juvenilia), published by
  Hodder and Stoughton (edition limited to 1,000 copies) in 1925.
The Spell. An extravaganza, first published by the Oxford University Press in 1931.
Legends of Angria. Compiled from the early writings of Charlotte
  Brontë, by Fannie E. Ratchford, Yale University Press and
  Milford, 1933. A most interesting study.
The writings of Charlotte and Branwell Brontë, between 1824
  and 1840, will appear, some of them for the first time, in *The
  Unpublished Works of the Brontës*, to be published in the Shakespeare Head Edition, Blackwell (Oxford).
For lists and accounts of Charlotte Brontë's Juvenilia see also
  Shorter II, Appendix V, and *The Brontës : their Lives, Friendships and Correspondence*, by Wise and Symington, Shakespeare
  Head Brontë, Blackwell, 1932.

The transition from Jane Austen, to whom the comedy of
manners was the supreme form of expression, and whose
temperate, rational spirit had little in common with the
writers of the Romantic Movement, to the Brontës, who had
one foot in the realist camp and the other in the romantic,
cannot be better explained than by quoting Charlotte
Brontë's opinion of *Emma* :—

" I have likewise read one of Miss Austen's works—*Emma*—
read it with interest, and with just the degree of admiration which
Miss Austen herself would have thought sensible and suitable.
Anything like warmth or enthusiasm, anything poignant, heart-felt,
is utterly out of place in recommending these works ; all such demonstration the author would have met with a well-bred sneer, would
have closely scorned as *outré* and extravagant. She does her business
of delineating the surface of the lives of genteel English people
curiously well. There is a Chinese fidelity, a miniature delicacy,
in the painting. She ruffles her readers by nothing vehement,
disturbs him by nothing profound. The passions are perfectly
unknown to her ; she rejects even a speaking acquaintance with that

stormy sisterhood. Even to the feelings she vouchsafes no more than an occasional graceful but distant recognition—too frequent converse with them would ruffle the smooth elegance of her progress " . . . . " Jane Austen was a complete and most sensible lady, but a very incomplete and insensible (not *senseless*) woman. If this is heresy, 1 cannot help it."

Whether we think this heresy or not, it is an excellent introduction to Charlotte Brontë's own temperament and the tone of her novels. Jane Austen began to write in the last decade of the eighteenth century and inherited its rational temper ; she died a year after Charlotte Brontë was born, and only five years after Byron had taken the country by storm with the first two cantos of *Childe Harold*. The Brontës, on the other hand, were growing up during the full tide of the Byronic cult, with its " men of loneliness and mystery," its Conrads and Manfreds, with their " foreheads high and pale," which " sable curls in wild profusion veil," and they were impregnated with the romantic revival. In Charlotte's adolescent stories there are many Byronic touches ; she endows her hero Zamorna with " ringlets dark and silken " and " lashes black as ebon," and flashes of spirit which " oft crossed his face like sullen lightning breaking." It is greatly to her credit that eventually she transferred her romance to the scenes of ordinary life—she is realist enough in her background of classrooms and parlours—but one can hardly imagine her writing with the *insouciance* of Susan Ferrier (in a letter about Byron as a lover) : " Did you ever read anything so exquisite as the new canto of *Childe Harold*? It is enough to make a woman fly into the arms of a tiger ! "

Charlotte and Emily must have drunk deep from romantic sources during their study of literature at Brussels ; it is thought that Hoffmann's story of *The Entail* may have influenced Emily's conception of *Wuthering Heights*. The difference between their outlook and that of Jane Austen or Susan Ferrier, however, is due to natural temperament as much as to the accidents of influence and experience. Charlotte was fundamentally ardent, introspective and romantic, in spite of the harsh schooling of a reality so much more meagre than her dreams, a schooling which she accepted courageously and to which she subjected her heroines, in their turn, with no little zest. Emily had the temperament of a mystic. Both depicted *grandes passions* in their novels, but Charlotte's lack of

normal satisfaction in life and Emily's spiritual aloofness informed their conceptions of love with an unusual quality,
perhaps never better described than as " passionate chastity."[1]
Few novels have made love glow upon the imagination as
Jane Eyre and *Wuthering Heights* do, and yet few great love
stories are less erotic.

The contrast between Charlotte's innate romance and
the cautious philosophy which forbade her to expect too much
from life is an interesting study. Naturally forward looking
(as are all introverts) and eager, Charlotte was yet afraid of
hope. Acknowledging an ideal bliss as a possibility, bestowed
on the " curled darling of Nature and Fortune " (as she called
Dr. John of *Villette*), she could yet look at personal limitations
with steady eyes, even embrace them with fanatical thoroughness : she sought courage in clear sight and candour rather
than in comfortable self-deception. This personal philosophy
of Charlotte's is embodied in Lucy Snowe, the heroine of
Villette. Lucy has no illusions about her own charms and
prospects, in fact she under-rates them, and needs rescuing
from what the modern would call an inferiority complex.
Describing how unfettered the handsome and gracious Dr.
John felt in her presence, Lucy does not mince the matter :—

" He accorded to my presence in the room just that degree of
notice and consequence a person of my exterior usually expects ;
that is to say, about what is given to unobtrusive articles of furniture,
chairs of ordinary joiner's work and carpets of no striking pattern."

In facing her prospects in life (an over-frequent exercise on
the part of all Charlotte's heroines) she concluded that " the
negation of severe suffering was the nearest approach to
happiness I expected to know." Therefore, she told herself:—

" About the present it is best to be stoical, about the future—such
a future as mine—to be dead. And in catalepsy and a dead trance,
I studiously held the quick of my nature."

In a similar strain Charlotte preached to herself when one of
her " rather fierce moods " was upon her, as when she wrote
to Ellen Nussey :—

" It is an imbecility which I reject with contempt, for women
who have neither fortune nor beauty to make marriage the prime
object of their hopes and wishes, and the aim of all their actions ;

[1] C. P. S. in *The Structure of Wuthering Heights*.

not to be able to convince themselves that they are unattractive, and that they had better be quiet, and think of other things than wedlock."

The fascination of Lucy Snowe's story lies in the revelation and gradual release of the keen " quick of her nature," brought about by the mercurial little professor, Paul Emanuel, who senses the fires damped down under her meek exterior and repressed manner. The quiet English teacher, whom the girls regarded as " a melancholy sober-sides," and Ginevra Fanshawe called Diogenes and Timon, is accused by M. Paul of being " more of a coquette than ten Parisiennes," given to *emportement* and *chaleur*, " live as gunpowder " when taken to task for a fault. He insists that she must, at a moment's notice, play the part of a foppish gallant at the school vaudeville for Madame Beck's fête :—

" Play you must. I will not have you shrink, or frown or make the prude. I read your skull that night you came ; I see your *moyens :* play you can, play you must."

So Lucy is forced to blossom. For this very fête she had chosen a crepe dress of purple-grey—" the colour of dun mist, lying on a moor in bloom " (even in describing a Brussels dress the imagery of the moorland comes first to Charlotte's mind)— turning from the prevailing gaiety as Charlotte herself did when she " had not the spirit nor the means to launch out at five shillings a yard " on the " beautiful silks of sweet, pale colours." Very soon, however, Lucy is wearing pink, and she enjoys sparring with M. Paul when he scolds her for flaunting about in a " scarlet gown " :—

" ' What fatal influence had impelled me lately to introduce flowers under the brim of my bonnet, to wear *des cols brodés*, and even to appear on one occasion in a scarlet gown—he might indeed conjecture, but, for the present would not openly declare.'
Again I interrupted, and this time not without an accent at once indignant and horror-struck.
' Scarlet, M. Paul ! It was not scarlet ! It was pink and pale pink, too : and further subdued by black lace.'
' Pink or scarlet, yellow or crimson, pea-green or sky-blue ; it was all one ; these were all flaunting, giddy colours ; and as to the lace I talked of, *that* was but a *colifichet de plus*.' And he sighed over my degeneracy. ' He could not, he was sorry to say, be so particular on this theme as he could wish : not possessing the exact names of these *babioles*, he might run into small verbal errors which would not fail to lay him open to my sarcasm, and excite my unhappily sudden and passionate disposition.' "

The scenes between Lucy and M. Paul are as good as anything Charlotte Brontë wrote. There is a pleasing one when, on one of his tempestuous mornings, the porteress dare not take an urgent message into his classroom, and Lucy is deputed to beard him, and only escapes unshattered because she knocks his valuable spectacles off his desk and they are smashed ; in the face of this real disaster, and her real distress for it, the choleric little man becomes suddenly mild and tractable. There is an engaging quality in his naïve vanity when he receives bouquets from the girls on his fête-day and exclaims three times, in tones of deepening tragedy, " *Est-ce là tout ?* " when he misses a contribution from Lucy, and in his corresponding pleasure when he is at last convinced that the watch-guard which he has seen her making was really intended for him from the first. Equally naïvely he informs her—" Don't suppose that I wish you to have a passion for me, Mademoiselle ; *Dieu vous en garde !* What do you start for ? Because I said passion ? Well, I say it again. There is such a word, and there is such a thing—though not within these walls, thank Heaven ! "

M. Paul soon knew his Lucy Snowe. In him Charlotte's humour, often acrimonious, is softened into whimsicality ; his pungent, forceful personality blows through the class-rooms of the Brussels Pensionnat like a fresh wind.

Lucy Snowe offers us a further study in psychology because she seems to be divided between two loves ; her first awakening to the call of romance takes the form of a secret adoration for the bright qualities of Dr. John, whose kindness suggests poignant visions of what his love might be :—

" He had still such kind looks, such a warm hand ; his voice still kept such a pleasant tone for my name ; I never liked ' Lucy ' so well as when he uttered it. But I learned in time that this benignity, this cordiality, this music, belonged in no shape to me, it was part of himself, it was the honey of his temper . . . Good-night, Dr. John ; you are good, you are beautiful, but you are not mine. Good-night, and God bless you ! "

Here we have one of Charlotte's apt phrases—" the honey of his temper." We gather that, had fortune favoured her, Lucy would have asked nothing better than to be loved by Dr. John : even after the testy little Professor, who, to borrow a phrase from *Jane Eyre*, suited her " to the finest fibre of her

nature," had harried her into the real love of her life, she still
had a romantic yearning when she thought of the Doctor.
The transference of her devotion has been a stumbling-block
to many critics (notably Harriet Martineau), who cannot be
convinced of her sincerity.   The problem is the more interesting because Charlotte introduces other cases of a transference of feeling : the child Polly in *Villette* has a passionate
adoration for her father which rings true, and is poignantly
represented, but within a short time of his leaving her she is
just as much absorbed in her big school-boy hero, Graham
Bretton.   Even Jane Eyre, in whom sincerity of passionate
love cannot be doubted, is strangely moved by St. John Rivers,
and her new life centres round him rather than round his
sisters, although she does nerve herself to break through his
influence rather than marry him in order to help him in the
mission field.   Charlotte's women, in fact, had a vital need to
spend themselves in love of an intensely personal kind, and
their own sex could not satisfy it ;   denied the ideal relationship, their imaginations must feed upon such material as life
offered them.   In Lucy's case even the normal affections of
family life were wanting, and she had no nourishment for
bright hopes in herself or her circumstances :   it was surely
natural that she should warm her starved senses with visions
of an ideal love, and see in Dr. John, in his strength, beauty
and charm, her ideal of a lover ?   Such a visionary passion often
first awakes the nature, and Charlotte was sufficiently a
realist to recognise that, even when a more satisfying emotion
has superseded it, the romantic memory may still be cherished
without disloyalty to the new love.

Villette and *Jane Eyre* are both based on the well-worn but
always appealing Cinderella motive ;   but Charlotte's Cinder-
ellas need rescuing from themselves, from voluntary repres-
sion and lack of expectation bred by the want of " natural
advantages," rather than from tyrannical relations.   They do
not represent beauty in distress, denied its natural sphere,
they are not even particularly lovable :   no one could call Jane
or Lucy " a charming girl," or long to meet them in real life,
as one does Elizabeth Bennet or Anne Elliot.   Jane and Lucy
have too much idiosyncrasy for pure charm.   Lucy's story is
the drama of an ardent—somewhat narrowly ardent—spirit,
at odds with a poor exterior and petty circumstances.   To

some modern minds it is a petty drama ; but many still find a moving power in what Birrell has described finely as " the well-nigh sunless landscape of Lucy Snowe's sad, passionate and valiant life." To realise passion and valour in petty circumstances is no mean thing.

Jane Eyre, which preceded *Villette* by six years, has a crudely powerful plot and some scenes more striking than anything in Charlotte's other novels, but it is not a particularly well constructed story. *Villette* is certainly Charlotte's best constructed work, although she herself admitted some inconsistency between the boy Graham Bretton and the man Dr. John.

Jane Eyre is an elfin creature, with her diminutive person, her green eyes, her timidity which breaks into mocking humour when she is at her ease. She faces life gallantly with no experience behind her but that of the charity school. The first meeting between her and Rochester, in the ghostly dusk of the winter lane where she sits on a stile as his great dog lopes by, silent as a shadow, sets the stage for their romance in a beautifully fitting manner. Elfin and yet demure, Jane's little frame conceals a spirit of fire and iron—fire in her intensity of feeling, iron in her resolute obedience to her principles, even when obedience almost kills her. No wonder conventional propriety in 1847 was shocked at her, when she could bare her heart so vehemently to Rochester on hearing that he intended to marry Blanche Ingram :—

" ' Do you think I can stay to become nothing to you ? Do you think I am an automaton ?—a machine without feelings ? and can bear to have my morsel of bread snatched from my lips, and my drop of living water dashed from my cup ? Do you think, because I am poor, obscure, plain and little, I am soul-less and heartless ? You think wrong !—I have as much soul as you—and full as much heart ! And if God had gifted me with some beauty and much wealth, I should have made it as hard for you to leave me, as it is now for me to leave you. I am not talking to you now through the medium of custom, conventionalities, nor even of mortal flesh ; it is my spirit that addresses your spirit ; just as if both had passed through the grave, and we stood at God's feet, equal—as we are ! '

' As we are ! ' repeated Mr. Rochester."

The powerful *Quarterly Review* had some very severe strictures for *Jane Eyre* : it asserted that the book dared to tilt against Providence with a murmuring against the comforts of the rich and the privations of the poor, which, so far as each individual is concerned, is a murmuring against God's appointment "; Jane, it is admitted, " does right and exerts great moral strength," but nevertheless she is " the personification of an unregenerate and undisciplined spirit . . . No Christian grace is perceptible upon her "—this, although, in resisting the temptation to stay with Rochester, Jane tells herself " I will keep the law given by God, sanctioned by man."

Charlotte Brontë, the quiet, high-principled Vicar's daughter, had had no idea that her novel could be thought shocking, that women like the good clergyman's sister she drew from life in *Shirley* (as Margaret Hall) could be taught to call *Jane Eyre* " a wicked book " ; that Harriet Martineau, for whom she had friendship and admiration, would accuse her of allowing her heroines to be obsessed by love beyond the reasonable and seemly ; that even Mrs. Gaskell would apologise for " the existence of coarseness here and there in her works, otherwise so entirely noble."

The Brontës had, fortunately, been born and bred in a remote part of Yorkshire where passions had not been watered down by polite conventions, they were used to strong meat in the stories which their father, Tabby, and probably Branwell too, told them ; there was nothing namby-pamby in their nurture, and it did not occur to them to be ashamed of representing raw nature, nor did they shirk the occasional intrusion of the brutal or the revolting (as in the description of the maniac in *Jane Eyre*).   Side by side with this robust quality, there is in Charlotte's books a tendency to make mountains out of mole-hills, to the modern there is far too much heart-searching for too little cause : but the modern has shaken off many of the inhibitions of the Victorian middle-class and finds it hard to enter into the mentality of heroines such as Lucy and Jane in their cramped circumstances. There is also something to be said for Harriet Martineau's point of view that other sides of life than the emotional are ignored ; but what other way of escape from drab monotony did life offer in the 1840 s to women in the position of Lucy and Jane ?

In *Jane Eyre* Charlotte Brontë showed the quality of her humour : after the perfectly modulated irony of Jane Austen her pungency sometimes makes the eyes smart, but when it is not too acrid it has a shrewdly tonic tang.   In Mr. Brocklehurst it is admirable : the whole description of the charity school at Lowood is a skilful blend of pathos and satire which avoids any taint of sentimentality and has become one of the classic pictures of literature. The " black marble " clergyman of the early part of *Jane Eyre* throws into admirable relief the white marble quality of the priest of the later chapters, St. John Rivers. The asceticism which he forces on himself as he might a straight jacket is strangely compelling, and if Jane had succumbed to the cold, steady penetration of his influence readers would not have found it incredible.

Shirley is, on the whole, a quieter and less powerful book than *Jane Eyre*. It used also to be thought inferior to *Villette*, but many moderns find it more readable : there is a greater variety of scenes and characters ; in place of concentration on the mental processes of one intense nature, living in cramped circumstances such as are scarcely known to-day, *Shirley* presents much of the life of the northern countryside during the last years of the struggle with Napoleon. Nevertheless, *Jane Eyre* and *Villette* were both more calculated to draw attention to the author's striking and intense quality than *Shirley*. The most dramatic scenes in *Shirley* are at Robert Moore's mill : when he is waiting by lantern-light for his new machinery, which has to run the gauntlet of machine-wreckers on Stillbro' Moor, the suspense is extremely well worked up to the climax of the return of the empty waggons. This and the attack on the mill later are amongst the most vivid side-lights on economic history to be found in fiction. Charlotte had heard such tales of times not long gone by at Roehead, and probably from her father. The Rev. Matthewson Helstone, too, was drawn from a parson of whom stories were still current at Roehead in her school-days.

Shirley herself is supposed to be drawn from Emily Brontë, as she might have been in happy, easy circumstances ; her nickname of Captain Keeldar is a memory of Emily being called the Major ; the incident of the dog bite is a true experience of Emily's. Shirley is not, however, quite a satisfactory flesh and blood girl : Charlotte uses her too much as a mouthpiece, she stands for the courageous and the intellectual in the feminine spirit and anticipates the dawn of a woman's movement, especially in the vision of a fuller life for women which she related in her theme for Louis Moore.

Very different is Caroline Helstone, drawn partly from

Ellen Nussey, a charming period portrait of a young girl in the
throes of an anxious love for a man who really loves her but
tries, not with consistent success, to wean himself from a sweet
folly which he cannot afford. Caroline may repay her lover
for a kindness by " an admiring and grateful smile, rather
shed at his feet than lifted to his face," but when his manner
to her changes she can rally pride and dignity to her support.
Charlotte shows how well she understood the price that must
be paid for love and pride when hope fails. Caroline has had
justification enough for falling in love, but a time comes when
she remembers with humiliation how she had asked for a
lock of Robert's hair :—

> " It was my doing, and one of those silly deeds it distresses the
> heart and sets the face on fire to think of—one of those small but
> sharp recollections that return, lacerating your self-respect like tiny
> penknives, and forcing from your lips, as you sit alone, sudden,
> insane-sounding interjections."

Fighting her battle alone, Caroline has little help from
circumstances. In true Brontëan style she tries to gain
courage and resolution by looking facts in the face, all too
closely. Life stretches before her aimless and unvarying to an
extent incredible to-day. Domesticity and charity are the
only fields of activity ; Caroline is too comfortably served by
her uncle's maids to have much scope for the one and too
diffident to be very successful in the other. No one will
listen for a moment to her proposal to leave home and launch
herself upon the one possible profession, that of governess.
She sees herself gradually growing old, unattractive and
lonely in the same daily round and, with sudden compunction,
hastens to call upon such of her neighbours as have already
reached this forlorn state. She determines to learn from one
of them, Miss Ainley, how to be useful in making others
happier, even though happiness is not for her. Yet these
conscientious efforts " brought her neither health of body nor
continued peace of mind." The two practical anodynes for a
disappointment in love—enforced activity and complete
change of circumstances—were hard for the girl of the period
to come by. Even so late as 1862 Trollope, in his novel *The
Small House at Allington*, gives a pathetic account of Lily
Dale's long illness and weary convalescence after the desertion
of Adolphus Crosbie, and irritates us into fretful impatience

because it never occurs to anyone to take her away for a change, or even to try to re-shape her daily round in any way : life was to go on just as it always had been, except that the hope which had made its supreme interest was dead. It was the same with Caroline Helstone, although circumstances did eventually come to her rescue : yet Caroline has a spirit of her own, and a clear sight such as Charlotte Brontë must bestow upon every heroine she cherished. This picture of " a nice girl " has more in common with Frances Henri in *The Professor* than with Jane Eyre or Lucy Snowe.

The Professor, Charlotte's first work (but not published until after her death), is the only one of her novels which is written from the view-point of a man : the hero tells his own story, and it is a pleasant change to see one of Charlotte's heroines from outside for once, instead of being admitted into her innermost thoughts ! Frances Henri is a softer and sweeter Lucy Snowe, and the slight sketch of her has a delicate charm. In *The Professor*, Charlotte showed that she was not afraid to make two men talk to one another, as Jane Austen has been accused of being. There is less of this, naturally, in the books which were written from the heroine's standpoint, but in *Shirley* there is talk between Robert Moore and Mr. Yorke at some length.

Apart from the heroines who embody so much of her own experience and philosophy of life, Charlotte Brontë gives us a bevy of excellent minor characters, in which her humour has full range. In *Jane Eyre* we have Mr. Brocklehurst, as well known to generations of readers as Jane Austen's Mr. Collins. Mrs. Fairfax, the poor relation housekeeper, is a pleasant picture of a simple-minded old lady. Charlotte's servants are all good, and never sentimentalised.

Shirley is particularly prolific in minor characters. There are the three curates, who call forth Charlotte's humour at its most biting : she maintained that her portraits of them were not caricatures, but it is difficult to believe this. The book opens with the sentence : " Of late years an abundant shower of curates has fallen upon the North of England," and Charlotte's pen is launched with acrimonious glee. The curates are at their best when diluted with other society, as on an evening visit to the Rectory with other guests. Mr. Donne aims at drawing attention to himself by lingering majestically

over his tea : the Rector grows suddenly impatient to leave
the table :—

" ' For whom are we waiting ? ' he asked.
' For me, I believe,' returned Donne complacently appearing to
think it much to his credit that a party should thus be kept dependent on his movements.
' Tut ! ' cried Helstone.   Then, standing up, ' Let us return
thanks,' said he, and did so forthwith, and all quitted the table.
Donne, nothing abashed, still sat another ten minutes quite alone,
whereupon Mr. Helstone rang the bell for the things to be removed.
The curate at length saw himself forced to empty his cup, and to
relinquish the rôle which he thought had given him such a felicitous
distinction, drawn upon him such flattering general notice."

The came Mr. Malone's turn to assert himself.   Approaching the sofa on which Caroline was seated he " deposited his
great Irish frame near her " and prepared to make himself
agreeable.   This induced extraordinary contortions :—

" In the course of his efforts to render himself agreeable, he
contrived to possess himself of the two long sofa cushions and a
square one ; with which, after rolling them about for some time with
strange gestures, he managed to erect a sort of barrier between
himself and the object of his attentions."

Caroline did not object to this barrier, but soon she crossed
the room, and Malone found himself " left entirely to his own
resources, on a large sofa, with the charge of three small
cushions on his hands."

The Rev. Matthewson Helstone is the type of man who
would probably have risen to high command in the army, a
natural leader in times of danger and difficulty, and enjoying
the same domination in society, but exacting docility and quiet
in the women of his own household.   What is right and
proper they shall have—he, was, we are told, liberal rather
than generous—but it is their duty to be quiet and content.
Yet he is humanised by a touch of genuine distress when his
niece is seriously ill, and is delighted when she reaches the
intelligible stage of asking him to send up some dainty from
his own plate for her supper.

In the Rev. Cyril Hall, Charlotte draws a clergyman of a
really good and saintly type, a very pleasing sketch.

Hortense Moore, with her passion for her superfine Belgian
method of darning, her scorn of an English servant's notions
of cooking and of the finicking ways of neighbours who smiled

when she went to Church in pattens, and her pride in possessing (and exercising) an *esprit positif*, is a strong, convincing portrait. She kept " a hot kitchen of it," as her mother had done in Antwerp, and found her refreshment of spirit in the occupation of " rummaging," which meant " arranging, disarranging, rearranging and counter-arranging " the contents of her drawers every day.

In *Villette* there is Madame Beck, a clever study of a capable, masterful woman who gained her ends by any means that served, but always with suavity. Ginevra Fanshawe, Lucy's only compatriot at the pensionnat, must surely have been drawn from life ; frivolous and selfish, enjoying and exploiting her own charms, she disarms her confidante by her frankness, which is genuine enough. Rosine, the porteresse, is a good thumb-nail sketch.

Amongst the characters with which Charlotte is less successful, it is difficult to believe in the Yorke family, although they were partly drawn from life ; Pauline de Bassompierre resembles Shirley in being too consciously a walking ideal ; Blanche Ingram, the society beauty who orders the footman to " cease thy chatter, blockhead," is appalling. Rochester is " stagey," but he lives, he is actually virile ; Louis Moore is attractive, but not so real a man as his brother Robert.

Of Charlotte Brontë's style it must be admitted that *at its best* it is excellent ; every reader can pick out phrases, real *mots justes*, to his taste to savour reminiscently. Unfortunately, she also indulged in flights of rhetoric, and most of her purple patches offend modern literary taste. Some allowance must be made for period again ; a certain formality, a preference for long words and consciously well turned phrases, was still the fashion. Here and there, Charlotte's descriptions remind us of the flamboyancy of Fanny Burney's, as in these few lines about Pauline de Bassompierre :—

" This was not an opaque vase, of material however costly, but a lamp chastely lucent, guarding from extinction, yet not hiding from worship, a flame vital and vestal."

Charlotte also put short essays into the mouths of her characters, particularly in *Shirley*, and she apostrophises the reader (a fashion also popular with Dickens) at considerable length. Her susceptibility to scenery is evident in her novels, although she does not make her scene glow upon the imagina-

tion as Emily did, least of all when she becomes rhetorical.
Yet who but a country-woman, with a loving eye for the detail
of hedgerow and field, could have written this description of
a wintry lane in *Jane Eyre* ? :—

"I was a mile from Thornfield, in a lane noted for wild roses
in summer, for nuts and blackberries in autumn, and even now
possessing a few coral treasures in hips and haws, but whose best
winter delight lay in its utter solitude and leafless repose. If a
breath of air stirred it made no sound here ; for there was not a
holly, not an evergreen to rustle, and the stripped hawthorn and
hazel bushes were as still as the white, worn stones which cause-
wayed the middle of the path. Far and wide, on each side, there
were only fields, where no cattle browsed : and the little brown
birds, which stirred occasionally in the hedge, looked like single
russet leaves that had forgotten to drop."

As regards Charlotte Brontë's world, we have travelled far
from the fashionable circles of the eighteenth century as
represented by Fanny Burney, with their glamour and their
dangers, the miniature tragedy and comedy of ballroom and
"public place." Almost as far removed are the social
standards of Jane Austen's drawing-rooms, with their comfortable and generally accepted certainties, according to which
"elegance" of mind and manner was a large part of feminine
duty. Charlotte Brontë's governesses are on a very different
social plane, although Shirley and Caroline have points of
resemblance to Emma Woodhouse and Anne Elliot. An
interesting study of the life of the early Victorian governess
could be founded on the contemporary evidence of Charlotte
and Anne Brontë. Governesses were almost a class apart ; no
testimony as to this is more forcible than that which Charlotte
puts into the mouth of Mrs. Pryor in *Shirley*. Although the
book is dated back to a period before Waterloo, Charlotte
embodies some genuine personal experiences in Mrs. Pryor's
indictment, and makes her use some of the very phrases which
had hurt her in the severe review of *Jane Eyre* in the *Quarterly*.
It is a bitter attack on the treatment of governesses. Mrs.
Pryor was given to understand that, as she was not the equal of
her employer's family, she must not expect their sympathy.
It was not concealed from her that she was a burden and
restraint in society ; the gentlemen regarded her as a "tabooed
woman," to whom they were "interdicted from granting the
usual privileges of the sex," and they were correspondingly

annoyed when she crossed their path in going about the house. Even the servants disliked her—her anomalous position made it difficult for them to know how to treat her, no doubt—and she was deliberately told that however much her pupils loved her, or she was interested in them, they could never be her friends. Worse still, the eldest daughter of the house explained to her with brutal frankness that governesses must always be kept in this sort of isolation in order to maintain " that distance which the reserve of English manners and the decorum of English families exacts." Finally the same lady informed her that the aristocracy needed the failures and mistakes of a certain number of gentlemen, which providentially sowed the seed " from which WE reap the harvest of governesses. . . . WE shall ever prefer to place about OUR offspring those who have been born and bred with somewhat of the same refinement as OURSELVES."

The same isolation is stressed in the case of Louis Moore, the tutor in *Shirley*, to whom Mr. Sympson, his employer, was austerely civil (except when in an irritable mood), and Mrs. Sympson, naturally a kind woman, was attentive and formal, while the grown-up daughters skilfully indicated by their manners that their brother's tutor did not live for them, but was " an abstraction rather than a man."

No doubt behind Charlotte's account of Mrs. Pryor's experiences there was a memory of " love the *governess*, my dear ! " and probably of a country-house visit on which Charlotte unwillingly accompanied her charges and their parents, when her ineptitude for her task and her " touchiness" very likely made her presence an awkward restraint on society. Nevertheless, even discounting Mrs. Pryor's as an extreme statement of the case, there is ample contemporary evidence of the wretched lot of the governess. Jane Austen supplies one example in Jane Fairfax's horror of " taking a situation," and the general pity for her excited by such a miserable necessity. Dickens furnishes more circumstantial evidence in the case of Ruth Pinch in *Martin Chuzzlewit*. Ruth's ambiguous position as neither family nor servant is shown by the ingenious footman who announced her visitors " with a nice discrimination between the cold respect with which he would have announced visitors to the family and the warm personal interest with which he would have announced visitors to the cook." When Tom Pinch enquires from the same footman " Pray does Miss Pinch live here ? " he receives the reply " Miss Pinch is governess here." His next attempt, " Pray is Miss Pinch at home ? "—is met with " She's *in*." While Ruth receives her guests in the school-room her pupil makes mental notes of all that is said for her mother, who " is interested in the natural history and habits of the animal called governess." The visit is, however, soon cut short by a warning message :—

" ' Missis's compliments to Miss Pinch,' said the footman, suddenly appearing, and speaking in just the same key as before, ' and begs to know wot my young lady is a-learning of just now ? ' "

Charlotte Brontë may be classed with Dickens as one who helped to improve the lot of the under-dog in society by frank exposure and well aimed satire. Mrs. Haldane, who died in 1925 at the age of a hundred, recorded in her reminiscences that men and women of her generation realised, as those born later could not be expected to do, what a debt humanity owed to Charles Dickens and Charlotte Brontë.

Side by side with her bitter reflections on the treatment of governesses, Charlotte opens up in *Shirley* the lot of girls in " sheltered homes " who did not marry, and whose fathers, having provided the homes, were aggrieved if their daughters could not be content to find their chief outlet in cooking and sewing in them all their days. Charlotte exclaims, " as if they had no germs of faculties for anything else—a doctrine as reasonable to hold as it would be that fathers have no faculties but for eating what their daughters cook, or for wearing what they sew." In Caroline Helstone's struggle to conquer a disappointment in love under these conditions Charlotte puts forward a very forcible case. When even Shirley suggests that hard work and learned professions are said to make women coarse and unwomanly, Caroline is goaded into the retort :—

" And what does it signify whether unmarried and never-to-be married women are unattractive and inelegant or not ? provided they are decent, decorous and neat, it is enough. The utmost which ought to be required of old maids, in the way of appearance is that they should not absolutely offend men's eyes as they pass them in the street ; for the rest, they should be allowed, without too much scorn, to be as absorbed, grave, plain-looking and plain-dressed as they please."

Here is a more modern note breaking in upon the standards of the Emma Woodhouses of society with the revolutionary suggestion that there may be circumstances in which inelegance " does not signify ! " Caroline brings forward arguments which are obviously the precursors of the woman's movement which was to come, but she could hardly be expected to imagine the independent woman of the future, who might even out-rival her busy and harassed married sister in smartness, culture and ready charm !

In conclusion, Charlotte Brontë's best work was based on personal experience, which she transmuted into something richer : hers was not a highly creative imagination, despite its intensity. To some readers her field is too limited : they admit that her novels have become classics, but they are only the classics of renunciation, introspection and the inferiority complex ; so far they have been kept alive by a throb of genuine feeling and a preserving salt of humour, but they are likely to seem more and more remote from modern experience. This is true to some extent, but it is not the whole truth : renunciation and introspection remain fundamentals of human nature, even if modern life offers new ways of escape from the inferiority complex, and the ultimate strength of Charlotte Brontë's appeal is that she stands for the triumph of love and individuality over scanty nurture and mean circumstances.

X

EMILY BRONTË'S NOVEL

Wuthering Heights, 1847.

In 1883 the first biography of Emily Brontë, by Mary F. Robinson, was published. She had been asked to write a life of Charlotte for the Eminent Women Series and replied that she would prefer to take Emily as her subject; the publishers gave a grudging assent, but stipulated that the fee offered for Charlotte's life must be considerably reduced for Emily's. Since then, Emily Brontë has come into her own, and is acclaimed as the greater genius of the two; in fact, some modern critics only allow Charlotte great talent, reserving genius for Emily. This is due to the fact that Emily's was a creative imagination, whereas Charlotte was dependent on experience and observation. Charlotte's material was largely autobiographical: Emily, both physically and spiritually isolated in the home she so seldom left, evoked passions and created characters which transcend normal experience, and which have not yet been laid to rest in the oblivion which so surely overtakes the second-rate in literature.

For some years only one voice gave Emily an adequate meed of praise, that of Sydney Dobell, in the *Palladium* of September 1850. Other individual appreciations were not wanting as time passed. Swinburne, in 1877, wrote as a poet of the love of the moors which " exhales as a fresh wild odour from a bleak shrewd soil, from every storm-swept page of *Wuthering Heights*." His verdict is that *Wuthering Heights* is not a book that everyone will like, but those who do will " like nothing much better."

M. Maeterlinck (in *Wisdom and Destiny*) made great claims for Emily.[1] Gradually, as the fog of mid-Victorian squeamishness lifted, the full force and originality of *Wuthering Heights* became apparent to more than the select few.

It is not often in literature that we are confronted by the conceptions of a powerful, daring, original mind which has

[1] See chapter on *The Lives of the Brontë Sisters*.

undergone so little toning-down or shaping by first-hand experience of life. Emily Brontë was something of a recluse : Charlotte wrote in her Preface to a new edition of *Wuthering Heights* :—

" I am bound to avow that she had scarcely more practical knowledge of the peasantry amongst whom she lived, than a nun has of the country people who sometimes pass her convent gates. . . . Except to go to church or take a walk on the hills, she rarely crossed the threshold of home. Though her feeling for the people round was benevolent, intercourse with them she never sought ; nor, with very few exceptions, ever experienced. And yet she knew them ; knew their ways, their language, their family histories ; she could hear of them with interest, and talk of them with detail, minute, graphic, and accurate ; but *with* them she rarely exchanged a word."

Emily heard these stirring and sombre tales of love, hate, and jealousy working themselves out in bleak, isolated places. She fed on them in her own mind, she had little actual contact with the normal world to modify her own vivid conceptions and intense feeling : she wrote spontaneously from imagination practically uncurbed by experience. The result, if she had been less than a genius, would have been intolerably crude, if not disgusting. *Wuthering Heights* is crude, but with a clean elemental crudeness which exhilarates rather than revolts.

It is not, however, on *Wuthering Heights* alone that Emily's modern reputation stands so high. Some of her poems are now recognised as the rare expression of a mystic experience such as very few in each generation know, but which to them is the most genuine thing in life. *The Prisoner* contains a description of a mystic vision or possession and its painful passing away :—

" But first, a hush of peace—a soundless calm descends ;
　The struggle of distress, and fierce impatience ends ;
　Mute music soothes my breast—unuttered harmony,
　That I could never dream, till Earth was lost to me.

Then dawns the Invisible ; the Unseen its truth reveals,
　My outward sense is gone, my inward essence feels ;
　Its wings are almost free—its home, its harbour found,
　Measuring the gulf, it stoops and dares the final bound.

Oh ! dreadful is the check—intense the agony—
　When the ear begins to hear, and the eye begins to see ;
　When the pulse begins to throb, the brain to think again
　The soul to feel the flesh, and the flesh to feel the chain.

> Yet I would lose no sting, would wish no torture less ;
> The more that anguish rack, the earlier it will bless ;
> And robed in fires of hell, or bright with heavenly shine,
> If it but herald death, the vision is divine ! "

For Emily's quality as a poet of love the poem *Remembrance* should be read.   Its stoicism, forcibly imposed on a passion denied earthly comfort and longing to be quenched in death, is expressed with simple realism in the two lines :—

> *Then did I learn how existence could be cherished,*
> *Strengthened and fed without the aid of joy.*

On this poem alone, the theory has been put forward that Emily must have loved, and in vain.   It has even been suggested that she was emotionally obsessed by her brother. On the other hand, her mystic verse has been used as an argument that she was on a plane above bodily desire.   The most illuminating analysis of these theories and of the real content of Emily's writing is to be found in an essay by Charles Morgan which appeared in *Great Victorians* (1932).   It was an inspired choice to commit the essay on Emily Brontë to the author of *The Fountain*.   He acknowledges a debt to May Sinclair for a clue to the nature of Emily's mysticism : it was not the fruit of " religious vocation," but it evidently brought her a spiritual exaltation which seemed to place her beyond the limitations and pressure of outward circumstances, her spirit tasted " the illusory nature of time and material things."[1]

Emily, in Charles Morgan's conception, was free of two worlds, that of her vision, to which she longed to escape with painful eagerness, and that of her domestic duties at Haworth Parsonage.   She is not to be pitied as being forced to spend in household drudgery time of which she might otherwise have made a golden use :   that very routine, occupying the body and making no demands on the spirit, induced the state of mind in which she could release herself from the temporal and the material and achieve that " spiritual ecstasy " which must be regarded as " the key to her art."   With the insight of understanding Charles Morgan writes :—

" She clung to her duties at the Parsonage as visionary and contemplative men cling always to the discipline that they have cultivated as an enablement of their vision."

This explains how the Emily who is the author of the poems

[1] May Sinclair in *The Three Brontës*.

could also write the prosaic memorandum of July, 1845, intended to be re-read three years later by herself and Anne, in which, after recording the blessings of good health in the family and no present anxiety about income, she concludes :—

" I am quite contented for myself : not idle as formerly, altogether as hearty and having learnt to make the most of the present and long for the future with less fidgetiness that I cannot do all I wish ; seldom or never troubled with nothing to do, and merely desiring that everyone should be as comfortable as myself and as undesponding, and then we should have a very tolerable world of it."

Charles Morgan regards the poems as conclusive evidence that Emily was the author of *Wuthering Heights*, despite the claims which have been made for Branwell :—

" Whoever wrote the poems wrote *Wuthering Heights*, the same unreality of this world, the same greater reality of another, being in them both, and in nothing else the human mind has produced. The poems and the novel are twins of a unique imagination. They have the same prosaic lapses, the same poetic transcendence ; they have the same obsession with the idea of imprisonment and of supernatural visitants ; the same swift alternation between two contradictory ideas of death."

The theory that Branwell wrote *Wuthering Heights* has its foundation in the statements of two of his friends—F. Grundy and F. A. Leyland—who both wrote books about him and his family. F. Grundy said that Branwell told him he was the author and that Emily bore it out. He did not publish the statement until twelve years after Charlotte's death, and his dates are inaccurate. F. A. Leyland said that Branwell told him he was writing a novel and actually read him some opening chapters, which he afterwards recognised in *Wuthering Heights*. Two other friends in the same circle corroborated Leyland's story : one of them—W. Dearden, a poet—wrote an article on the subject in the *Halifax Guardian* for June, 1867.

Branwell may have appropriated his sister's MS. as a practical joke for the moment : on the other hand, there is no improbability in his having had a part in the writing, especially of the earlier chapters. He certainly influenced Emily's mind : some phrases in the book are more or less adopted from Branwell's expressions in letters ; but this is not necessarily evidence that he incorporated them himself, Charlotte appropriated one of her best phrases—when Jane Eyre assures Rochester that he suited her " to the finest fibre of my nature, sir "—from a poem of her father's.

Alice Law[1] argues ably that Emily spurred Branwell on to begin a novel in order to rescue him from inaction and despair, and that later she co-operated with him in the writing. E. F. Benson puts forward the theory that Branwell wrote the opening chapters and Emily then took over the book. It is tempting to accept this. The clumsy and poorly co-ordinated structure of the story suggests that it was begun on one plan and finished on another. The first narrator, Lockwood, is drawn at the beginning as if he were intended for a larger part, there is even a hint that he might lose his heart to the younger Cathy and so become an actor instead of a mere listener. When Nelly Dean becomes the narrator, Lockwood almost drops out of the picture for the greater part of the book. There is also a conspicuous change of style : of course, it is natural that Nelly Dean should tell her story in a simpler and more straightforward way than the educated man of leisure and property, but Lockwood's speech at the beginning is so pedantically stilted and ornate, and Nelly's so direct and yet graphic, that it is difficult to believe that the author who could achieve Nelly's would have borne with Lockwood's at all. Moreover, when Lockwood does take up the tale again at a later stage his language is rather simpler.

When Nelly takes over the story her style seems exactly the right medium for it : Emily would, of course, be at home in reproducing this kind of speech, with which she was familiar in Haworth Parsonage ; but Branwell might well have given her the character of Joseph.

The one safe conclusion seems to be that, despite Charlotte's assertion that Branwell was not taken into his sisters' confidence about their novels, he did know that Emily was writing *Wuthering Heights* and had some influence on its composition. It is, however, beyond doubt that the greater part of the book, and above all its atmosphere, are of Emily's creation. Branwell—a male writer—would not have made Catherine at once so clear-sighted about her love for Heathcliff (" Nelly, I *am* Heathcliff ") and able to contemplate marrying Edgar Linton in order to " aid Heathcliff to rise "—his present " degradation " being the one barrier to marriage with him. Also, as Emily's first biographer—Mary Robinson—pointed out, " only an

---

[1] *P. B. Brontë and E. J. Brontë and the Authorship of Wuthering Heights.*

imagination of the finest and rarest touch " would have wrought poetic justice on Heathcliff not by subjecting him to " common horrors " and " a vulgar Bedlam frenzy " but by causing him to die of joy, his " panther nature " worn down by " the torturing apprehension of a happiness never quite grasped." Haunted by the imminence of re-union with the dead Catherine, constantly imagining himself just about to be in her presence, he lets the culmination of the revenge he has pursued so long and so relentlessly slip from him ; he forgets to breathe for half a minute together, and when he stretches out his hand to take food his fingers clench before they reach it, and he is rapt in a new ecstasy of expectation.

Wuthering Heights is too involved and full a story to be analysed in a short essay, but the two outstanding features which have made it live are the saturation of its characters, above all Catherine Earnshaw, in the very spirit of the moorland, and the vivid presentation of the passion which burns out both her and Heathcliff with an almost unearthly fire which owes nothing to sensuality.

One scene, in which Catherine forces her confidences about her love upon the outraged Nelly, illustrates both these features. Catherine has been describing a dream in which she thought she was in heaven :—

" Heaven did not seem to be my home ; and I broke my heart with weeping to come back to earth ; and the angels were so angry that they flung me out into the middle of the heath on the top of Wuthering Heights, where I awoke sobbing for joy. That will do to explain my secret as well as the other. I've no more business to marry Edgar Linton than I have to be in heaven ; and if the wicked man in there had not brought Heathcliff so low, I shouldn't have thought of it. It would degrade me to marry Heathcliff now ; so he shall never know how I love him ; and that, not because he's handsome, Nelly, but because he's more myself than I am. Whatever our souls are made of his and mine are the same ; and Linton's is as different as a moonbeam from lightning, or frost from fire. . . . If all else perish and *he* remained, *I* should still continue to be ; and if all else remained and he were annihilated, the universe would turn to a mighty stranger : I should not seem a part of it. My love for Linton is like the foliage in the woods : time will change it, I'm well aware, as winter changes the trees. My love for Heathcliff resembles the eternal rocks beneath : a source of little visible delight, but necessary. Nelly, I *am* Heathcliff. He's always, always in my mind : not as a pleasure, any more than I am always a pleasure to myself, but as my own being."

Here is Heathcliff after his night's vigil while Catherine
died :—

> " He was there—at least a few yards further in the park ; leant
> against an old ash tree, his hat off, his hair soaked with the dew that
> had gathered on the budded branches and fell pattering round him.
> He had been standing a long time in that position, for I saw a pair
> of ousels passing and repassing scarcely three feet away from him,
> busy in building their nests, and regarding his proximity as no more
> than that of a piece of timber."

His hand and forehead were stained and Nelly saw splashes
of blood on the tree where he had dashed his head against the
knotted trunk in an attempt to dull his agony.   He resents the
suggestion that Catherine is at peace : his temper has always
been vengeful, since, as a boy, he brooded on his wrongs to
Nelly :—

> " ' I'm trying to settle how I shall pay Hindley back. I don't
> care how long I wait, if I can only do it at last. I hope he will
> not die before I do ! '
> ' For shame, Heathcliff ! ' said I. ' It is for God to punish wicked
> people ; we should learn to forgive.'
> ' No, God won't have the satisfaction that I shall.' "

Love, hate, revenge, brutality—all surge in *Wuthering
Heights*, sometimes melodramatic, occasionally ludicrous, often
fine : and through it all the ears of its tempestuous characters
are always open for the note of the moor-lark, the flow of the
distant beck, as it sounded " On quiet days following a great
thaw or a season of steady rain," noting when it was possible
to distinguish its girding at the large stones it could not cover,
regretting it when " the murmur of summer foliage " drowned
its music.   Even in delirium Catherine evokes the spirit of the
moor about her bed by plucking the feathers from her pillow :—

> " And here is a moor-cock's ; and this—I should know it among
> a thousand—it's a lapwing's. Bonny bird ; wheeling over our
> heads in the middle of the moor. It wanted to go to its nest, for
> the clouds had touched the swells, and it felt rain coming."

And, finally, when revenge has lost its savour for Heathcliff,
the two last representatives of the families he has all but
ruined come together in a fresh, sane love, and the grim story
ends on a new note : one of the last pictures is that of the
younger Cathy picking the primroses of *Wuthering Heights*
to stick them in Hareton Earnshaw's porridge.

XI

ANNE BRONTË'S NOVELS

Agnes Grey, 1847.
The Tenant of Wildfell Hall, 1848.

Anne Brontë's novels would probably be quite neglected to-day if it were not for her sisters' fame, and yet there is some good material in them, competently handled in a style which is neither laboured nor slip-shod. *Agnes Grey* provides interesting evidence of the trials of the early Victorian governess. Anne Brontë's experience seems to have lain chiefly amongst families in which the children were still reared on the principle that to thwart a child is to impair the fearless and independent nature desirable in a boy or the sense of dignity and position with which a " young lady " should be fortified. We are more accustomed to associate with early Victorian up-bringing such maxims as " spare the rod and spoil the child," and " children should be seen and not heard," but evidently Anne Brontë found in the early eighteen-forties that the comfortable features of Rousseau's doctrine had outlived its artificially-natural severities and produced a crop of indulgent mothers, in the same tradition as Jane Austen's Lady Middleton, who, when her little boy snatched Miss Steele's pocket-handkerchief and threw it out of the window, remarked, " John is in such spirits to-day ! He is full of monkey-tricks."

The description of poor Agnes' arrival at her first " situation," a gentle, diffident girl of eighteen who had never left her happy Vicarage home before, must surely be autobiographical. She was benumbed with cold after her five hours' coach journey, unable to change her mud-splashed dress and heavy boots because her boxes had not yet been brought to her room, and after " clomping " downstairs in a nervous agony was called upon to wrestle, with fingers still stiff, with a plateful of very tough beef-steak, and half cold potatoes, under the sternly appraising eye of her formidable mistress. She dare not leave the meat and at last she " des-

perately grasped the knife and fork in her fists, like a child of
two years old, and fell to work with all the little strength she
possessed." Then came the ordeal of introduction to Mrs.
Bloomfield's spoiled darlings. Tom was described to her by
his fond Mamma as " a generous, noble-spirited boy, one to be
led, but not driven," but she soon formed her own impression
of him as " a consequential little gentleman." On her first
day she finds it impossible to keep the children, whom she is
to " lead but not drive " (she was forbidden to punish them),
out of the dirtiest part of the garden, and incurs the displeasure
of Mr. Bloomfield, who sees her for the first time as he rides
up the drive and stops his horse to shout at the children, and
order her to take better care of " Miss " and " Master "
Bloomfield. On a subsequent occasion when the children
have escaped her and are rampaging in the snow, and her
best attempt at " grim looks and angry words " are hopelessly
ineffectual, Mr. Bloomfield comes raging upon the scene and
roars, " Come in with you, you filthy brats, or I'll horse-whip
you every one." They obey at once, and he turns to Agnes
with scornful severity, " There, you see ! They come at the
first word ! " Once Agnes ventured to threaten that they
should not have their supper until they had cleared up the
litter on the nursery floor, whereupon Tom immediately ran
to the table and threw the bread and milk all over the carpet,
struck his sisters and caused such a pandemonium that Mrs.
Bloomfield appeared, crying, " what is the matter with my
boy ? " When the trouble was explained to her she rang for
the nursery-maid to put the room in order and bring Master
Bloomfield another supper, to which he settled down with a
truculent " there now ! "

Agnes Grey's second venture—with the Murrays—was
little better. Mrs. Murray, a society woman, did not trouble
her much, after a plea for gentleness in the treatment of " dear
little Charles," reinforced by a mild complaint that the
governesses she has sampled hitherto have all failed in this
respect—" they wanted that meek and quiet spirit, which
St. Matthew, or some of them[1] says is better than the putting
on of apparel—you will know the passage to which I allude,
for you are a clergyman's daughter." Agnes needed the meek
spirit indeed, for the young Murrays gave their own orders and

[1] St. Peter.

expected her to fall in with them : sometimes they insisted on
having the schoolroom dinner up before it was half cooked,
sometimes they left it on the table for over an hour.   If they
had a fancy to get lessons over before breakfast they sent a
servant to wake Agnes at 5.30 a.m., but when she came down
to an unlighted fire and an undusted schoolroom at 6 o'clock,
she would find they had changed their minds and were still
snug in bed.

Agnes Grey is eventually " made happy ever after " by an
admirable curate, whom she first sees in the throes of a hopeless adoration for lovely Rosalie Murray.   One regrets that he
could not come to Agnes's rescue earlier, and that when she
relieved her feelings by talking of her home to him and
exclaimed " I think I could not live but for the thought of
it ! " he only has the coldest comfort to offer her :—

> " ' Oh, yes, you could,' he said, with a thoughtful smile, ' the
> ties which bind us to life are tougher than you imagine.   You might
> be miserable without a home, but you could live, and not so miserably
> as you suppose.   The human heart is like india-rubber :   a little
> swells it, but a great deal will not burst it ' "

from which he leads her on to his conclusion that " the best
of happiness is the power and will to be useful."   In this there
is a sad reminder of Anne's last reflections when she realised
she was dying, and permitted herself one regret—that she
could not now fulfil one or two projects she had of doing
something useful in the world.   There are many pathetic
bits of self-revelation in Agnes Grey, such as the incident when
the curate offers to share his umbrella with Agnes in an unexpected shower—" ' No, thank you, I don't mind the rain,'
I said.   I always lacked common-sense when taken by
surprise."

Anne Brontë wrote The Tenant of Wildfell Hall under the
agony of watching Branwell's terrible surrender to drink and
drugs, unable to reach him by any appeal.   She intended the
book as a vicarious expiation ;   she hoped to wring some good
out of his wasted life by turning the dearly-bought experiences
into a warning for others.   Hence it came about that she
produced a book in which some of the scenes and language do
violence to all our conceptions of her nature.   The Tenant of
Wildfell Hall, however, has scarcely had its due, although it
has received one tribute of praise from a high source—the late

George Moore considered that it has been seriously under-rated. It is certainly a readable story, and the character of the wastrel Huntingdon is exceedingly well done—he is gay and gallant when he first comes on the scene, and there is no difficulty in understanding his attraction for the high-souled, but not impassive, Helen Lawrence, because we feel it ourselves. In his deterioration, he still has a lingering hold on our sympathy, especially in his ironic outbursts when his wife has given him too heavy a dose of virtuous solemnity. Anne Brontë showed in this book that she could draw real men ; the lively hobble-de-hoy Fergus is good work, and so is the sketch of Hattersley, Huntingdon's boon-companion ; the scene in which the latter, rather more than half-drunk, takes his wife on his knees and teases her to tell him why she is crying is convincing, and has just enough saving grace to make it bearable. We can believe in Hattersley's ultimate reform, which is not over-strained.

Genius is not claimed for Anne Brontë, but she cannot be denied talent, and there is a surprisingly disciplined quality about the construction and style of her work.

BOOKS ABOUT THE BRONTËS

The following list does not include all the numerous books which have been written on the Brontës but only those which are likely to be in public libraries or those which, though not easy to procure, may be of interest to students specialising in the Brontës. Practically no articles from periodicals, no papers from the Brontë Society Annual Transactions, and no limited editions printed for private circulation only, are included. The volumes of the Brontë Society's Transactions can be purchased from the Curator, Brontë Parsonage Museum, Haworth, Yorks. The Museum Catalogue (price 1s.) contains useful lists and descriptions of periodicals, newspaper cuttings and private editions, all of which may be seen in the Brontë Society's excellent library at the Museum. A Bibliography of the works of all the members of the Brontë family, and of Brontëana, is to be published in the Shakespeare Head Brontë (Blackwell, Oxford, 17s. 6d.).

1857–1900.

N.B.—All authors writing before 1913 were unaware of Charlotte Brontë's letters to M. Heger, except Mrs. Gaskell.

**The Life of Charlotte Brontë. Mrs. Gaskell, 1857. This is recommended as one of the great biographies of English literature and the book which made the Brontës live in the imagination of a wide and sympathetic public. It should be read in conjunction with a modern study of the Brontës, as there are misrepresentations and omissions in it which need a commentary.
Charlotte Brontë : a Monograph. T. Wemyss Reid, 1877.
*A Note on Charlotte Brontë. Algernon Charles Swinburne, 1877.
*Essay on Emily Brontë. A. C. Swinburne in Miscellanies.
Haworth : Past and Present. Horsfall Turner, 1879.
Pictures of the Past. Francis Grundy (Griffiths and Farran) 1879. Francis Grundy was a railway engineer who became the friend of Branwell Brontë when he was acting as a railway clerk at Luddenden Foot. He gives a picture of Branwell in 1841–1842, and some later glimpses, and declares that Branwell told him he wrote a great part of Wuthering Heights. His dates are inaccurate.
*Emily Brontë. A. Mary F. Robinson (Madame Duclaux).
Eminent Women Series, 1883. An interesting and well-written study. M. Robinson, however, repeats some of the assertions Mrs. Gaskell had to withdraw, such as that the Brontë children were not allowed meat.

The Brontë Family, with Special Reference to Patrick Branwell Brontë. F. A. Leyland, 1886. F. A. Leyland, the sculptor, was a friend of Branwell's. He states that Branwell read him a fragment of a novel which he professed to have written and the scenes and characters were those of *Wuthering Heights.*

*The Life of Charlotte Brontë. *Augustine Birrell,* 1887.

The Brontë Country : its topography, antiquities and history. Erskine Stuart, 1888.

Literary Shrines of Yorkshire. Erskine Stuart, 1892.

The Brontës in Ireland : or, Facts Stranger than Fiction. W. Wright, 1893.

Charlotte Brontë's Place in Literature. Frederic Harrison, 1894.

*Charlotte Brontë and Her Circle. *Clement K. Shorter,* 1896. C. K. Shorter was the first great authority on all connected with the lives of the Brontës ; he knew Mr. Nicholls and Miss Ellen Nussey and received much material from them. He was unable to publish copyright letters at this date but made as complete a study as he could in this useful volume which is to be found in most public libraries.

The Brontës : Fact and Fiction. Angus Mackay, 1897.

The Sisters Brontë. Mrs. Oliphant (Women Novelists of Queen Victoria's Reign) 1897. See May Sinclair in *The Three Brontës* for strictures on Mrs. Oliphant's attitude to Charlotte.

The Father of the Brontës. W. W. Yates, 1897.

Thornton and the Brontës. W. Scruton, 1898.

1900–1933.

Charlotte Brontë, George Eliot and Jane Austen. Henry H. Bonnell (Longmans, Green), 1902. H. H. Bonnell presented a large number of Brontëana (including childish manuscripts of Charlotte's, autographs, Emily's writing-desk) to the Brontë Parsonage Museum at Haworth, where they occupy the dining-room in which the girls lived and wrote.

The Challenge of the Brontës. Edmund Gosse, 1903.

The Brontës, double number of the Bookman, October, 1904.

The Key to Charlotte Brontë's " Wuthering Heights." John Malham Dembleby, 1911. For a refutation of J. M. Dembleby's argument that Charlotte wrote *Wuthering Heights,* see *Appendix* to May Sinclair's *The Three Brontës.*

**The Brontës : Life and Letters *(2 vols.). C. K. Shorter (Hodder and Stoughton)* 1908. These two volumes contain a full compilation of correspondence and other evidence about the Brontës' lives available in 1908. They are still a standard work, and the matter in them is incorporated in *The Brontës : their Lives, Friendships and Correspondence* (4 vols.) by Wise and Symington (1932).

*The Three Brontës. *May Sinclair,* 1912. *Later Edition, with Preface referring to the publication of the Brontë-Heger letters in* 1913 *(Hutchinson)* 1914. This is a book of great literary charm and insight, especially in regard to Emily Brontë. It approaches Mrs. Gaskell's biography in spirit.

In the Footsteps of the Brontës. Mrs. Ellis Chadwick, 1914.

Charlotte Brontë : A Study. Maude Goldring, 1915.

Charlotte Brontë in Brussels. M. H. Spielmann, 1916. It was M. H. Spielmann whom the son and daughter of M. Heger consulted as to the publication and disposal of the four Brontë-Heger letters in 1913.

Jane Eyre and Wuthering Heights. Virginia Woolf in The Common Reader, 1916. *Reprinted as an Essay, Hogarth Press,* 1925.

The Symbolism of " Wuthering Heights." Colman Kavanagh, 1920.

Patrick Branwell Brontë. Alice Law (Philpot) 1923.

P. B. Brontë and E. J. Brontë and the Authorship of "Wuthering Heights." Alice Law (Old Parsonage Press, Altham, Accrington), 1925. Alice Law is an exponent of the theory that Branwell wrote at least a great part of *Wuthering Heights.*

The Structure of Wuthering Heights. C. P. S. (Hogarth Essay) 1926. Analysis of pedigrees, dates, etc., showing their absolute consistency.

Haworth Parsonage. Isabel Clarke (Hutchinson) 1927. A readable book. I. Clarke takes the view that Emily was in love with William Weightman.

The Brontë Sisters. Ernest Dimnet (Jonathan Cape) 1927. *Translated from a French edition of* 1910. A pleasant study, with one or two minor inaccuracies.

All Alone : The Life and Private History of Emily Jane Brontë. Romer Wilson (Chatto and Windus) 1928. The private history is founded on assumptions based on the study of Emily's poems and on psychological arguments. Some of the suggestions are interesting and even helpful, but they are necessarily a matter of conjecture and private opinion.

A Short History of the Brontës. K. A. Sugden (O.U.P.) 1929.

*Emily Brontë. Charles Simpson (Country Life Ltd.) 1929. This book is principally concerned with the influences of locality on Emily's work, and gives some interesting descriptions of scenes and houses which were evidently familiar to her round Haworth and Law Hill, and of which details are used in *Wuthering Heights.* It is illustrated by attractive sketches of the Brontë country.

The Brontë Sisters. Emilie and Georges Romieu (Skeffington) 1931. These authors make a particularly dismal drama of the Brontës' life in death in the " sepulchre " of Haworth Parsonage. Imagination is given free play, beyond the warrant of evidence, in high-flown language. One or two of Mrs. Gaskell's discarded statements are repeated.

**The Life of Charlotte Brontë. E. F. Benson (Longmans) 1932. Witty in style, this book avoids casting any false glamour over the Brontës and may be thought too little sympathetic to Charlotte. It is excellent in sifting evidence on various controversial theories, particularly in its summing-up and commenting on the arguments that Branwell wrote *Wuthering Heights.*

***Great Victorians. Essay on Emily Brontë. Charles Morgan (Nicholson and Watson)* 1932. This essay by an author who has real understanding of the mystic temperament is as satisfying and illuminating as anything that has been written on Emily Brontë. In the same volume see the essay on *Charlotte Brontë* by Rebecca West.

***The Brontës : Their Lives, Friendships and Correspondence* (4 *vols.*). *T. J. Wise and J. A. Symington (Shakespeare Head Brontë, Blackwell, Oxford)* 1932. This compilation by T. J. Wise, a well-known specialist in Brontë " lore " and collector of Brontëana, and J. A. Symington, Brotherton Librarian and formerly associated with the Brontë Parsonage Museum, incorporates all the material used by C. K. Shorter in his *Life and Letters* (2 vols., 1908) and a number of letters by or to members of the Brontë family which have been brought to light since. The aim of the Shakespeare Head edition is " to achieve finality." These four volumes are limited to 750 copies and the price is £3. On this account the references in this book are to C. K. Shorter's *Life and Letters*, which is easily accessible, and contains all that the average student needs, with the notable exception of the Brontë-Heger letters which were unknown in 1908.

***The Brontës. Irene Cooper Willis. (Great Lives Series, Duckworth),* 1933. A very readable and trustworthy short biography at the modest price of 2s.

PLAYS ABOUT THE BRONTËS.

The Tragic Race, M. B. Linton.

The Bride of Quietness and Other Plays, Oscar W. Firkins.
See the Play with the title *The Purple Moors.*

The Brontës, Alfred Sangster.

Wild Decembers, Clemence Dane.

Jane Eyre. A drama in Five Acts, adapted from the novel by *John Brougham.* French's American Drama, Acting Edition No. CXXXVI.

Emily Brontë, Alice Law.

The Brontës of Haworth Parsonage, John Davison.

XII

THE LIFE OF ELIZABETH CLEGHORN GASKELL

(1810–1865)

Thackeray wrote of "those fair creatures we love in Reynold's portraits, and who still look out on us from his canvases, with their sweet, calm faces and gracious smiles." The description might have been written for Richmond's portrait of Elizabeth Gaskell, which is surely one of the most charming faces, and the most suggestive of a sweet and happy nature, in the National Portrait Gallery.

Elizabeth Cleghorn Stevenson was born on September 29th, 1810, in Lindsey Row, now part of Cheyne Walk (the actual house is No. 93), in Chelsea. Her father came of a Border family connected with the sea, and said to be of Norwegian origin, but he early decided to be a Unitarian minister : for a time he both served a Chapel and taught in Manchester, then, owing to religious doubts, he gave up these appointments and took to farming near Edinburgh. He now married Elizabeth Holland, of Sandlebridge, near Knutsford, Cheshire, whose home is the original of Hope Farm in Mrs. Gaskell's story *Cousin Phillis*, which is so fragrant with the very breath of country life. The Hollands were a good sound family to spring from ; one of Elizabeth's uncles, Dr. Peter Holland, was a well-known figure in Knutsford, and one of her cousins became a distinguished physician and a Fellow of the Royal Society, Sir Henry Holland, ancestor of Lord Knutsford.

William Stevenson soon found farming unsatisfactory and moved into Edinburgh, where his wife kept a boarding house for students, while he secured both teaching and journalistic work : he wrote for some good periodicals and in 1803 became editor of the *Scots Magazine*. Eventually, this work was given up on the offer of the post of keeper of the Treasury Records in London. Meanwhile, Mrs. Stevenson had had seven children, of whom only one—a boy—survived early childhood, before the birth of Elizabeth. When Elizabeth was thirteen months old, her mother died at the age of forty.

The baby girl was sent into Cheshire to be under the care of her mother's sister, Mrs. Lumb, at Knutsford. Here was passed the childhood which bore such fine fruit in *Cranford* and *Wives and Daughters*. Elizabeth Stevenson grew up in a roomy red-brick house looking out upon a heath, and became familiar with several households of gentle, elderly ladies who made a high vocation of living with refinement on small incomes, and with the good old servants who managed and loved their mistresses as if they were their children, and the raw young ones, fresh from country cottages, whose training was so puzzling to themselves and so interesting to the ladies. Mrs. Gaskell has recorded that she was afraid to put all the little Knutsford scenes she could remember into *Cranford*, in case she should be accused of exaggerating. Elizabeth also accompanied her uncle, Dr. Peter Holland, on his rounds in a dog-cart, and many village scenes and characters were stored up in her mind, as well as a vivid impression of a country doctor's life, which served her well in drawing Dr. Gibson (of *Wives and Daughters*). She had the advantage of learning French from M. Rogier, who also gave dancing lessons and had taught William Pitt. He suggested the charming little story she wrote called *My French Master*.

At fourteen Elizabeth was sent to a good boarding-school at Stratford-on-Avon for two years. The house, since destroyed, was said to have been the home of Shakespeare for a short time in 1602, and had previously belonged to Benedictine monks. At Clopton Hall near Stratford she heard a ghost story which she afterwards used, and perhaps it was now that her love of ghosts and mysteries began to develop.

In 1827, Elizabeth returned to Knutsford, but she was soon summoned to join her father's household in London, now presided over by a step-mother who had a son and daughter of her own. At this time Elizabeth's own brother, who was in the merchant service, disappeared in India and was never traced. This must have suggested the disappearance of Peter Jenkins in *Cranford*. The two years spent in London were unhappy and difficult, and Elizabeth had just learned to care for her father when he died, in 1829. After this her relations seem to have thought that she needed a change and experience of a wider life, and it was arranged for her to spend two winters with a family named Turner in Newcastle, where Mr. Turner was a Unitarian minister. Here she had stimulating and literary society ; to be a Unitarian at this date was to be one of an intellectual circle which justly claimed considerable freedom and liberality of thought. With Mr. Turner's daughter, Ann, Elizabeth visited Edinburgh, of which she wrote later : " Edinburgh, compared to London, is like a vivid page of history, compared to a dull lecture on political economy." Her beauty was already striking at this period, and she sat for a miniature and a bust to artists who delighted in such a model.[1]

At the house of Mr. Turner's married daughter, Mrs. Robberds, whose husband was minister of Cross Street Unitarian Chapel in Manchester, Elizabeth Stevenson first met William Gaskell, who was the junior minister of the Chapel and also Professor of English History and Literature at the Manchester New College (a theological training college for Unitarian Ministers, the ancestor of Manchester College, Oxford). He was a man of fine appearance, six feet tall, described by a contemporary as walking "with stately graciousness." His high-minded seriousness did not prevent his winning the heart of the beautiful, happy-tempered and yet spirited Elizabeth Stevenson, and in August, 1832, they were married in Knutsford Church (there were no marriages in chapels then). On the bride's twenty-second birthday they returned from their honeymoon in North Wales to take up the burden of a busy life in Manchester, which was to be their home for thirty-two years.

As Mrs. Gaskell was one of the group of writers who published novels dealing with what Carlyle called the " condition-of-England question," then a strange, new field for fiction, it is essential to understand the Manchester scene of which she became such a close and sympathetic observer. In the thirties the working-class was in the trough of that great wave of mechanisation known as the Industrial Revolution, which had swept across England leaving its deposits of machinery, mine and mill, all over a country which, almost up to the middle of the eighteenth century, could have been

[1] The miniature painter was Thompson, the sculptor Dunbar, a pupil of Chantry.

described as primarily a granary and a sheep-fold. English life had suffered what might be called *a steam-change*. Starving hand-loom weavers still walked the streets, reminders of the days when every farm-house or substantial cottage was a little independent hand-worked factory. To the old life of country parish and small market-town was now added that of the mushroom cities which sprang up about the coal and iron fields, of which it could be fairly said :—

"These towns were precisely what they looked. They were settlements of great masses of people collected in a particular place because their fingers or their muscles were needed on the brink of a stream here or at the mouth of a furnace there." [1]

Unfortunately the small, supple fingers of children were particularly suitable in handling the early types of machines, and the work-houses a ready source of supply ; child-labour at low wages became an established practice, and often the father of a family would be unable to get work himself and had to act the part of slave-driver to his children. One father, giving evidence before a Parliamentary Commission, said that the children often came home too tired to eat and fell asleep " with the victual in their mouths," and then they had to be roused again with daylight and sent—or even carried—back to the mill.

Town government was a matter of chance, town planning did not exist : there is a record of a street in Manchester in which the houses were deliberately built to utilise a deep, undrained ditch for cellars, which were rented to poor families as homes. In fact, the development of industrialism had outstripped man's control : checks and regulations were not yet accepted as a necessary accompaniment of industrial expansion, and both mill-owner and workman were swept along helpless in the relentless race to keep pace with the amazing growth of machinery, wealth and population.

The backwardness of reform and readjustment to the new conditions was partly due to the facts that the Reign of Terror in the French Revolution had set back progressive movements in England by a quarter of a century, and that for twenty years the national energy had been absorbed in keeping Napoleon in check. Fortunately, however, during the thirties the ills of the country brought other crusaders into the field

[1] Hammond in *The Town Laborer*.

as well as writers, and all strengthened one another's hands.

In 1832 the Reform Bill brought in a first, meagre instalment of democracy : the middle-classes gained the vote, the great new towns won the right to elect members of Parliament, and manufacturers took their seats beside country squires in the House of Commons. Shortly afterwards, the first public grant was made to education, the Poor Law was harshly reformed, but beneficially in the painful long run, and town government was established by the Municipal Corporations Act. Meanwhile, Sadler, Oastler and Ashley (Lord Shaftesbury) were fighting in the cause of the factory workers, especially the children, and in 1833, the first effective factory act was passed, appointing Government inspectors. Of Ashley's fine work it has been said that " he did more than any single man or any single Government in English History to check the raw power of the new industrial system.[1] " Robert Owen helped to found the short-lived Grand National Consolidated Trade Union in 1834, and in 1838 the People's Charter was drawn up and accepted with blind enthusiasm by working-men, especially in the industrial North, who pinned their faith to a more democratic Parliament as their salvation. The Chartist leader O'Connor assured his followers in 1841 that " six months after the Charter is passed every man, woman and child in the country will be well-fed, well-housed, and well-clothed " : but the " hungry forties " stretched before them.

In the same year that the Charter was put forth, the Anti-Corn-Law League was founded, and soon Cobden and Bright were launched on their campaign for the cheap loaf. In the year of the collapse of Chartism, which led F. D. Maurice and Charles Kingsley to preach Christian Socialism, free trade triumphed.

All through the eighteen-thirties and forties, England was in travail, and in Manchester the very core of the distress, and the resentment and pitiful delusions which it bred, could be seen in their naked reality by all who had eyes to see. Mr. and Mrs. Gaskell were amongst these. Both did all they could to help individual cases, and Mr. Gaskell served on a voluntary Public Health Committee which endeavoured to take preventive measures against the visitations of cholera, and on

[1] Hammond in *Life of Lord Shaftesbury*.

another committee which aimed at improving conditions with regard to drink, and as Chairman of the Portico Library he presided over lively discussions of social questions. These years were very full indeed for both husband and wife : Mr. Gaskell had his work as minister, as lecturer at Owens College (forerunner of the Victoria University of Manchester) and as Principal of the Unitarian Home Missionary College, and Mrs. Gaskell was fully occupied with her house and family, which consisted of four little girls and one boy. Nevertheless, she played her part graciously and well both in their interesting circle of friends and amongst the poor with whom her husband's position brought her in contact. It shows great mental vitality that she also tried her hand at literary work, first collaborating with her husband in *Sketches among the Poor* (1837) for *Blackwoods*', which stopped short after the first sketch. Encouraged by William and Mary Howitt, Mrs. Gaskell also wrote three short stories, which were later published in the Howitt's *Journal*.

In 1843, a tragic blow fell on the Gaskells. Two of the children had been taken to North Wales and there caught scarlet fever, and the baby boy died. Mrs. Gaskell was struck down very low by this loss of her only son and hardly knew how to pick up life again. The first thing that roused her from her overwhelming grief was the trouble of others. She had been trying to preach patience to a mill-worker and was met with the reply : " Aye, ma'am, but have yo' ever seen a child clemmed to death ? " The words struck home, she could not forget them, her mind dwelt more and more on the distress and poverty around her, and eventually came the impulse to make it known to the world in the form of a story, and so she came to write *Mary Barton : A Tale of Manchester Life*.

Although it was begun soon after Mrs. Gaskell's loss, *Mary Barton* was not published until 1848. It at once roused both sympathy and controversy. Amongst the tributes of admiration she received was a letter of high praise from Carlyle, and Dickens at once recognised a kindred spirit and a writer of fine possibilities. Although the book had serious faults it " touched strings that were ready to vibrate to the chord which reached them."[1] On the other hand, there were plenty of

[1] E. Haldane in *Mrs. Gaskell and Her Friends*.

hostile articles and reviews, saying the book was unfair to employers, and the *Manchester Guardian* of February 28th, 1849, complained of " the morbid sensitiveness to the conditions of the operatives " which Mrs. Gaskell showed in common with would-be reformers amongst " the gentry and landed aristocracy."

Now Mrs. Gaskell was drawn into the literary world : Dickens insisted upon her writing for the new magazine he was launching—*Household Words*—and she was a guest at a dinner he gave in celebration of the publication of *David Copperfield*, at which she met the Carlyles, Thackeray, and other literary men. She could not fail to form interesting friendships ; as Charlotte Brontë recorded, she well deserved " the epithet which I find is generally applied to her— charming " ; those who once met her generally wanted to do so again, and found a ready response. An enlargement of her life followed : the Gaskells had inherited some money, the poverty around them was growing less acute, and they felt justified in taking a more spacious and attractive house— 42, Plymouth Grove—which became a place of happy memories to many, including Charlotte Brontë. Here Mrs. Gaskell lived up to the most exacting Victorian ideals of a wife and mother, with an occasional outburst to an intimate friend when a multiplicity of cares overwhelmed her. Writing from Ambleside in 1852, she allowed herself one of these :—

" Well, I'm here ! *How* I came, I don't seem to know, for of all the weary, killing, wearing out bustles in this life that of the last week passed all belief. Thackeray's lectures, two dinners, one concert, card party at home, killing a pig, *my* week at the school which took me into town from 9 till 12 every morning—company in the house, Isabella leaving, William too busy to be agreeable to my unfortunate visitors (Mr. and Mrs. Wedgwood, Dot and Jane, their servant, Annie and Ellen Green[1] closely packed !) so I had to do double duty and talk aesthetically (I dare say) all the time I was thinking of pickle for pork, and with a Ruskinian face and tongue I talked away with a heart like Martha's."

The " double duty " which falls to the wife of a very busy man if she also has activities of her own was never shirked, and Mrs. Gaskell's rich home life imparted a lovable, tenderly human quality to her writing, but only in a comparatively small proportion of her work did she achieve real art. She was

[1] The Miss Greens were friends of her schoolgirl daughters.

the only one of the novelists included in these essays who was both a wife and a mother, and as the wife of a minister she had a rôle to play in her husband's work too ; her friend, Miss Winkworth, said that her literary work was done *after* " all possible social and domestic claims had been satisfied." Moreover, her own social gifts and charming appearance gave society a natural attraction for her, nor could she be satisfied not to dress herself and her daughters with a taste which required thought and time ; Miss Winkworth describes how she called upon her one day in " radiant spirits," evidently partly due to her new " *espiègle* French bonnet." Meanwhile her husband became more and more immersed in his work (especially the preparation of sermons and lectures) and more loth to be uprooted or disturbed, although he generally made himself acceptable in society if he did go out ; on one occasion Mrs. Gaskell said that she had enjoyed a visit more than usual, partly on account of William " being very jolly." As a rule, however, she had to pay her visits by herself ; she stayed at Sir James Kay Shuttleworth's house in the Lake District when Charlotte Brontë was there too, was Florence Nightingale's guest at Lea Hurst and Embley, went to London from time to time, found an occasional welcome respite from her busy round at Silverdale, on Morecambe Bay, and she also travelled in Europe, often with a daughter. When at home her writing was done in the family dining-room, often on a corner of the breakfast table. The first story she produced for *Household Words* was *Lizzie Leigh*, and she wrote to a friend (Miss Fox) :—

" Do you know they sent me £10 for *Lizzie Leigh* ? I stared and wondered if I was swindling them (i.e. the editor of *Household Words*), but I suppose I am not ; and William has composedly buttoned it up in his pocket. He has promised I may have some for my Refuge ! "

Although William's buttoning up her earnings in his pocket gives a shock to the modern, Mrs. Gaskell was evidently always sufficiently in command of funds to make her visits and live as she wished. During 1851–1853 *Cranford* made its appearance in parts in *Household Words*, and Mrs. Gaskell thereby won her abiding place in English literature. She had intended to bring it to a close with Captain Brown's death, but was persuaded to continue the series. More short stories, varying from those with a highly moral tone intended for her Sunday-school girls to tales of ghosts and robbers, followed rapidly, and in 1853 she produced another novel with a purpose—*Ruth*. This book, which is the story of a young unmarried mother, raised an outcry against her. The conventional morality of the period was outraged because both the author and a leading character in the story, a Nonconformist minister, showed too much tenderness for the unfortunate heroine. When *Ruth* appeared Josephine Butler's brave campaign had not yet influenced opinion, although that was to come in the near future; Florence Nightingale was only on the brink of her plunge into the thick of a fight against a cholera epidemic in London, of which many of the victims were "fallen women," one of whom, described by her as "loathsomely filthy," she held in her arms to ease her in dying. Mrs. Gaskell had the courage of liberal-minded convictions too, but she suffered deeply, nevertheless, when she was accused of being unwomanly and setting a low moral standard, and even heard of fathers of families whom she knew throwing her book into the fire !

Despite the trouble which *Ruth* brought upon her, Mrs. Gaskell was writing another novel in 1854, again with a purpose—an attempt to do justice to the industrial employer without losing sight of the workers' point of view. The book was called *North and South*, and had a secondary theme in showing the great differences of life and outlook between the industrial north and the agricultural south. It was in order to help her to leisure for writing this novel that Florence Nightingale invited her to stay at Lea Hurst, her family's beautiful Derbyshire home, and remain there by herself when the Nightingales moved south. Her letters from Lea Hurst, with their interesting details about Florence Nightingale's way of life and characteristics, and her family's attitude to these before she had become a national heroine, are well worth reading.[1] In particular she notes how, once Florence Nightingale has achieved her freedom, she" takes up one thing at a time and bends her whole soul to that "; when that phase of her life was closed and she had passed on to the next she had a lack of interest or sympathy for her old causes which seemed almost inhuman.

[1] See *Mrs. Gaskell and her Friends*, by E. Haldane.

In 1855 came the death of Charlotte Brontë, and Mr. Brontë's desire that Mrs. Gaskell should write her biography. The spirit of consecration in which she set about this task, her conscientious labour, combined with a too ready credulity and rash expression of it (from which it seems strange that her husband did not save her, but probably he was much too busy, and rather required her attendance upon his own work !) have been described in the essay on *The Lives of the Brontë Sisters*. When at last the book was finished she shrank from reviews because she might be doubly hurt—by any aspersions or misunderstandings concerning Charlotte Brontë or by disparagement of the effort which had cost her so much.   Accordingly she set off for Rome where she spent a memorably happy time staying with the William Storys.   On her return she was faced with the storms raised by the biography, including the libel actions threatened by Mrs. Robinson's solicitors and the defenders of the Rev. Carus Wilson and the Cowan Bridge School.   The worry told upon Mrs. Gaskell's health and spirits, and except for the usual output of short stories for magazines she did not embark on any new work for the present.

In 1858 Mrs. Gaskell and a daughter travelled in Germany, and she paid one of a number of visits to Madame Mohl (née Clarke, of Scottish-Irish birth), the eccentric and witty wife of a distinguished French specialist in oriental studies.   Odd, untidy, clever, with a supreme gift for drawing the best out of the interesting men and women whom she attracted to her *salon* in the house where Madame Récamier had lived and Chateaubriand died, Madam Mohl was a congenial and faithful friend to various notable Englishwomen, including Florence Nightingale and Elizabeth Blackwell, one of the pioneer women doctors, who qualified in America before a woman could do so in England.   She often drew Mrs. Gaskell to Paris, and other parts of France were visited too : on one occasion Mrs. Gaskell and her daughters made a Sévigné pilgrimage, following in the footsteps of the great letter-writer.

Meanwhile a holiday in Whitby in 1859 had given her the theme for a new novel—*Sylvia's Lovers*—which required a certain amount of historical research, and was not published until 1863.   It was in a new vein, not intended to serve any moral purpose, but to be a dramatic " tale of love and daring."

During the years 1862-3 Manchester suffered seriously from a cotton famine, due to the fact that the American Civil War prevented the gathering and shipping of the cotton crops. Mrs. Gaskell threw herself into the relief work which was organised until the strain became too much for her health. In 1863 she took another holiday in Rome, there meeting Landor and Swinburne. The following year Mr. George Smith, the publisher, sent her a Valentine which represented her as a dairy-woman (one of her home interests) and himself on his knees before her begging for a manuscript ! Eventually a bargain was made between them by which he promised her the then generous price of £2,000 for seven years' copyright of her next novel, which was to appear first as a serial in the *Cornhill*. Thus her last and, with the possible exception of *Cranford*, her best work was undertaken in conditions of ease and leisure which she had not hitherto felt justified in creating for herself. *Wives and Daughters* is worthy of the privileged circumstances for its composition which had not been accorded to any of her former books. Part of it was peacefully written away from home distractions in Pontresina ; but complete concentration was never to be a possibility for her, and even this book had to be interrupted owing to the illness of one of her daughters.

Now, too, Mrs. Gaskell indulged in the realisation of a castle in the air by buying a charming Southern country home at Holybourne, near Alton, in Hampshire. Messrs. Smith and Elder advanced her some of the money for the purchase, and the transaction was kept secret from Mr. Gaskell ; it was intended to let the house furnished for three years, by which time the mortgage would be paid off, and then to offer it to him as a place of retirement when he was ready to give up his strenuous life in Manchester.

In November, 1865, Mrs. Gaskell had a small family house-party, consisting of her daughters and a son-in-law, at this new home, called The Lawn. She went to service at the village Church on Sunday, November 12th. On the same afternoon, as she was presiding over the tea-table, she suddenly collapsed, and was found to be dead. No doubt her over-full life had taken its toll of her strength for many years past.

Mrs. Gaskell herself had the true Victorian love of somewhat sententious quotations fitted to persons or events ; perhaps that is why it seems irresistible to choose the final comments on her life from the Bible and from Browning. The first quotation that insistently suggests itself is that she was " lovely and pleasant in her life " ; the second that no one had more right to say to a Recording Angel, " Write me down a lover of my fellow-men."

XIII

NOVELS.

Mary Barton, 1848.
Ruth, 1853.
Cranford, 1853.
North & South, 1855.
Sylvia's Lovers, 1863.
Wives & Daughters, 1866 (published after Mrs. Gaskell's Death).

BIOGRAPHY.

Life of Charlotte Brontë, 1857.

SHORT STORIES.

Mrs. Gaskell's short stories may be read in various volumes, differently grouped in different editions. The *Knutsford* edition of her works in 8 volumes is a fine one, but the following list is taken from the *World's Classics* edition :—

Cousin Phillis and Other Tales, including Cousin Phillis, Mr. Harrison's Confessions, The Sexton's Hero, Clopton House, Company Manners, French Life, Modern Greek Songs, An Italian Institution.

Lizzie Leigh, the Grey Woman and Other Tales, including Lizzie Leigh, The Well of Pen-Morfa, The Heart of John Middleton, The Old Nurse's Story, Traits and Stories of the Hugenots, Morton Hall, My French Master, the Squire's Story, The Grey Woman, Curious if True, Six Weeks at Heppenheim, Libbie Marsh's Three Eras, Christmas Storms and Sunshine, Hand and Heart, Bessy's Troubles at Home, Disappearances.

Round the Sofa, including Round the Sofa (an introduction), My Lady Ludlow, An Accursed Race, The Doom of the Griffiths, Half a Lifetime Ago, The Poor Clare, The Half-Brothers.

Right at Last and Other Tales, including Right at Last, The Manchester Marriage, Lois the Witch, The Crooked Branch, A Dark Night's Work, The Schah's English Gardener, Cumberland Sheep-Shearers, Sketches among the Poor, Bran, The Scholar's Story, A Christmas Carol, Preface to *Mabel Vaughan,* Preface to *Garibaldi at Caprera,* How the First Floor went to Crowley Castle, Two Fragments of Ghost Stories.

N.B.—In the *World's Classics* edition, *The Moorland Cottage* and *The Cage at Cranford* are bound up with *Cranford.*

In an Introduction by Anne Thackeray Ritchie to an edition of *Cranford* published in 1891, there are some significant para-

graphs in which she discusses the difference between Jane
Austen's world and Mrs. Gaskell's. She found the clue to
that difference in a French critic's article on Mrs. Gaskell.
M. Montégut argued that every age has a force of its own—it
may be intelligence, or passion or determination, and he went
on to enquire what was the predominating force in his own age,
which was also that of Mrs. Gaskell :—

" It certainly is not will, nor is it brilliant intelligence, as in the
age of Voltaire. It is a quality which, for want of a better word,
we will call the *force of sentiment*. . . . ' People,' he continued, ' have
little confidence in systems, a man with a hobby is immediately
a butt, but a man who is not obliged to be right in order to guard
his vanity, has but to describe in a few simple and true sentences
some fact, some moral wrong which needs redressing, and see the
effect, and the silent help which immediately follows, and for this
reason it is that in literature we have seen of late the almost exclusive
reign of fiction.' "

Here we certainly have, straight from her contemporaries,
two clues to a real comprehension of Mrs. Gaskell's art : she
belonged to an age dominated by " the force of sentiment,"
and her tenderly sympathetic nature could not resist the call—
to her it must even have seemed a duty—to turn her literary
gift to propaganda at a time when the condition-of-England
novel was one of the most effective influences in stimulating
social reform. Her best work, however, only yields to sentiment so far as is natural and inevitable to the characters, time
and place of the story, sentiment does not encroach upon art ;
in her best work, too, she wrote to please herself, stories that
needed no building up because they were in her and of her,with
no ulterior motive of propaganda. *Cranford*, *Cousin Phillis*,
Sylvia's Lovers and *Wives and Daughters* are stamped with their
period, but it is only a background, an aroma, clinging about
scenes and characters which represent enough of the essential
drama of human nature to appeal to one generation after
another. The same cannot be said of *Mary Barton*, *Ruth* and
North and South, which are chiefly interesting to the student of
social and industrial history, although confirmed lovers of Mrs.
Gaskell will find in them some flowering of the fair personality
which even propaganda and over-strained moral earnestness
could not swamp entirely.

In *Mary Barton* we have a very valuable picture of home life
in the mean streets of Manchester on the eve of the " hungry

forties," when the raw force of the Industrial Revolution had not yet been brought under humanitarian control : a beginning had been made by factory acts, poor law reform and education sponsored by Parliament, but so far these often seemed to impose more burdens than they relieved. The book is one of those which paint the background of Chartism, as did Kingsley's *Alton Locke* and Disraeli's *Sybil*, and of the three authors Mrs. Gaskell was the best qualified to draw her scenes from actual life. She *lived in Manchester*, and as a Minister's wife, concerned with the relief of the poor and needy, whereas Kingsley was by up-bringing and choice a countryman, spending the greater part of his time in a Hampshire village, and Disraeli had to "getup" his industrial background from Chartist papers and spasmodic investigation. His was an honourable labour in a statesman of the period whose life had lain as far apart from factory and slum areas as that of his hero Coningsby, to whom Manchester, where " even his bedroom was lighted by gas," was a revelation of a new world of which the Dantesque quality left him with " no appetite and a whirling head." Disraeli, however, could not venture to describe what the average mill-hand would find in the cupboard that served him for a larder as Mrs. Gaskell could, with the certainty of personal knowledge. None of the grim scenes of *Alton Locke* or the rhetorical descriptions of *Sybil* bring home to the reader the condition of average life in the mean streets of an industrial town as do Mrs. Gaskell's bare statements that provision shops sold *ha'porths* of tea, sugar, butter, and even flour, to accommodate their customers, and that parents sat up in their clothes by the fireside the whole night for seven weeks together so that the children might have the only bedding.

Mrs. Gaskell did not, however, confine herself to bare statements. Her descriptions of the Davenports' cellar home, and of one wretched death-bed after another, would seem too extreme to be believed if they could not be compared with Lord Shaftesbury's reports on London slums, which provide parallels to this account of a Manchester street :—

" It was unpaved : and down the middle a gutter forced its way, every now and then forming pools in the holes with which the street abounded. Never was the old Edinburgh cry of *Gardez l'eau* more necessary than in this street. As they passed women from their doors tossed household slops of *every* description into the gutter ; they ran into the next pool, which overflowed and stagnated ; heaps of ashes were the stepping-stones, on which the passer-by who cared in the least for cleanliness, took care not to put his foot.   Our friends were not dainty, but even they picked their way, till they got to some steps leading down to a small area, where a person standing would have his head about one foot below the level of the street, and might at the same time, without the least motion of his body, touch the window of the cellar and the damp muddy wall right opposite.   You went down one step even from the foul area into the cellar in which a family of human beings lived.   It was very dark inside.   The window-panes, many of them, were broken and stuffed with rags, which was reason enough for the dusky light that pervaded the place even at mid-day."

Barton enters with some bread for the famished children :—

" In that dim light, which was darkness to strangers, they clustered round Barton, and tore from him the food he had brought with him. It was a large hunch of bread, but it vanished in an instant . . . Wilson had done what he could at Davenport's home . . . . He had opened a door, but only for an instant ; it led into a back cellar, with a grating instead of a window, down which dropped moisture from pig-styes, and worse abominations.   It was not paved ; the floor was one mass of bad-smelling mud.   It had never been used, for there was not an article of furniture in it ; nor could a human being, much less a pig, have lived there many days.   Yet the ' back apartment ' made a difference in the rent.   The Davenports paid three-pence more for having two rooms."

Such scenes in *Mary Barton* would be more effective if Mrs. Gaskell had been more sparing of them.   The book had been inspired by the starkly simple question of a working-woman whom she was trying to encourage—" Have you ever seen a child clemmed to death ? "—and the shadow of the death-bed lies heavy on it from beginning to end ; and while Mrs. Gaskell shows very clearly the cumulative, relentless force of circumstances turning John Barton first into a trade union leader, then into a Chartist and finally into a murderer for the cause, all the scenes are interlarded with a moral purpose and a sentimental piety which suggest the tract.   The plot has its exciting phases, graphically dealt with, as Mrs. Gaskell liked a good, strong plot and was sometimes tempted into melo-drama.   It is not, however, either on account of the story or the descriptions that no student of social history can afford to neglect this " tale of Manchester life " : it is because Mrs. Gaskell could penetrate and reveal the workings of the minds of the poorest victims of the overwhelming, mushroom growth of industrialism at a time when it outstripped man's control. In all the literature of Chartism (whether genuine documents or fiction) there is nothing which brings out so vividly all that the great Chartist petition of 1839 stood for in the minds of the working people of the industrial North, and all their mental reactions both to the distress and the infant reforms of the day, as the scene in *Mary Barton* in which John Barton's friends and neighbours come to have a few last words with him before he leaves for London as one of the Chartist delegates who were to present the great petition to Parliament—a band of " life-worn, gaunt, hunger-stamped men." As John Barton sits by the fire puffing at his pipe and his daughter is washing his two shirts for the great march on London, the neighbours collect and press their opinions upon him. One begs him to ask for the destruction of all machines ; another tells him to be sure to put in a few words for the Short Hours Bill ; a widow begs him to explain to " the Parliament folk " how hard the law which keeps children under ten out of the factories bears on mothers with sturdy boys, with whom " porridge seems to go no way," especially when they can't afford to send them to school. Another tells a story of his mother's, when she was a laundry-maid and discovered that fine gentlemen sometimes wore two shirts a day, and he suggests that if they could be made to have calico ones " 'twould make trade brisk, that would, wi' the power of shirts they wear " ; to which another replies that John should ask Parliament to set trade free, then all the poor weavers who only have a rag for a shirt, and don't know how to buy another when that's done, could use up the calico now lying in the mills fast enough. The scene is a brilliant commentary on the struggles and distress of the late thirties and the " hungry forties."

John Barton returned from London a broken man. The Petition, after a delay which caused the Chartists great difficulties, was rejected by 235 votes to 46, and the delegates were not permitted to speak at the bar of the House of Commons. This is, however, history rather than literature, and the interest of *Mary Barton* and *North and South* is historical rather than literary.

In *Ruth* (published in 1853), Mrs. Gaskell produced a

M

different type of social-problem novel ; the theme is not the condition of England but the particular fate meted out to the unmarried mother who wishes to re-establish herself in respectable society. The heroine is a pretty dressmaker's assistant, rather too innocent and ignorant at the outset to be convincing, who, after the desertion of her lover and much further tribulation, redeems her ruined life by becoming a hospital nurse—then an occupation not far short of degrading and disgusting in many institutions—and spending herself to the uttermost in an epidemic of typhoid. Unfortunately Mrs. Gaskell's sentiment and underlining of morals rather irritates the modern reader than enlists his sympathy for Ruth and her illegitimate baby (referred to as " the noble child ! ") and she concludes the story in an orgy of moral justice and expiation by making Ruth's betrayer one of the typhoid victims whom she nurses, then taking the infection herself and dying of it.

There are, however, good things in *Ruth*. The minister who befriends her—Thurston Benson—is a finely drawn character, although the morality of the day was shocked by Mrs. Gaskell's allowing him to pass Ruth off as a young widow in order to give her the only possible chance of recovering respectability. From this deception there springs a train of disasters which surely point the moral sufficiently thoroughly to excuse the author, at least, if not the minister ! In her own day, however, Mrs. Gaskell was reviled for an over-light and even unwomanly treatment of this moral and social problem, and the book was banned by various circulating libraries. Now we are as much shocked at the state of society which made such a deception practically essential, if the young mother was to rise at all from the outer darkness of a " fallen woman," as at the minister's being a party to it. One modern critic's[1] comment is that " a similar book published to-day would be thought prudish."

In *North & South* (published 1855) Mrs. Gaskell was influenced by the fact that various Manchester friends, besides critics in the press, had complained that *Mary Barton* was unfair to employers. The hero of *North & South*—John Thornton—is an employer who is proud of his own capacity and of the progress of industry, in which he wishes his firm

[1] Stanton Whitfield in *Mrs. Gaskell* (Routledge, 1929).

to play a notable part ; in the course of the story he gradually grows into more sympathy with his men, realising that they, too, have a stake in industry, and in the firm which employs them.   The book, however, gives no complete picture of the relations of masters and men as a whole, except, perhaps, to show up the lack of co-operative spirit between them.   There are some strong incidents, and students of industrial history will find interest in the accounts of a strike, of the persecution of the men who refused to join the struggling trade unions and of an attack on Thornton's mill.   Another striking feature of *North and South* is the way in which it brings out the extraordinary differences in working life and outlook between the industrial North and the agricultural South, and between the well-to-do manufacturers of the factory towns and the landed gentry of the Southern counties.   Disraeli gave his novel *Sybil* the sub-title of *The Two Nations*, meaning the rich and the poor ; it would have applied equally well to *North and South*.   *North and South* is readable and its side-lights on industrial life worth study, but it was written with a purpose and has not the attraction of spontaneous art.

Meanwhile *Cranford* had been appearing as a series of sketches in Dickens' new periodical *Household Words*, and with it Mrs. Gaskell entered her own kindgom.   She had lived in Cranford (the Knutsford in which much of her youth had been passed), and she was intimate with its little " elegant economies," all planned to serve the great and all-absorbing art of *keeping up appearances*.   Snobbery is too harsh a word for this practice of the Cranford ladies, many of them the last representatives of families which had seen " better days " : their brave attempts not to fall too far below the standards of fair and dignified living which they felt they had in trust from their ancestors was then as fine an art as it would be a vulgar one in the present democratic age of easier manners and robust frankness.   Through Mrs. Gaskell's own sensitive response to these ideals of a class on the eve of passing away, we catch for a moment the delicate aroma given off by such words as " genteel " and " elegant " on the lips of the elderly ladies of Cranford.   We feel an impulse to shield Miss Matty and her friends from exposure to the keen air of modern criticism ; the scenes of Cranford should be—metaphorically speaking— laid up with sprigs of lavender between layers of tissue paper.

The only criticism which does not seem too rude a jar for Miss Matty and her world is such as Ruskin's, who wrote : " I have just been reading out *Cranford* to my mother . . . the first time I tried I flew into a passion at Captain Brown's being killed and wouldn't go any farther—but this time my mother coaxed me past it, and then I enjoyed it mightily."

At last Mrs. Gaskell had cut free of the trammels of propaganda and moral purpose, her story welled up into her mind from the very roots of her own being, and she carries her readers back with her into the small country-town as she knew it in the eighteen-thirties and forties (when it really was both country and town) and into its old-maids' parlours, where life was still brave and touching even in its pastel setting of fading colours. How living Cranford and its households were to those whose own childhoods held some similar memories is testified by many of Mrs. Gaskell's contemporaries. A particularly charming picture is that of Thackeray's daughter almost tremulously placing in his hands the number of *Household Words* containing the account of Captain Brown's death, and watching him read it under the gas-light in his dining-room in Young Street. The watching girl, who felt as if she had actually seen the " most touching and heroic deed," longed for her father's sympathy and, although she was " a grown girl," she had " a feeling that even yet he might avert the catastrophe."

Captain Brown was a sacrifice to the requirements of the magazine ; Mrs. Gaskell's *Cranford* series was supposed to end much earlier than it did—but, owing to the success of these first sketches Dickens was anxious for her to continue them and she consented. As a book it loses a little in unity from having been cast in serial form, which requires a distribution of interest through all the parts that is less satisfactory when it is read as a whole.

It is superfluous to quote from *Cranford*, of which most people can find a copy, if not in their own houses in that of a parent or an aunt. Some of the incidents are already classic : Miss Betsy Barker's Alderney cow going to the field in its coat and drawers of grey flannel, after its unlucky fall into a lime-pit had burned off its hair ; Miss Matty rolling an indiarubber ball under her bed every night to make sure that no obstructing burglar is in hiding there, her hand meanwhile on the bell-

rope and her lips forming the names " John ! " and " Harry ! "
to give the impression of a staff of men-servants within call ;
the cat swallowing Mrs. Forrester's priceless old lace which
had been put to soak in milk, and its being given an emetic and
kept a prisoner in a top-boot until it took effect ; the laying of
newspapers on the floor to save the new carpet from fading,
and the little paths of newspapers laid down from the door to
the principal chairs on the occasion of a tea-party.

The ladies themselves are not the only delectable characters ;
there is Miss Matty's country servant Martha, who, on being
instructed that when waiting at table she must hand the
dishes to the ladies first, comments regretfully, " I'll do as
you tell me, ma'am, but I like lads best." The same girl,
when Miss Matty has lost her money in the bank failure and
explains to her that she must listen to reason and leave a house
where she can no longer be paid wages, replies with equal
sturdiness, " I'll not listen to reason, reason always means
what someone else has got to say."

So, despite the worship of birth and the sacrifices made to
fulfill its obligations, in spite of the lady who boasted of her
cousin Mr. ffoulkes, who " looked down upon capital letters,
and said they belonged to lately-invented families," and did
not marry until he was fortunate enough to meet an eligible
Miss ffaringdon, there is plenty of genuine humanity in
Cranford. It is, however, a *genre* piece, which limits its appeal
to something less than that of the greatest books, which rise
above the boundaries of period and place in their universal
interest. The particular *genre* represented by *Cranford*
becomes more and more old-fashioned and strange in an
increasingly free and democratic age, and there is some danger
that what used to be thought so touching may in time be called
petty or even contemptible : but this can never apply to Miss
Matty, the central figure of the book, whose gentle dignity and
unexpected courage and initiative in misfortune will always
win over detractors of Cranford standards.

After *Cranford* and the group of social-industrial novels
Mrs. Gaskell's next important piece of work was her *Life of
Charlotte Brontë*. Enough has been said about this bio-
graphy, and the trouble it cost her, elsewhere in this book.[1]
It is likely to remain one of " the noblest few of English

[1] See *The Lives of the Brontë Sisters* and *The Life of E. C. Gaskell*.

biographies,"[1] despite its departures from strict accuracy and its suppressions, none of which really impair Mrs. Gaskell's incomparable picture of the Brontës and their home. Perhaps its worst flaw is that it does less than justice to Emily, and also to Mr. Nicholls ; but her picture lies at the foundation of the Brontë cult which has proved so fascinating to many people of many types.

During the whole of this period Mrs. Gaskell wrote a large number of short stories and sketches for magazines, some of which—or at least parts of them—are in her best style, others marred by the over-stressed morality of the tract or by a melodramatic choice of plot. Of one—*The Moorland Cottage* —Charlotte Brontë wrote happily that " it opens like a morning daisy, and closes like a herb—a balsamic herb, with healing in its leaves." The heroine, Maggie, foreshadows one of Mrs. Gaskell's best creations—Molly Gibson in *Wives and Daughters*—and her mother is not unlike Molly's step-mother. Early in the story she instructs her daughter how to behave on a visit :—

" Of course you'll never think of being helped more than twice. Twice of meat and twice of pudding, is the genteel thing. You may take less, but never more."

Maggie's attention wanders from her mother's exhortations as they approach the town :—

" 'Oh, mamma ! How beautiful Colehurst spire is with that cloud behind it ! ' exclaimed Maggie, as they came in sight of the town.
' You've no business with Colehurst spire when I'm speaking to you. I'm talking myself out of breath to teach you how to behave, and there you go looking after clouds, and such-like rubbish. I'm ashamed of you.' "

A story which has for title *The Moorland Cottage*, and opens on these lines, has no business to end with an elaborately worked up shipwreck, in which the ne'er-do-weel who is ruining Maggie's life is conveniently drowned, and her lover providentially turns up in the steerage just in time to save her life. It is a violation of art ; the most satisfying stories draw to an end which more or less harmonises with the beginning.

In the stories which represent the daily life of weekly

---

[1] Quiller-Couch in *Charles Dickens and Other Victorians*.

wage-earners the details of Mrs. Gaskell's pictures ring true, even when over-laid too thickly with morals. Few writers not born and bred in a poor street could have ventured so certainly on describing the little sewing-woman's change of lodgings in *Libbie Marsh's Three Eras*, or have entered so graphically into the Whitsuntide holiday spirit of the Man- chester workpeople streaming out of the town to spend the fine summer day in Dunham Park.

Another group of Mrs. Gaskell's short stories deal with ghosts, robbers, mysteries and even horror, subjects which had a great fascination for her, and in which she showed a strong sense of drama. *Lois the Witch* is a graphic and tragic tale of the persecution of an English girl, who, left an orphan, goes out to join her uncle and his godly community in New England. The mentality of the settlers is most convincingly drawn : it seems inevitable that they should cling to their narrow creed as the one certain salvation in their precarious hold on this new world, where the illimitable forest which hems them in makes the mystery and fear of the unknown (from Indians to evil spirits) a haunting oppression from which they cannot shake themselves free. Simply and vividly Mrs. Gaskell brings that oppression home to us in her description of " the great wood with its perpetual movement of branch and bough, and its solemn wail, that came into the very streets of Salem when certain winds blew, bearing the sound of the pine trees clear upon the ears that had leisure to listen."

The Grey Woman is a fine mystery tale with a touch of horror, as good as anything Mrs. Gaskell wrote in this line. Other short stories in her list of thirty are in the *Cranford* vein, amongst them *Mr. Harrison's Confessions* and *My Lady Ludlow*. *My French Master* has the same old-world touch with a difference.

In 1863 Mrs. Gaskell published a novel which contains some of her best work, *Sylvia's Lovers*, the first half of which is an enthralling story beautifully told. The opening description of Monkshaven (Whitby) sets the scene for a drama of the press-gang, with its reactions upon the romance of the lovely little Sylvia Robson of Haytersbank Farm, whom we first meet walking into the town with her friend Molly Corney, with butter and eggs to sell in the market. Sylvia's head is full of the stuff for a new cloak which she is to buy in Monkshaven, and the great problem whether it shall be grey or scarlet duffle. Even while the girls wash their feet in the last stream which crosses their path she is still chattering about it. Once in Monkshaven the girls are soon caught up in the excitement which holds the whole town in grip, for the first whaler has just come home from Greenland and can be seen beyond the bar waiting for the tide to come in :—

" The fresh, salt breeze was bringing up the lashing, leaping tide from the blue sea beyond the bar. Behind the returning girls there rocked the white-sailed ship, as if she were all alive with eagerness for her anchors to be heaved.

How impatient her crew of beating hearts were for that moment, how those on land sickened at the suspense, may be imagined, when you remember that for six long summer months those sailors had been as if dead from all news of those they loved ; shut up in terrible, dreary, Arctic seas from the hungry sight of sweethearts and friends, wives and mothers. No one knew what might have happened. The crowd on shore grew silent and solemn before the dread of the possible news of death that might toll in upon their hearts with this up-rushing tide. The whalers went out into the Greenland seas full of strong, hopeful men ; but the whalers never returned as they sailed forth . . . Many a heart swelled with passionate, unspoken fear, as the first whaler lay off the bar on her return voyage."

Scarcely had the men landed when the press-gang was upon them ; they were unprepared, for there had been a long period of freedom from the cruel kidnappers, but now Napoleon was threatening the very shores of England and there was a shortage of experienced sailors to man the war-ships, so the strongest and finest of the home-coming seamen were torn from the arms of their sweethearts, wives and mothers and marched off under a strong guard which dare not indulge them with any opportunity for leave-takings. No one knew when—or whether—they would come back ; the chances of sending news by letter were few and costly, the risks of war and foreign service incalculable.

So the scene is set for a powerful and moving story, to which Mrs. Gaskell brings a quality of description (of which the extract quoted, a very fair sample of her prose, gives evidence), characterisation and dramatic force which leaves little to be desired. She marshals her material well in the first part of the book : there is a hero—Charley Kinraid— wounded in a fight with the press-gang and left for dead, to be idolised by the girls of Monkshaven and to win the young heart of the adorable Sylvia, and there is Sylvia's cousin—Philip Hepburn—who has loved her with patient perseverance and looks to her as the crown of a laborious career in which he has risen from shop-boy in a prosperous draper's to the near prospect of a partnership. Meanwhile the last cruel boat of the press-gang still lurks amongst the rocks, although the Monkshaven fishermen believe that all the gang have left the neighbourhood. The inevitable capture of Kinraid, the hero with a reputation of being a light-of-love, to whom Sylvia has just pledged herself, follows, and Hepburn is the only witness ; had the will been there he might even have saved him by a timely warning. By him Kinraid sends a solemn message to Sylvia that he will come back and marry her. Hepburn, sore and indignant that circumstances should force him to be the messenger of Kinraid, in whose sincerity he has no faith, delays to report the capture. Meanwhile Kinraid's hat, ornamented with Sylvia's ribbon, is picked up on the rocks, it is taken for granted he is drowned, and Hepburn decides to hold his peace.

Here is ample material for a genuine tragedy, only needing time and circumstances to bring Sylvia to marry Hepburn, and then Kinraid's inevitable return, to complete it ; but too much that is anything but inevitable is dragged in ; Sylvia is reduced to marriage with Hepburn by the extreme method of seeing her father tried and hung for interfering with the press-gang ; Hepburn stands by the wife and daughter in their agonising ordeal, and she gives herself to him half in gratitude and half in the listlessness of despair. Then Kinraid returns. Hepburn, his treachery revealed, disappears and enlists, but Sylvia, a mother now as well as a wife, cannot join her life to Kinraid's. Unfortunately Mrs. Gaskell's ingenuity is still unsatisfied : there must needs be one of those irresistible coincidences to enable Hepburn to save Kinraid's life, and then he must return, disabled and almost penniless, to live on the outskirts of Monkshaven and be given food as a beggar by his own little girl. Finally he saves her life too, and then dies in Sylvia's arms in a thick odour of retribution and piety. Sylvia is also brought to an early death. In this fashion Mrs. Gaskell defaces what is very nearly a masterpiece. *Sylvia's Lovers* is, nevertheless, a most moving story and the first half of the book finely conceived and beautifully executed.

In 1865 Mrs. Gaskell, in Edmund Gosse's phrase, " con-
quered the pastoral episode in *Cousin Phillis*," a short, sad
idyll of unfulfilled love in a country setting, redolent with the
remembered fragrances of Sandlebridge Farm near Knutsford, where her mother had been born and bred.   In this
story Mrs. Gaskell's prose is at its best and purest, with a
lyric quality, and the boy Paul, Phillis's cousin, who tells
the story of her love for another man, is so natural that a
critic remarked that Mrs. Gaskell seemed to be able to get
inside the skin of a youth of eighteen.   Phillis's father, an ex-
Nonconformist minister and something of a classical scholar,
turned farmer, was no doubt suggested by Mrs. Gaskell's own.
Of *Cousin Phillis* Quiller-Couch says :—

" It beats me to guess how any true critic can pass it over and
neglect a thing with all that is best in Theocritus moving in rustic
English hearts.   And it is not *invented*.   It has in all its movements
the suggestion of things actually seen . . . each in its turn a little
flash of light upon the steady background of rural England.   It is
English and yet pure Virgil."

The sad charm of *Cousin Phillis* is akin to that of *Cranford*
in that it is born of an age that is past.

At the time of her death Mrs. Gaskell was just drawing
near the conclusion of *Wives and Daughters* as a serial in the
Cornhill.   Her last work was her best : *Wives and Daughters* is
an unspoiled harmony of story, characterisation and style, it
is, in fact, to many readers, as good and as dear as any novel by
any nineteenth century woman writer, except Jane Austen.
Its quiet key, which is an essential part of its charm, has kept it
from being a really popular success : it lacks the sparkling
irony which is such a preservative in Jane Austen's books, and
the dynamic force of *Jane Eyre* and *Wuthering Heights* ;
the canvas is not so wide as that of *The Mill on the Floss*.

Wives and Daughters fully justifies its sub-title of *An
Every-day Story*.   The incident is confined to a little girl's
unsatisfactory day on the happily anticipated occasion of the
annual visit of the Hollingford school-visitors to the " great
house " of the neighbourhood ;   her relations with her father ;
his second marriage ;   a very young girl's entanglements
between three lovers ;   a young man's not knowing his real
mind as soon as he might have done, and a secret marriage on
the part of a minor character.   Out of these materials Mrs.

Gaskell has made a living drama of character. We watch these people creating their own story simply by being what they are, and to do this we have to become intimate with their daily round. We are with them on their walks, at the table, in the drawing-room, at the Hollingford parties, in those days when evenings were so long after the early dinner, and journeys of rare occurrence. We do not " quiz " them, as Jane Austen might have led us on to do, or penetrate their reserve to the innermost core of feeling as we might if they were in Charlotte Brontë's hands, or subject their emotions to deliberate pyschological analysis such as George Eliot used : when Cynthia locks her bedroom door on Molly we are locked out too. Yet we feel the relief when Molly can escape from the vapid chatter of her step-mother and the deft millinery of her lovely step-sister to be alone for a little while in her own small room.

Mr. Gibson, the busy country doctor of Hollingford, who covers so many miles on horseback and finds so few neighbours to match him in intelligence, is one of Mrs. Gaskell's best portraits. We see him first as a widower, facing the disconcerting problems of having a daughter growing up with no woman as head of his household. An old friend has persuaded him to take his son as a pupil, the youth falls in love with Molly Gibson, who is not quite seventeen, and Mr. Gibson intercepts his first love-letter to her. He sits down at his writing-table to compose a prescription, headed " Master Coxe," which is to accompany the returned letter. The ingredients are *verecundia*, *fidelitas domestica* and *reticentia*, the whole to be taken *ter die in aqua pura*. The envelope is addressed to Edward Coxe, Esq., and it is delivered by the groom instead of a maid-servant, as a concession to the young man's pride. The little incident both reveals the man and prepares the way for his story.

We see Mr. Gibson's second wife, the widow who had hardly borne to change her poetic maiden name of Hyacinth Clare for that of Hyacinth Kirkpatrick, and was now called upon to make the further descent to Gibson, both through his eyes and Molly's, and our sympathy is equally divided between them. Like Mr. Bennet in *Pride and Prejudice*, Mr. Gibson takes refuge in satire when the shallow airs and graces and the succession of petty ambitions which are the breath of life to Mrs. Gibson become oppressive. Her

relations with the Earl of Cumnor's family at the Towers, with
whom she had been a governess and who still have both uses
and kindly patronage for " Clare," are excellently drawn.
One typical incident is when she lunches at the Towers after
her marriage :—

" At lunch Mrs. Gibson was secretly hurt by my lord's supposing
it was her dinner, and calling out his urgent hospitality from the
very bottom of the table, giving as a reason for it, that she must
remember it was her dinner. In vain she piped out in her soft,
high voice, " Oh, my lord ! I never eat meat in the middle of the
day ; I can hardly eat anything at lunch." Her voice was lost, and
the duchess might go away with the idea that the Hollingford doctor's
wife dined early ; that is to say, if her grace ever condescended to
have any idea on the subject at all, which pre-supposes that she
was cognisant of there being a doctor in Hollingford, and that he
had a wife, and that his wife was the pretty, faded, elegant-looking
woman, sending away her plate of untasted food—food which she
longed to eat, for she was really desperately hungry after her drive."

Mrs. Gibson exercised great finesse to encourage Osborne
Hamley, the heir to Hamley, in attentions to her daughter
Cynthia, while equally discouraging the younger brother,
Roger.   When the two young men have sent bouquets to the
girls before the Hollingford ball, which they themselves cannot
attend because they are in mourning, Osborne disclaims the
entire credit, which Mrs. Gibson thrusts upon him :—

" ' Oh,' said Osborne, ' you must not thank me exclusively.
I believe it was my thought, but Roger took all the trouble of it.'
' I consider the thought as everything,' said Mrs. Gibson, ' thought
is spiritual, while action is merely material.' This fine sentence
took the speaker herself by surprise ; but in such conversation as
was then going on, it is not necessary to accurately define the meaning
of everything that is said."

We become as familiar with Mrs. Gibson's foibles as her
husband and Molly, and soon know that when she has anything unpleasant or inconvenient to announce she will take an
opportunity to do so when a visitor is present, so that family
comment is restrained until the first shock of the proposition
has passed off.   Yet even Mrs. Gibson has her saving graces,
and in this she is superior to Jane Austen's Mrs. Bennet :
when she has goaded her husband into some caustic remark
which she cannot understand she says pathetically to Molly,
" poor papa seems tired," and goes off to order some favourite
dish for his dinner.

Cynthia Kirkpatrick is a complex character very well drawn ; her charm is really there, we do not only see its effects on the other characters in the story while we ourselves must take it on trust. The lack of principle due to her up-bringing, which she herself genuinely regrets even while she continues to act as nature and training dictate, is not so serious as to destroy affection, either in Molly or the reader. She is, in fact, a skilful blend of opposite characteristics into a thoroughly convincing personality.

To draw Molly Gibson needed the touch of genius. She is a straightforward, undistinguished, thoroughly nice girl, and to make her so lovable, and her quality so good, while barely lifting her out of the ruck of average nice girlhood, was no small feat. These two girls are examples of Mrs. Gaskell's art at its best, such as Georges Sand must have had in mind when she said to Lord Houghton :—

" Mrs. Gaskell has done what neither I nor other female writers in France can accomplish ; she has written novels which excite the deepest interest in the man of the world, and yet which every girl will be the better for reading."

Mrs. Gaskell's best work is the fine flowering of a charming, lovable, well-balanced personality, with a wide but mainly happy experience of life. Her humour, especially, is the sound, sweet fruit of a life of happy relationships : she can command irony, as in the character of Mrs. Gibson in *Wives and Daughters*, but she has none of Charlotte Brontë's acerbity, and not even a touch of cynicism, such as there is in Jane Austen's satire.

Mrs. Gaskell's prose is not exceptionally distinguished or very individualistic ; it is pleasant, clear, graphic and sometimes lyrical. Sometimes the influence of period is evident in long words where short, simple ones would be more fitting, and in rather formal or grandiose phrases ; sometimes there are slovenly or ill-considered passages, which is not surprising in a writer who was so prolific in the midst of such a busy life. On the whole her stories gain in grace and charm by her manner of telling them, and when she gives the conversations of working men and women, whether of town or country, she is seldom at fault.

We can well believe the testimony of a friend that she herself was " like the best things in her books," that is, "full of gracious and tender sympathies, of thoughtful kindness, of pleasant humour, of quick appreciation, of the utmost simplicity and truthfulness."

BOOKS ABOUT MRS. GASKELL

By Mrs. Gaskell's own wish, consequent on the trouble caused by her *Life of Charlotte Brontë*, no biography of her was permitted for many years. Therefore the best early accounts of her life and work are to be found in *The Dictionary of National Biography* and in the excellent biographical and critical prefaces to the *Knutsford edition* of her works (8 volumes) : all these articles were written by *Sir A. K. Ward*.

Women Novelists of Queen Victoria's Reign. Article on Mrs. Gaskell by A. E. Baily (*Edna Lyall*).

Le Roman Social en Angleterre (1830–1850) *Cazamian* (*Paris*) 1903. Chapter on Mrs. Gaskell under the title *Mrs. Gaskell : L'interventionisme Chretien.* Cazamian's account of the development of the condition-of-England novel is excellent.

Mrs. Gaskell and Knutsford. G. A. Payne (*Manchester Press*) 1905.

Mrs. Gaskell : her Haunts, Homes and Stories. Mrs. Ellis Chadwick, Revised edition. 1913.

Mrs. Gaskell. G. A. Payne (*Manchester Press*) 1929.

Elizabeth Gaskell, with a *Bibliography.* C. S. Northup (*U.S.A.*) 1929.

*Mrs. Gaskell. A Stanton Whitfield (*Routledge*), 1929. A useful and readable book of moderate length. There are good biographical and chronological appendices.

**Mrs. Gaskell and Her Friends. Elizabeth Haldane (*Hodder & Stoughton*) 1930. A complete and scholarly biography containing extracts from letters hitherto unpublished.

XIV

CHARLOTTE MARY YONGE AND HER NOVELS
(1823–1901)

Contributed by Dorothea Blagg

The following are the principal novels by Charlotte Yonge, of which the first was published in 1844 and the last in 1900 :—

Abbey Church (1844), *Scenes and Characters, Henrietta's Wish, Kenneth, The Two Guardians, The Heir of Redclyffe, Castle Builders, Heartsease, The Lances of Lynwood* (for young people), *The Daisy Chain, The Trial* (*More Links of the Daisy Chain*), *Dynevor Terrace, Hopes and Fears, The Young Stepmother, The Clever Woman of the Family, The Dove in the Eagle's Nest, The Prince and the Page* (for young people), *The Chaplet of Pearls, The Caged Lion, The Pillars of the House, My Young Alcides, The Three Brides, Love and Life, Unknown to History, Stray Pearls, The Armourer's Prentices, Nuttie's Father, Chantry House, A Modern Telemachus, A Reputed Changeling, Grisley Grisell, That Stick, The Long Vacation, Modern Broods* (1900).

In the year 1844 Richard Church, a young Oxford don, afterwards Dean of St. Paul's, was talking to a friend about a book which had just come out. " It is a very clever book," he said, " and the young lady will write well in future." " Oh, why ? " said his companion. " Because every character, however simple, is perfectly distinct and living."

Probably few people now alive have read *Abbey Church*, Charlotte Yonge's first published book ; but Dean Church's critical insight discovered in it the outstanding characteristic which is Charlotte's chief claim to merit as a novelist : her characters are " perfectly distinct and living." In this one respect there is no writer of English fiction who excels her.

But a writer cannot be placed in the front rank by virtue of one gift alone ; and there were serious defects in Charlotte Yonge's work. These were not fully recognised by her contemporaries, for she had not to wait, like Jane Austen, until after death for her full meed of praise ; and for many years posterity has been busy redressing the balance. In truth it has done the work too thoroughly.

In one respect Miss Yonge is at a disadvantage as compared with other women novelists. She lived to be nearly eighty, and was writing constantly for half a century; whereas all the great women writers of the 19th century died comparatively young, and not one of them wrote more than six complete novels. Can we suppose that if they had lived to be nearly eighty they would have kept up their level as we know it?

It is impossible to resist comparing Jane Austen and Charlotte Yonge. Their circumstances were curiously similar. Both lived in Hampshire villages, both belonged to the "upper middle-class" of English society. Hence they had a similarly limited outlook. They wrote of what they knew, and let the rest of the world alone. Both concerned themselves largely with the life and doings of young girls. But there the resemblance ceases. Charlotte Yonge's girls live in a new atmosphere, an atmosphere of earnest purpose. They have discovered the possibility of other interests besides water-colour drawing, morning calls, walks in the shrubbery, balls and assemblies, all continually pervaded by thoughts of possible husbands. They know the enthusiasm of devoting one's life to a cause. Young men had been fired with high ideals in the days of the French Revolution, but they had not communicated the fire to young ladies—not at least to the young ladies of Jane Austen's circle. The Napoleonic war did not touch them except when it brought fascinating officers to their assemblies or carried off beloved brothers to the high seas. About half a century separated Jane Austen's novels from those by which Miss Yonge made her name, and there is quite half a century's difference in their outlook. We shall be able to develop this point more fully as we consider some of the individual books.

Yet the contrast between Charlotte Yonge and her contemporaries is almost greater. They were akin in that they all belonged to the romantic and idealistic age, whereas Jane Austen had not really emerged from the classical eighteenth century; but the refined restraint of Charlotte Yonge seems to have more in common with her than with the fierce emotions of the Brontës, the social propaganda of Mrs. Gaskell, or the psychological subtleties of George Eliot.

Charlotte Yonge's books may be divided into three main classes; Family Chronicles, Historical Romances, and Novels of Contemporary Life. Of these, the two first contain by far her best work. In both she may be said to have worked in a medium of her own, and used it with remarkable skill. Even her third class was more or less of an innovation, for it was something between a girls' book and a full-blown novel. It proved very attractive at the time, but these books belong more exclusively to their period and contain more of her characteristic weaknesses than the others. Yet it was one of these, *The Heir of Redclyffe*, which made her fame. Moderns who want to make acquaintance with Miss Yonge's work should not begin with *The Heir of Redclyffe*. They will almost certainly not like it, and it may prevent their reading others which they would enjoy. How, then, can we explain its remarkable success when it was published in 1853 ? It cannot be dismissed lightly as a typical instance of a best seller, appealing to the low-brow public. It was not merely gushing girls who admired it. Serious critics like M. Guizot praised it. The young Pre-Raphaelites, William Morris and Dante Rossetti, " took Guy as their hero-model." The book seems to have been read quite as much by men as by women. Miss Yonge's brother Julian found that nearly every officer in his regiment had a copy, and when Charlotte visited Oxford in 1865, it is recorded that the enthusiasm for her among the undergraduates was surprising. Clearly there must have been a quality and a power in the book which modern readers miss because they are not *en rapport* with its spirit. It was a product of the age, and it evoked a response from the best spirits of the age. The youth of to-day will no more paint like the Pre-Raphaelites than they will read *The Heir of Redclyffe :* nevertheless the P.R.B. were serious artists, whose judgment on a work of literature is worthy of respect. On the face of it, it does not seem as if there were much affinity between Miss Yonge's work and theirs. But the Brotherhood was in the direct line of descent from the Romantic Revival, which was also conspicuous in the ancestry of the Oxford Movement : and Charlotte was a child of the Oxford Movement, a disciple of John Keble, who prepared her for confirmation and was her spiritual guide until his death.

The germ of *The Heir of Redclyffe* was supplied to Charlotte by her friend Miss Dyson, who said there were two characters she wanted to see brought out in a story—the essentially

N

contrite and the self-satisfied. There were plenty of heroes who were subdued by the memory of some involuntary disaster, but the " penitence of the saints " was unattempted. It was a good idea, but unfortunately Charlotte could not bring herself to make her hero do anything very wrong, and therefore his repentance is overstrained and exaggerated. All he did was to give way to fierce rage against his cousin for a few hours under intense provocation, but he succeeded in forgiving him before the sun went down. If only he had done Philip some injury in the heat of his anger, the story might have been a much finer one.

One thing which Charlotte Yonge achieved by *The Heir* and kindred books was that she made goodness interesting. Jane Austen's heroes were nice young men, but they were never in any danger of becoming too good for this world. It was for Charlotte Yonge to depict a more exalted and heroic type of character, involving the spirit of self-sacrifice, and coming near to the standard of the saints, while at the same time so attractive that her girl-readers fell in love with it.

Other novels of contemporary life which followed were *Heartsease, Dynevor Terrace, The Young Stepmother*, and *The Clever Woman of the Family*. *Heartsease* was much liked in its day (by Charles Kingsley for one), but most people would probably find *Dynevor Terrace* more attractive. It contains a charming young man, and shows more of Miss Yonge's gift of humour than appears in the two previous books. *The Young Stepmother* is noteworthy for having kept Tennyson awake at night. F. T. Palgrave thus relates the incident[1] :—

" One bedroom with two huge four-posters was allotted us ; and Tennyson lay in his with a candle, reading hard the book which on this trip he had taken for his novel-companion, and at every disengaged moment opened whilst rambling on the moor. This chanced to be one of Miss Yonge's deservedly popular tales, wherein a leading element is the deferred Church Confirmation of a grown-up person. On Tennyson read, till I heard him cry with satisfaction, ' I see land ! Mr. —— is just going to be confirmed ! ' after which darkness and slumber."

The heroine of *The Clever Woman of the Family* bears some resemblance to Jane Austen's *Emma* ; but it is significant of the changed conditions that, whereas Emma's mistakes are

[1] *Alfred Lord Tennyson: A Memoir.* By his son, Hallam Lord Tennyson, p. 456.

concerned with matchmaking, Rachel's relate to philanthropy and social experiment. A later novel, *The Three Brides*, published in 1876, is decidedly inferior to any of these : but it contains passages which are highly entertaining in the presentation they give of the opinions of those days. Here is an instance. A disastrous fire has occurred in the town, and a public meeting is held to consider, amongst other things, how to meet the distress due to a number of women having been thrown out of employment through the destruction of a paper-mill. A scheme is proposed, and a lady present asks a question throwing doubt on its practicability.

" ' Do you wish any expedient to be proposed ? ' asked the Chairman, in a sort of aside.
' Yes, I have one. I spent yesterday in collecting information.'
' Will Captain Duncombe [her husband] move it ? ' suggested Raymond.
' Oh no ! he is not here. No, it is of no use to instruct anybody ; I will do it myself, if you please.' And before the astonished eyes of the meeting, the gold pheasant hopped upon the platform, and with as much ease as if she had been Queen Bess dragooning her parliament, she gave what even the astounded gentlemen felt to be a sensible practical exposition of ways and means . . . She finished off in full order, by moving a resolution to this effect."

The resolution was carried without opposition, but this is how the incident was discussed by the society of the neighbourhood afterwards :—

" ' She should have got her husband to speak for her,' said Mrs. Poynsett.
' He was not there.'
' Then she should have instructed some other gentleman. A woman spoils all the effect of her doings by putting herself out of her proper place.'
" Perfectly disgusting ! ' said Julius."

One member of the party, however, takes up the cudgels for the absent.

" Rosamond exclaimed, ' Ah ! that's just what men like, to get instructed in private by us poor women, and then gain all the credit for originality.'
' It is the right way,' said the mother. ' The woman has much power of working usefully and gaining information, but the one thing that is not required of her is to come forward in public.'
' Very convenient for the man ! ' laughed Rosamond.
' And scarcely fair,' said Cecil.

'Quite fair,' said Rosamond, turning round, so that Cecil only now perceived she had been speaking in jest. 'Any woman who is worth a sixpence had rather help her husband to shine than shine herself.'

'Besides,' said Mrs. Poynsett, 'the delicate edges of true womanhood ought not to be frayed off by exposure in public.'

. . . 'You were forced to thank her,' said Cecil.

'Yes, in common civility,' said Raymond ; 'but it was as much as I could do to get it done, the position was a false one altogether.' "

Rosamond's jesting remarks show that the author saw it was just possible to take another view ; and it is interesting to note that in one of her much later books she had advanced so far that she made one of her woman characters (without adverse comment) take up the career of a public lecturer.

Between the publication of *Heartsease* and *Dynevor Terrace* came *The Daisy Chain*, which was published in 1856. This was the first of the family chronicles, unless we include *Scenes and Characters*, an earlier work of little importance apart from the fact that it introduces us to the Mohun family, whom we meet again later.

In these family chronicles we have Miss Yonge's specially characteristic contribution to English literature. Family chronicles are to-day a familiar form of fiction. John Galsworthy and Hugh Walpole would probably have been surprised at being told that they were following in the footsteps of Charlotte Yonge ; but the fact remains that she was a pioneer in that art. These books are a class by themselves. They have no plot, any more than the true history of a family has a plot. Each book is simply a slice out of the life-story of a large family, extending over a considerable number of years. Further events in the same family are related in later books. As they have no plot, so they have properly no hero and heroine. Certain members of the family assert themselves and come inevitably to the fore, but that is all. This type of book was extraordinarily well suited to Charlotte Yonge's special talents ; for she had very little power of construction, but her great gift was in the creation of living characters. To the genuine lover of Miss Yonge the characters in *The Daisy Chain* and *The Pillars of the House* are real people ; to dip into one of these books for an hour is to spend that hour on a visit to personal friends. Of these two books, Miss Yonge stated that *The Daisy Chain* had always had the largest sale of any of her books, but that on re-reading them she herself preferred *The Pillars of the House* as being brighter and less pedantic. Unquestionably they are the two best of her family chronicles.

The two outstanding creations in *The Daisy Chain* are Dr. May and his daughter Ethel.   The character of Dr. May is thought by many people to be the best thing Charlotte ever did.   Certainly the book is worth reading for that alone.   The author at first intended Margaret to be the chief girl character, but happily Ethel took the law into her own hands ; for Margaret is a rather tiresomely perfect character who gives wise counsel from her sofa.   It is Ethel's enthusiasm about Cocksmoor which shows how far we have travelled since the days of Elizabeth Bennet and Anne Elliot.   And it is no sentimental glamour which moves her ; there is not much glamour about tramping rough country roads in all weathers to teach an unruly horde of children in a neglected hamlet.   But Ethel sees in Cocksmoor a real need, and having seen it she proceeds to action.   The children are neglected and untaught, and she can teach them ; and the teaching must of course be founded upon religion, therefore they must have a school and as soon as possible a church, and she will never rest until that end is reached.   Mrs. Romanes has pointed out in her book on Charlotte Yonge that she is a true Romantic, for she sees all the glory and beauty that lie behind the dull routine of life. It is because Ethel May knows what is the real inner heart of her Cocksmoor work that she sticks to it through all difficulties. The other great enthusiasm of *The Daisy Chain* is foreign missionary work, to which the clever brother, Norman, consecrates his life.   The proceeds from the sales both of this book and of *The Heir of Redclyffe* were given to the Melanesian Mission.   It had been decided, when Charlotte began to publish, that it would never do for her to keep the proceeds of her writings for her own benefit ! and it was not until comparatively late in life that she broke through this rule.

The Daisy Chain amuses us at times by the light it throws on the social conventions of those days.   It was deemed impossible for Margaret, aged eighteen, to take part in an afternoon walk with the rest of the family if young Mr. Ernescliffe were going too—although the governess and any number of young brothers and sisters were of the party ! This is an astonishing contrast to the free-and-easy days of Jane Austen, when a mamma would encourage and exhort a girl to go for a solitary walk with a young man. The unhandy Ethel commands our sympathy when we realise the difficulties she had to contend with in the matter of dress—trying to pin up a heavy crape skirt on a muddy day with only a common pin !

The Trial, although a continuation of *The Daisy Chain*, can hardly be included in the family chronicles, for it has quite a thrilling plot, turning on the subject of a murder, for which the hero is tried and condemned to death, the sentence being commuted in view of his youth. Eventually his innocence is established and he is released, but he has been in prison for years, and there is an atmosphere of sadness over a great part of the book. It is an example of Miss Yonge's thoroughness that she went with Judge Coleridge to visit Portland prison, in order to get her details correct with regard to the treatment of the prisoner.

Part of *The Daisy Chain* had appeared in *The Monthly Packet*, the magazine which Charlotte Yonge founded in 1851, and continued to edit for almost half a century. Among her many works which appeared first in it was *The Pillars of the House*, the other family chronicle already mentioned. It was written in the early seventies, when Miss Yonge was about fifty, and it bears the marks of a maturer mind. Again it is the history of a large family—there were eleven Mays, there are thirteen Underwoods. Charlotte thoroughly understood the ways of large families, as in her young days she used to pay annual visits to her numerous cousins in Devonshire. In *The Pillars of the House*, even more strongly than in *The Daisy Chain*, we are shown the flower of heroic goodness blossoming in circumstances of commonplace drudgery. For the thirteen young Underwoods are left fatherless, with an invalid mother, to face the battle of life under conditions of real poverty.

Every one of the thirteen stands out clearly as an individual character. The author's own favourites, we feel sure, are Felix and Lance, and so she makes most of her readers like them the best ; Felix, the eldest brother, who has to shoulder the responsibilities of the family, giving up all thought of the University and Holy Orders to take a post in a printer's and bookseller's shop (a bitter pill for one of Miss Yonge's well-born young men to swallow ! but he does it without any fuss) ; and Lance the musical genius, brighter and livelier than the steady-going Felix, who has had most of the liveliness knocked out of him by his family cares.   But the merry young Lance does not fall behind Felix in the matter of self-sacrifice, for he sticks to the shop and resists the lure of a possible musical career.   There is plenty of humour shown in the drawing of the various characters and their inter-action upon one another.   But most readers will probably agree with Mrs. Romanes in seeing no reason why the author should have killed Felix in the end.   One of her weaknesses is that she is too fond of illnesses and death-bed scenes.   In the history of large families we are bound to have some of them, but they are too long-drawn-out, with too much detail ; the picture would be more effective if drawn with fewer strokes.

We turn now to Miss Yonge's other class of stories—the historical romances.   In view of these books, critics might demur to the statement that Charlotte Yonge wrote of what she knew and let the rest of the world alone.   But she did move so familiarly among the people of bygone periods that it may really be said that she wrote of what she knew.   Doubtless she was not always correct as to facts, but it was not for want of taking pains.   Even in her girlhood she and her young friends talked about obscure historical characters with the same allusive familiarity with which other people discuss their relations.   And in her historical romances she achieved the rare feat of making her historical personages as completely alive and real as her fictitious characters.   This is the chief merit of *The Caged Lion*.   The hero is a moderately interesting young man named Malcolm Stewart, but the real charm of the book is in the characters of Henry V and his brother John of Bedford, and James I, the captive king of Scotland—captive yet friend of the English king.   The description of King Henry's last hours, and the picture of John of Bedford in his desolation taking up the reins of government on behalf of his baby nephew, are full of pathos.   But Charlotte Yonge's best historical romances are *The Chaplet of Pearls* and *The Dove in the Eagle's Nest*.   *The Chaplet of Pearls* has a really good plot. The scenes are laid in France and England at the period of the St. Bartholomew massacre, and the story recounts the perils and adventures of a young pair who are parted for years but find one another again at last.   *The Dove in the Eagle's Nest* is a story of German history, giving a vivid picture of the contrast

between the half-savage robber barons in their mountain
fortresses and the highly-civilised burghers of the towns. Both
these books contain scenes of great beauty and pathos.

Miss Yonge wrote numerous other historical tales, most of
them shorter and slighter than these. Some, like *The Little
Duke*, were simply stories for children. In that category *The
Little Duke* is admirable. After the seventies she wrote
very little of any solid merit ; but two of her later historical
romances, *Unknown to History* and *A Reputed Changeling*, are
well worth reading. The plot of the former centres on an
imaginary daughter of Mary Queen of Scots and Bothwell.
A Reputed Changeling deals with the Revolution of 1688, and
introduces some interesting local colour, notably at Port-
chester Castle, and Blackgang Chine in the Isle of Wight.

There is a prevalent notion that Miss Yonge's books are of
the nature of religious propaganda. This is true of some of
her smaller books, written expressly for young people ; and
here it should be mentioned that she wrote a whole series of
village tales which are remarkably good of their kind, and
interest village children of to-day as thoroughly as they
interested their grandparents. But in her larger and more
important works there is no direct propaganda. The only
influence they exercise is through atmosphere. It must be
remembered that reserve in religious matters was a marked
characteristic of the Tractarians. The principles of the
English Church are present as a background, but even in *The
Pillars of the House*, which deals more intimately with distinctive religious practices than any of her other stories, the
allusions spring naturally from the narrative because it happens
to be a record of people to whom these things were of
paramount importance.

Miss Yonge's method of work was curious ; it was her habit
to have three works on hand at the same time, *e.g.*, one novel
and two other works, and to write a page of each in turn,
leaving the first to dry while she wrote the next. In this way
she wrote *The Pillars of the House* and the *Life of Bishop
Patteson*, and announced one day at luncheon that she had had
a dreadful morning—she had killed the Bishop and Felix !
She left a quantity of other writings besides novels, but we
are concerned with her here only as a writer of fiction. That
her work had numerous weaknesses must be clear to anyone

who has read thus far.   Her literary style was not usually very good, and at its worst it was very bad.   It became absolutely slipshod in her later years.   Allied to this fault was her lack of constructive power.   The deterioration in her later work is easily explained.   It was not only that her powers were naturally failing, but her life, which had always been secluded, became increasingly isolated owing to the fact that she had an invalid friend living with her, which prevented her from travelling about or receiving visits from other friends. It was seldom that she had the pleasure of intellectual companionship at Otterbourne.   One such rare occasion was a visit from Miss Wordsworth , who has left a charming record of it[1] in which she speaks of her hostess as " looking like a French Marquise," a description borne out by her portraits. Her work suffered from lack of contact with the outer world, and from the absence of that bracing criticism which she might have had through association with abler intellects than her own.   But perhaps what has been set down here may serve to convince some, who have never hitherto thought much about her, that her work is not merely a curious relic of bygone days, but a serious contribution to English literature.

BOOKS ABOUT CHARLOTTE YONGE

The Life and Letters of Charlotte Yonge.   Christabel Coleridge, 1903. *Charlotte Yonge : an Appreciation.   Ethel Romanes,* 1908.

---

[1] In *Charlotte M. Yonge : an Appreciation*, by Mrs. Romanes.

XV

THE LIFE OF GEORGE ELIOT

(1819–1880)

Mary Ann Evans—to give her the correct baptismal name—was born at Arbury Farm, near Griff in Warwickshire, in November, 1819, the year of Queen Victoria's birth. Her father, Robert Evans, was the son of a carpenter and small builder who lived in the village of Ellastone in North Staffordshire, and his superb physique was matched by the efficiency of his keen, practical mind. Capable, reliable, knowledgeable in all that pertained to local mines and plantations, Robert Evans became land-agent to Mr. Francis Newdigate, and moved with him when he inherited the Newdigate estate in Warwickshire. Thus Mary Ann Evans was born and bred a child of the English Midlands. She grew up for twenty-one years in the rich, but not spectacular or stirring, county of Warwickshire, in a comfortable red-brick, ivy-covered house with farm buildings attached, and a wide range of heart-of-England farms and fields lay open to her observant eyes and reflective mind as she drove about the countryside with her father.

This childhood of George Eliot's belonged to the old countryside, before the application of scientific methods to agriculture had made great inroads upon the faith and practice of farmers and their labourers, who chiefly thought of towns as mere markets for butter, cheese and hay, and did not concern themselves much with politics. In girlhood she became familiar with the manufacturing town, with its trade unions, its election riots and the dissenting chapels which meted out grim comfort to poorly paid hand-loom weavers, referring good and ill alike to predestination. In womanhood she was keenly absorbed in the scientific and speculative thought which challenged the educated mind in the 'fifties.

Early family impressions sank deep into Mary Ann Evans' mind. Her father was the model for Adam Bede and Caleb

Garth ; her mother had a strain of Mrs. Poyser, anu ₁rom her family the Dodsons were drawn ; the contrast between herself and Chrissie suggested that between Dorothea and Celia Brooke ; her hero-worship of her brother Isaac gave her material for the childhood relations of Tom and Maggie Tulliver ; her aunt, Mrs. Samuel Evans, was the inspiration for Dinah Morris.

The chief feature of Mary Ann's childhood was her passionate devotion to her brother, and her first taste of tragedy was when his first pony superseded her for a time in Isaac's affection. Like Maggie Tulliver, she had an intense need for affection, and to be first with someone ; and yet, also like Maggie, she could not altogether sink her individuality in another, she was not content to give without receiving, and could rebel against her adored. This phase of her life is beautifully illustrated by the *Brother and Sister* sonnets (1869), and it is the foundation for the early part of *The Mill on the Floss* ; her sister Chrissie was the Lucy Deane type of little girl.

Her school-days revealed Mary Ann as a promising pupil, whose essays were a source of pride to her teachers. Owing to her mother's failing health she was sent early to a small school at Attleboro', then to Miss Wallington's school at Nuneaton, and finally to the Miss Franklins' at Coventry. Miss Wallington's school supplied her with a friend in Miss Lewis, the head " governess," with whom she corresponded for many years, and who had a strong evangelical influence upon her. Miss Franklin's father was her model for Rufus Lyon in *Felix Holt*, the dissenting minister whose dignity and spiritual quality are finely manifested in spite of a quaint, insignificant appearance.

It was characteristic that Mary Ann's one enduring school friendship was with a mistress : to the girls she appeared so mature that one of them said it was impossible to imagine that she had ever been a baby ! This was partly due to her appearance—she was a large, plain girl with a massive head—and partly to her naturally earnest cast of mind.

Mary Ann's mother died when she was sixteen, and soon afterwards her sister married a doctor, and at seventeen she became her father's housekeeper. It was no light task to run a farm-house with the same Dodson-Poyser efficiency which came natural to her mother and sister, but Mary Ann was determined to rise to the occasion, and she succeeded. She made the cheese herself, and was always proud that one of her hands became permanently larger than the other in consequence ; she stood over boiling jelly and damson cheese until she trembled with the tension, she made excellent mince pies, she devoted hours to the household sewing. Meanwhile, however, the craving for intellectual interests could not be subdued ; she read voraciously, and she had one master from Coventry to teach her Italian and German and another for music-lessons. Emily Brontë made bread with a German book propped up before her, and yet, we are told, the bread was always light. Mary Ann Evans' German did not spoil her damson cheese and mince pies, and she was sincere when she said that she liked a clean kitchen better than any other room. These two women of genius certainly proved that a keen mind can be applied in more ways than one.

A passage in a letter to Miss Lewis at this period conveys a staggering sense of her wide, undirected reading :—

" My mind presents an assemblage of disjointed specimens of history, ancient and modern ; scraps of poetry picked up from Shakespeare, Cowper, Wordsworth, Milton ; newspaper topics ; morsels of Addison and Bacon, Latin verbs, geometry, entomology, and chemistry ; reviews and metaphysics—all arrested, petrified and smothered by the fast-thickening everyday accession of actual events, relative anxieties and household cares and vexations."

No wonder that her husband, J. W. Cross, wrote that she had " a limitless persistency in application ! "

At this period she held strict, evangelical views, did not allow herself to read novels or go to theatres, and despised the vanities of dress. She acknowledged later that she went about like an owl. On a visit to London with Isaac she read the Bible in her hotel bedroom while he went to the theatre. Isaac developed High Church views, and the breach between them widened. Yet her religion did not satisfy every part of her nature, and, like Charlotte Brontë, she chafed and longed to *do something*. She was voicing this girlhood's pain when she wrote in *Daniel Deronda*—" You may try, but you can never imagine what it is to have a man's force of genius in you, and to suffer the slavery of being a girl."

When Marian (as she now chose to spell her name) was

twenty-one, her father handed over the management of the Newdigate estate to Isaac and retired to a villa in Coventry. Miss Franklin, her old headmistress, told friends there that Marian was a remarkable girl and was sure to " get up " something or other : when she duly got up a clothing club in a poor district it was felt that she had amply fulfilled the prophecy. Now a new world opened to her, and in it she found a mental and spiritual liberation, at least for a time. Amongst her new friends were the Brays, a well-to-do ribbon manufacturer and his wife, and at their pleasant house—Rose-hill—she met intellectual society for the first time, including that of Mrs. Bray's brother and sister, Charles and Sarah Hennell. Their circle was deeply interested in the changing thought of this time of upheaval, when so many long respected ideas were challenged, and the sense of a coming conflict between science and religion already oppressed many minds and hearts. The title of Charles Kingsley's first novel— *Yeast* (published in 1848)—was an apt one to typify the economic, social and spiritual ferment of the middle of the nineteenth century. Charles Hennell had written a book called *An Enquiry Concerning the Origin of Christianity*, published in 1838, which had been warmly praised by Strauss. Marian Evans was deeply interested, and soon she was plunged into all the heart-burning of religious doubt ; emotionally she always clung with affection to the old, hallowed beliefs and to the Bible, but intellectually she could not accept the doctrines of any Church. A time came when she felt she must give up going to Church. Her father was outraged, and proposed to sell their house and go to live with Chrissie, and Marian contemplated finding a post as a governess. Eventually she and friends came to the conclusion that she was not justified in breaking up the home, and she decided to conform on Sundays as long as her father lived. Religion remained her primary interest, and through the Hennells she undertook the heavy labour of translating Strauss's *Life of Jesus* from the German. She was weary and sick in mind long before it was finished, and refreshed her spirit by gazing at an ivory statuette of Thorwaldsen's Christ which she kept on her desk. At last the book was done, and it brought her considerable appreciation of her scholarship.

At this time holiday journeys with the Brays were her chief

refreshment ; but another change in her life was coming. Her father fell seriously ill, and she nursed him devotedly for months, until his death in May, 1849. Marian now had to face life anew, at thirty, with only a small annuity (£80–£100) for her support. She travelled for some time with the Brays, and then stayed at a *pension* in Geneva. After her return to Rosehill she secured work in reviewing books for the *Westminster Review*, and eventually met Chapman, the editor, who encouraged her to go to London and stay at his house in the Strand. It was a Bohemian household, but the intellectual friendship which grew up between the admittedly susceptible Chapman and Marian Evans caused trouble with Mrs. Chapman, and after some time Marian established herself in rooms of her own. She was now launched on a journalistic career, became Chapman's assistant editor, and was called by Mrs. Carlyle " the strong woman of the *Westminster Review*." She met a number of interesting and distinguished people, and amongst them Herbert Spencer, who became a real friend. Spencer had just published *Social Statics*, in which he had set out to interpret ethics and politics through science ; it was he who originated the phrase " the survival of the fittest," which Darwin adopted from him. He was soon engaged on his *Principles of Psychology*, which opened up a largely uncharted field of thought to his generation.

Spencer's friendship was very stimulating to Marian Evans, who walked with him in Chapman's Thames-side garden day after day, and wrote to Sarah Hennell that she " always felt the better for being with Herbert Spencer." On his side he confessed that " the greatness of her intellect, conjoined with her womanly qualities and manner, generally kept me by her side most of the evening." Unfortunately his predilection did not ripen into anything warmer. Marian, on the other hand, began to find Platonic friendship a strain ; she was naturally ardent in emotion and always longed for reciprocity. She realised the position, fought her battle with her own feelings bravely, and succeeded in keeping Spencer's sincere friendship through life, although in a less intimate key.

Herbert Spencer introduced his friend George Lewes to his friend Marian Evans, and he, again, quickened her interest in science, and helped her to resolve her religious problem. As J. W. Cross wrote :—

" Her whole soul was imbued by, and fired with, the scientific spirit of her age, by the constant, rapid development of ideas in the Western world, and she felt that, as yet, no completely sufficient religious formula had been reached, or any political system that was likely to be final."

She was now content to leave faith at that, while still clinging to her reading of the Bible : as Lytton Strachey remarks, it was a period when " even the atheists were religious." Marian Evans, however, could not live long by interest in scientific progress and faith in the future, she needed a warm, intimate human relationship even more than most women do. Her thoughts and affections soon began to centre more and more round G. H. Lewes.

George Lewes, the grandson of a sufficiently successful comedian, was small and ugly—Douglas Jerrold called him " the ugliest man in London "—and his kaleidoscopic career as clerk, rover, preacher, medical student, actor and author, proved versatility rather than depth. Marian's moral earnestness was alien to his nature, and on the face of it she appeared on too massive a scale for him in every way. Lewes, however, had a quick imagination which could appreciate qualities he did not possess himself. In literary work his talent differed from hers just as much ; he was a first-rate populariser, informing every subject he took up with liveliness and point, achieving his effects largely through brilliancy of imagination and intuition, while she went to work with deep reflection, and her imagination has been described as " intellect sodden."[1] It was, however, his dynamic quality which fired her genius, and his vivacity and quick wit had for her the strong attraction of opposites. Mrs. Lynn Linton, who knew him personally, has recorded that " wherever he went there was a patch of intellectual sunshine in the room." Before he met Marian Evans he had achieved considerable success with his popular *Biographical History of Philosophy*, and had produced two novels.

Unfortunately George Lewes had married unhappily and was separated from his wife, who had first deserted him with Thornton Hunt. Lewes had to arrange for the education of three sons and pay his wife an allowance, all from the earnings of his pen. Divorce was beset with practically insuperable

[1] Anne Fremantle in *George Eliot* (Duckworth, 1933.)

difficulties : at this period (1854) a divorce could only be obtained by a special Act of Parliament, with legal preliminaries, and the cost was prohibitive to all but the wealthy. By the time the law was changed Lewes' union with Marian Evans was an accomplished fact, and a divorce would still have been extremely difficult.

Marian was wrought up to the pitch of deciding to live with Lewes when he had an illness, and was very wretched. After her father's death she had written that her one desire was " to have given me some woman's duty—some possibility of devoting myself where I can see a daily result of pure, calm blessedness in the life of another." Self-dedication and home-making had always had a compelling attraction for her, and Lewes was in sore need of just what she longed to give. It was, however, no light-hearted decision : before taking the final step, Marian visited Mrs. Lewes abroad and found out that there was no chance of her returning to her husband. She wrote to Mrs. Bray that the relation was to be a " profoundly serious " one—" light and easily broken ties are what I neither desire theoretically nor could live for practically." She adopted the rôle of mother to the three boys with great tenderness and success, and nursed the second one devotedly when he was invalided from abroad to die at home. Yet, in spite of determination to carry her burden proudly, she suffered very much from the taboo which her action brought upon her. She was much displeased with friends who failed to address their letters to Mrs. Lewes, and dedicated her books " to my dear husband "—a mid-Victorian touch. There is a pathetic detail in J. W. Cross's account of her first meetings with him and his family, when she was in Rome with Lewes : she always came in, he says, with " a very loving, almost deprecating look at my mother." This unsureness with other women was not lightly borne.

Henceforth, the life of George Eliot, as she shortly became, and George Lewes was an exceedingly busy one of writing, trying one house after another, as health or improved fortunes prompted a move, and frequent journeys abroad. Lewes' study for his successful *Life and Works of Goethe* took them to Germany, and it was in Berlin that George Eliot showed him a manuscript she had found amongst her papers, containing a sketch of Staffordshire countryside and peasants. He saw at once her latent literary power and persuaded her to begin the sketches which developed into *Scenes of Clerical Life*, published in 1857. *Adam Bede* followed in 1858, *The Mill on the Floss* in 1860, *Silas Marner* in 1861. Then a visit to Italy inspired *Romola*, an effort which " ploughed into her " almost as much as her translation of Strauss years before : next came *Felix Holt the Radical*, and then an excursion into poetry (*The Spanish Gypsy*, 1868), and then the great canvas of *Middlemarch* was filled in. Her final novel was *Daniel Deronda*, 1876.

During her literary labours (with her they generally were labours) George Eliot drew half her own vitality from Lewes' buoyant and galvanic spirit, though both had to struggle against poor health. Lewes managed all her business, and shielded her even more than was wise from all that might worry or disturb her, including adverse reviews, which he never allowed her to see. Gradually her genius, and the stability of her relation to Lewes, overcame much of the moral prejudice against her, and there are many accounts of the Sunday receptions, in which she received eager and distinguished guests like a stately goddess. J. W. Cross has described how she struck the in-coming visitor as he first saw her seated in her low armchair beside the fire :—

" On entering a visitor's eye was at once arrested by the massive head. The abundant hair, now streaked with grey, was draped with lace, arranged mantilla fashion, coming to a point at the top of the forehead. . . . She had a great dislike to raising her voice, and often became so wholly absorbed in conversation that the announcement of a visitor sometimes failed to attract her attention ; but the moment the eyes were lifted up, and recognised a friend, they smiled a rare welcome—sincere, cordial, grave—a welcome that was felt to come straight from the heart."

It is not surprising that John Morley thought that she looked like a bishop. Fortunately Lewes had just the social gifts that she lacked, and while the highly privileged took their turns to sit beside George Eliot for a *tête-à-tête* the others found their host a continual fount of wit and gaiety ; he could talk to thirty people as easily as to one, whereas, to quote J. W. Cross again, " it was difficult for her, mentally, to move from one person to another." Amongst the guests to be found at the Sunday receptions at the Priory (in Regent's Park), were

Tennyson, Meredith, Turgeniev, Trollope, Rossetti, Lord Acton and Burne-Jones.

Henry James has left an interesting account of a visit to their last home, at Witley in Surrey, on a stormy winter day. He was a great admirer of George Eliot's work, and even owned himself " a Deronda of the Derondists," and he was a little nervous about the meeting, feeling " that there couldn't be a single thing in the world on which the Leweses weren't almost scientifically particular." There was nothing very reassuring in his first sight of his " bland, benign, commiserating hostess, sitting by the fire in a chill desert of a room." He felt that they were glad he had come to pay his respects, but would return with satisfaction to their solitude *à deux*. There was very little of the paraphernalia of reading and writing about the room—" not to speak of that of tea, a conceivable feature of the hour, but which was not provided for." He left with the impression that, from the moment of " catching my celebrities sitting in that queer, bleak way," he had been raised on to a plane of rare intellectual detachment—" *there* " he reflected, " was the lift of contemplation ! "

The peace and intellectual detachment of the Witley home were not to last for very long : in 1878 Lewes died, and George Eliot (now fifty-nine) was desolate indeed. His eldest son, Charles, was very helpful, but he now had a family of his own. She was induced to persevere in bringing out her book of essays—*The Impressions of Theophrastus Such*—and she founded a scholarship in memory of Lewes. Her neighbour, J. W. Cross, helped her in her labours, and before long she became very dependent upon him—the nature which she herself had described many years ago as " ivy-like " had to reach out for a new and exclusive support. In May, 1880, George Eliot and J. W. Cross were married. Charles Lewes gave her away, and the marriage brought about a reconciliation with her brother Isaac. They travelled and then returned to Witley. Altogether George Eliot had seven months of calm happiness as Mrs. Cross, although she wrote to an old friend : " Deep down below there is a hidden river of sadness, but this must always be with those who have lived long." One joy she had with J. W. Cross which had been wanting with Lewes—they read the Bible together.

In the December of 1880 she had a return of an old ailment,

and after a few days' illness she died, at 4, Cheyne Walk. One of her last visitors was Herbert Spencer.

George Eliot had splendidly surmounted " the slavery of being a girl," which Marian Evans had felt such a check upon the " man's force of genius " within her ; she had also had much of the joy of being a woman.   Probably the best phase of her life was the twenty-five years spent with Lewes, of whom she wrote in 1865 : " How I worship his good humour, his good sense, his affectionate care for everyone who has claims on him ! That worship is my best life."

GEORGE ELIOT'S NOVELS

Scenes of Clerical Life, 1857.
Adam Bede, 1858.
The Mill on the Floss, 1860.
Silas Marner, 1861.
Romola, 1862.
Felix Holt, 1866.
Middlemarch, 1872.
Daniel Deronda, 1876.

At the opening of the third chapter of *Daniel Deronda*, George Eliot wrote :—

" A human life, I think, should be well rooted in some spot of a native land, where it may get the love of tender kinship for the face of earth, for the labours men go forth to, for the sounds and accents that haunt it . . . a spot where the definiteness of early memories may be inwrought with affection, and kindly acquaintance with all neighbours, even to the dogs, may spread not by sentimental effort or reflection, but as a sweet habit of the blood."

It was such a childhood, such a deep-seated " sweet habit of the blood," which gave its distinguishing quality to her best work : she was amply justified in claiming for *Adam Bede* that it should be redolent of hay and the breath of cows, and Mrs. Poyser's dairy (only matched in literature by that of *Tess of the d'Urbervilles*), is drawn with lovely retrospection by the hand which had grown broad in the making of butter and cheese. Apart from this refreshing pervasiveness of country earth and air, which Mrs. Gaskell also achieved in *Cousin Phillis*, George Eliot's work has other general characteristics which differentiate it from that of the earlier women novelists. She took to fiction when her mind was already fully matured, and thoroughly imbued with the scientific and psychological thought which prevailed in the circle of Herbert Spencer and George Lewes : she formed her style amidst the intellectual stir of the eighteen-fifties, and *Adam Bede* was published in the same year as Darwin's *Origin of Species*. Thus both temperament and environment inclined her to deep reflection, and even when she was drawing upon pure memory and autobiography (as in her creation of Maggie Tulliver) she was pre-occupied with the psychological analysis of her own experience. The force of life as it has actually been lived still pulses in Maggie Tulliver, as it does in Jane Eyre and Lucy Snowe, but George Eliot's self-revelation is a deliberate psychological study, whereas Charlotte Brontë's psychology wells up spontaneously—and, as it were, accidentally—through her passionately sincere attempt to reproduce what she herself has felt and borne. This difference between the two is well illustrated by Birrell's statement that George Eliot was a woman of intellect with a touch of genius, whereas Charlotte Brontë was a woman of genius with a touch of intellect. Nevertheless in Maggie Tulliver genius took the reins and intellect was kept within its proper sphere. There are other cases in which intellect predominated—notably in *Romola*—and genius was almost crowded out of the picture, and George Eliot's appeal to posterity has suffered in consequence, as reflection dates more than feeling.

In one feature of analytical and psychological fiction, George Eliot has not been surpassed—her power of showing a character *in growth*. In the early chapters of *The Mill on the Floss* we do not so much read as watch a living, developing childhood : Maggie Tulliver plays and frets and grows before us from child to girl, and girl to woman, and it is only in the mature phase of her life that we can have any doubt as to her complete reality. We see the same actual growth, with its spiritual and mental growing-pains, in Dorothea Brooke, and even in Gwendolen Harleth—probably this was the attraction which made Henry James admit that he was " a Deronda of Derondists."

Given the psychological and analytical bias, it was inevitable that in telling her stories George Eliot should interpolate general reflections and moral judgments, a habit which out-rages modern literary taste unless it is done with a very light hand, or a well-pointed wit. George Eliot both embodied her conclusions in humour (uncommonly well) and presented them naked and unashamed, and, again, some of them are extremely good, and if only the verbiage could be judiciously pruned, the golden apples of her wisdom would shine out conspicuously.

In another respect, George Eliot reflected the temper of her age : moral purpose was always in the forefront of her mind as she wrote, and, as her latest biographer[1] pithily expresses it, she believed that " the wages of sin are paid C.O.D." She herself admitted that she wrote to illustrate " the inexorable law of human souls, that we prepare ourselves for sudden deeds by the reiterated choice of good or evil which gradually determines character." So far as this she is in line with most great writers (Jane Austen's dramas of character illustrate the same law very neatly), but the purpose was sometimes over-laboured in George Eliot, the choices presented to her unfortunate characters too extreme, and their doom too drastic. Few in real life are confronted with such choices as Tito Melema and Gwendolen Harleth, and the tragedies of Hetty Sorrel and Maggie Tulliver seem out of proportion to their sins. The biographer quoted above holds that George Eliot's heroines were " her scapegoats, her sin-eaters," in whose persons she avenged all that Marian Evans had done that she ought not to have done, and rewarded all that she had not done that she ought to have done. It is probable that because she " lived in sin " with George Lewes, and gained far more by it than she lost, she was almost morbidly anxious to show that she did not condone such lapses because she herself happened to be a fortunate exception to the law of retribution, and in consequence she was harder on her characters than she might have been otherwise. Be that as it may, with George Eliot we pass out of the sphere of the second and third rate Victorian women novelists, who were apt to dispense justice like some Great Agrippa, ever on the watch to pounce on the wrongdoer with the appropriate punishment ; her genius saves her from the crudity and melodrama into which even Mrs. Gaskell fell at times ; in her the artist does transcend the moralist.

George Eliot's first work—*Scenes of Clerical Life*—shows all her qualities in small doses : there is wise, reflective character-drawing, conversation in which the individual reveals himself with pleasing irony, humour which she can manipulate either to scathe or to arouse sympathetic tenderness. She confesses in the first " scene "—*The Sad Fortunes of the Rev. Amos Barton*—that she had all her life " had a sympathy for mongrel, ungainly dogs, who are nobody's pets : " accordingly she takes for her hero a curate, middle-aged, poor, partially bald

[1] Anne Fremantle.

and with a habit of sniffing. He is inept even in his choice of
the dressing-gown he wears at his own fireside—a maize-
coloured one, which does not suit his complexion and is particularly prone to soil—and his religious doctrine is dry and
grim. He offends Mrs. Patten, one of his well-to-do
parishioners, by over-much stress on her sins and her need of
mercy, and she has to reassure herself by telling her friends
" if I'm not to be saved, I know many as are in a bad way."
The same comfortless doctrine is meted out to the inmates of
the Workhouse with equal severity.

Yet the Rev. Amos Barton has his sense of duty and a soul
which reaches upwards bravely in spite of the pressing material
worries of keeping a wife and six children on £80 a year ; and
George Eliot endows this " nobody's pet " with a lovely,
serene Madonna-like wife, the type of loving woman whose
whole world is within the four walls of her home. Gradually
we come to see Amos Barton anew through her love, and after
the tragedy of her death we feel that we, too, like the
parishioners of Shepperton, should have rallied round
him with a new sympathy, remembering how she would
have thought and felt about him. So her care envelops
him still after her death.

In this " scene " as in the other two, George Eliot sketches in
almost too much leisurely detail, sufficient to supply a background for a much longer story : but few of the minor
characters could be spared, certainly not Mrs. Hackit, an
understudy of Mrs. Poyser, whose knitting was always handy,
and yet " in her utmost enjoyment of spoiling a friend's self-
satisfaction, she was never known to spoil a stocking."

The second " scene "—*Mr. Gilfil's Love Story*—is the best
constructed of the three, and gives a touching account of a
passionate young girl crossed in love. The Cheverels of
Cheverel Manor, drawn from the Newdigates and Arbury
Hall, seem like old pictures come to life for us. The sketch of
Mr. Gilfil when he had grown elderly, catching his forgotten
spurs in his surplice as he mounted into the pulpit, is masterly ;
in fact, his young self is a shadow beside the portrait of him as
he grew old, and just in the same way the portrait of old Sir
Christopher Cheverel dwarfs that of his popinjay heir.

Janet's Repentance, the third scene, has scarcely substance
enough to carry its detail, but, like all George Eliot's work, it

yields a harvest of telling thumb-nail character sketches and wise reflections.

The *Scenes* were all founded on fact, the first two on actual stories of past Rectors of Chilvers Coton, where George Eliot had been christened. *Adam Bede* also owed its origin to a story which she heard from her aunt Mrs. Samuel Evans, who had played a part such as Dinah played to Hetty to a girl condemned for the same crime.

The glories of *Adam Bede* are, first it gives us the freedom of the lovely village of Hayslope (drawn from Staffordshire Ellastone) and of the Poysers' farm and dairy, the very ideals of what a farm and a dairy should be, and, second, the immortal portrait of Mrs. Poyser, with her keen-edged tongue and her conscious superiority as the perfect housewife. The picture is beautifully complete, with lovely seventeen-year-old Hetty displaying her pretty arms to such advantage in the dairy, and fat, little toddling Totty helping everybody to mind their business and also developing plenty of her own. George Eliot cannot be matched for delicious, natural children, perfectly fitted into the background of kitchen, farm or cottage, just as one would find them in real life. Timothy's Bess's Ben, playing his own momentary part in the gathering on the village green to hear the pretty Methodist girl preacher, is an inimitable sketch, and just occupies our attention as long as such little diversions do in actual life. Where *Adam Bede* fails to hold the modern reader is in the portrait of Dinah Morris, who is obviously meant to be a central figure, but is quite overshadowed by poor, pretty, betrayed little Hetty. Dinah's sermon on Hayslope green, given in full in an early chapter, is tedious, and she never seems either to grip our affections or to give us a sense of actuality, although George Eliot knew her dissenting world so well. Adam's eventual marriage to Dinah shocked many readers at the time, and certainly is not altogether pleasing.

The minor characters in *Adam Bede* are extraordinarily good, from Adam's whining mother to the high-born parson, Mr. Irwine, of whom Mrs. Poyser said : " It's summat-like to see such a man as that i' the desk of a Sunday ! As I say to Poyser, it's like looking at a full crop of wheat, or a pasture with a fine dairy o' cows in it ; it makes you think the world's comfortable-like." Mrs. Poyser herself would bear much quoting :

amongst a few of her best *bons mots* are her reply to old
Martin's remark that it's a poor look-out when the old folk
don't like the young ones—" Ay, it's ill livin' in a hen-roost
for them as doesn't like fleas "—and her comment on Chown's
wife's complaint that the weather has spoiled her cheese—
" there's folks as 'ud stand on their heads and then say the
fault was in their boots."

Adam Bede has its full share of George Eliot's characteristic
faults, it bears too clearly the marks of conscientious intellectual labour, and sometimes chapters or passages are obviously
introduced to give her an opportunity of " writing up " some
particular subject, such as the chapter on Adam attending the
night school. A beautiful descriptive passage is introduced
by the ugly phrase " it was a scene to sicken for with a sort of
calenture in hot and dusty streets," and the style is often
lengthy and involved ; but much may be forgiven her for the
sake of such a scene as that in which Hetty, in her bedroom,
unlocks her drawer to bring out her hoarded treasures—two
short bits of wax candle, a box of matches and a shilling
looking-glass *without blotches*—and proceeds to revel in her
own lovely image, which even her cheap green cotton stays
cannot spoil. Many such scenes of George Eliot's workman-
ship are as faithful and clear-cut as those of the old Dutch
masters.

Probably the majority of George Eliot's admirers would say
that *The Mill on the Floss* is her masterpiece. It presents a
wonderful study of childhood and adolescence, within the
limitations of Maggie Tulliver's period and environment. It
is redolent in turn of riverside meadows, beeswax, plumcakes
in the oven and steaming gravy, the mustiness of the attic and
the chill air of a shrouded spare bedroom. George Eliot's
humour is never better than in her drawing of the Dodson
sisters, with their Forsytean reverence for property (especially
linen and china) and their cherished family traditions in house-
keeping :—

" A female Dodson, when in ' strange houses ' always ate dry
bread with her tea, and declined any sort of preserves, having no
confidence in the butter, and thinking that the preserves had probably begun to ferment for want of due sugar and boiling."

Tom and Maggie Tulliver perched in a tree sharing their
last jam-puff make a classic picture :—

" . . . The knife descended on the puff and it was in two, but the result was not satisfactory to Tom, for he still eyed the halves doubtfully.

At last he said—

' Shut your eyes, Maggie.'

' What for ? '

' You never mind what for. Shut 'em, when I tell you.'

Maggie obeyed.

' Now, which'll you have, Maggie—right hand or left ? '

' I'll have that with the jam run out,' said Maggie, keeping her eyes shut to please Tom.

' Why, you don't like that, you silly. You may have it if it comes to you fair, but I shan't give it you without. Right or left, you choose, now. Ha-a-a ! ' said Tom, in a tone of exasperation as Maggie peeped. ' You keep your eyes shut, now, else you shan't have any.'

Maggie's power of sacrifice did not extend so far ; indeed, I fear she cared less that Tom should enjoy the utmost possible amount of puff, than that he should be pleased with her for giving him the best bit. So she shut her eyes quite close, till Tom told her to ' say which,' and then she said ' left-hand.'

' You've got it,' said Tom, in rather a bitter tone.

' What ! the bit with the jam run out ? '

' No ; here, take it,' said Tom firmly, handing decidedly the best piece to Maggie."

She tried to make him change, but it was no use : for a time all went well, and Maggie was happily " lost to almost every-thing but a vague sense of jam and idleness," but Tom finished first, still " feeling in himself a capacity for more " :—

" ' O, you greedy thing ! ' said Tom, when she had swallowed the last morsel. He was conscious of having acted very fairly, and thought she ought to have considered this . . .

Maggie turned quite pale. ' O, Tom, why didn't you ask me ? '

' I wasn't going to ask you for a bit, you greedy. You might have thought of it without, when you knew I gave you the best bit.'

' But I wanted you to have it—you know I did,' said Maggie in an injured tone."

The scene ends with Tom jumping down and going off with his dog, leaving Maggie to bitter and resentful tears. Tom, of true Dodson blood, was generally " conscious of having acted very fairly," and often with justice ; his usual mode of viewing his past actions was " I'd do just the same again," whereas Maggie " was always wishing she had done something different."

Mr. and Mrs. Tulliver are excellent : the poor, bewildered Dodson-born mother whining over her unbusiness-like husband and her brown-skinned, temperamental daughter, with her unruly curls and scorn of patch-work, and the father whose unintelligent peremptoriness was always softened for " the little wench," with whom he instinctively made common cause against the Dodson strain in wife and son. Mrs. Pullet, the mildest of the Dodsons, is delightful, whether she is showing her new bonnet, with solemn reflections on how often she may wear it, or indulging in a still greater luxury of woe over her physic-bottles :—

" Pullet keeps all my physic-bottles—did you know, Bessy ? . . . He says it's nothing but right, folks should see 'em when I'm gone. They fill two o' the long store-room shelves a'ready—but,' she added, beginning to cry, ' it's well if they ever fill three. I may go before I've made up the dozen o' these last sizes."

The end of *The Mill on the Floss* is not good enough for it. Swinburne said that Maggie's running away with the lover of her cousin Lucy, who had been so good to her, is one of the instances in which George Eliot " violates the truth of the heart," in a way that none of the Brontës would have done. Maggie repents and turns back almost at once, but the mischief to Lucy has been done. It is certainly not the development one expects of the high-souled Maggie, and Stephen Guest is such a tailor's dummy of a man that he does not help us to find her aberration convincing. George Eliot herself admitted that there was not adequate preparation for the final tragedy.

The last of George Eliot's stories of the countryside was the exquisite idyll *Silas Marner*, all the more charming from the contrast with Silas's early bitter experience in the town Chapel community of Lantern Yard. It is a book of pictures, such as few other writers except Thomas Hardy have given us, pictures drawn with tender insight into the hearts and minds of the villagers of Raveloe, as they were a hundred years ago. George Eliot is equally at home in the bar of the Rainbow, at Squire Cass's, in Dolly Winthrop's cottage as in Silas Marner's, when the poor miser, robbed of his gold, has one of his cataleptic fits and comes round to see the golden curls of the baby waif, Eppie, who has strayed into his home and his heart in place of the lost sovereigns. It is remote from the modern world in the same way as *Cranford*, and has the same type of charm.

Silas Marner was followed by *Romola*, a story of life in mediæval Florence. George Eliot's reading and research for this book aged her, she felt, by almost ten years, and, although it is a well-constructed, powerful, clever story, the student in her on this occasion mastered the artist. Yet, scrupulously correct though the detail may be, the spirit is English and Victorian rather than Italian and Renaissance.

George Eliot next attempted the social-political novel in *Felix Holt the Radical.* The best thing about this book is its preface, an incomparable retrospect in which is pictured the England of the eighteen-thirties, in which George Eliot grew up from child to girl. No student of economic and social history should neglect to read it. There is also a graphic account of an election, founded on a memory of her school-days, reinforced by a meticulous study of the daily newspapers of the period she was describing. Felix Holt is unconvincing, his radicalism bears so little practical fruit, and that at a time when new movements must have offered him a field, and he has a decided tincture of both the prig and the pedant. Rufus Lyon, the minister, is excellent, and so is the aggrieved Mrs. Holt, whom her son will not allow to continue the sale of the quack medicines which have been her support. The novel is readable, with its quota of good character-sketches and interesting reflections, but again George Eliot's genius was largely in abeyance.

In *Middlemarch* there is some of her best work, but the book is so cumbrous, with its subsidiary plots, and its attempt to portray the many-sided life of a country town, that it baffles many readers. It is as though we were required to gain a grasp of the lives and households of the Mayor of Middlemarch, at least two of the doctors and four of the neighbouring clergy, the chief banker, a squire and a baronet on the outskirts, a rich old miser and his circle of greedy relatives, a land-agent and his family, and—thrown in—an account of the politics of the town and the latest agitations about a new hospital and a projected railway. It has justly been called a saga of middle-class life, complicated just as life in a country town is complicated.

Nevertheless, *Middlemarch* well repays an effort to grapple with it : it presents two psychological problems which are of enduring interest, the conflicts of Dorothea Brooke, trying to find an outlet for spiritual and mental gifts which her relations think mere eccentricities, and of Lydgate, an intellectual young doctor eager to serve the jealous Gods of research and reform and thwarted by the equally strong craving of his pretty, socially ambitious wife for a sphere for her own powers.

Dorothea Brooke is a fine creation. An embryo Saint Theresa, noble-minded and dignified in bearing, her beauty was at its best in the plain garments of her choice " which, by the side of provincial fashion, gave her the impressiveness of a fine quotation from the Bible—or from one of our elder poets—in a paragraph of to-day's newspaper." Dorothea, who was something of an heiress, tried to satisfy herself in building model cottages, but her ideas were first over-ruled by Mr. Brooke, her uncle and guardian, and when an amiable baronet allows her to experiment on his estate it is a bitter blow to find that he is actuated by love rather than by philanthropy. Mr. Brooke, who thrust her ignorance of political economy as an extinguisher over all poor Dorothea's lights, and said young ladies were too flighty to be allowed amongst his documents, is one of George Eliot's best satirical sketches. His habits of " inordinate travel " and of " taking too much in the form of ideas," enabled him to say of almost any subject " Ah, I've been into that myself a good deal at one time," and proceed to lay down the law to experts. It is not surprising that Dorothea's starved intellectual energy and idealism find a strong appeal in the scholarly, elderly clergyman, Mr. Casaubon, who is engaged upon a monumental *Key to all Mythologies* ! She had once thought what a fine vocation it would have been to marry the judicious Hooker and save him from that wretched mistake he made in matrimony, or Milton in his blindness ; now, here was a modern Hooker, who seemed to think she might serve him in some humble way in his great work. Poor Mr. Casaubon (for he is to be pitied too) appeared at exactly the right moment to fire " the fine, inflammable material of Dorothea's youthful illusions." Her sister Celia, with whom she is admirably contrasted, points out that Mr. Casaubon scrapes his spoon disagreeably on his soup-plate and blinks before he speaks, and when Dorothea replies that only the commonest minds notice such things, Celia retorts, " then I think the commonest minds must be rather useful. I think it is a pity that Mr. Casaubon's mother had not a commoner mind ; she might have taught him to eat better."

Dorothea is not to be saved : she marries Mr. Casaubon, only to find out in time that he is but a dilatory pedant, her inferior in intellect, and, moreover, that most of the work he laboriously tinkers at has already been done by German theologians, whose books he has not read. His consciousness that she has seen through him, and the young, impetuous energy with which she tries to key him up to efforts of which he is incapable, make him withdraw into a cold reserve—he feels that she is " too young to be on the formidable level of wifehood." Nevertheless, Dorothea achieves some gleams of tenderness in the last phase of her mistaken marriage : when death threatens her husband, a divine pity overcomes her former sense of aggrieved frustration, and he responds to it.

The man Dorothea should have married is Lydgate, who finds in her some of the inspiration and sympathy he needs in his struggle to establish the new hospital. He tells her that he is handicapped because his chief supporter has religious views which Middlemarch in general dislikes—" ' That is all the stronger reason for despising such an opposition ' said Dorothea, looking at the affairs of Middlemarch in the light of the great persecutions." Unfortunately, Lydgate had not known what belonged to his peace :—

" Lydgate, in fact, was already conscious of being fascinated by a woman strikingly different from Miss Brooke . . . Miss Brooke did not look at things from the proper feminine angle. The society of such women was about as relaxing as going from your work to teach the second form, instead of reclining in a paradise with sweet laughs for bird-notes, and blue eyes for a heaven."

So Lydgate tries to realise his paradise by marrying lovely Rosamond Vincy, and is soon wrestling with his own shattered illusion. In the end her craving for self-expression, and her social and maternal ambitions, overcome his : first debt robs him of his independence and self-confidence, and finally he is driven to give up his high ideals of reform and his dreams of research and make the comfortable income Rosamond requires as a doctor in a fashionable watering-place. It is an excellent study of an eternal problem, which has also been ably treated by H. G. Wells in *Marriage* and Sinclair Lewis in *Martin Arrowsmith*.

George Eliot's last novel—*Daniel Deronda*—was her worst. In Deronda she tried to portray her ideal man and only succeeded in creating an abstraction, an assemblage of virtues without the breath of life. The study of Gwendolen Harleth is good, but it is some time before the reader likes her sufficiently to be interested in her development under the ordeal of marriage to Grandcourt. The Jewish part of the story is not of strong interest, although fore-seeing in parts. Few people could now read the book without frequent " skipping."

Amongst the general verdicts on George Eliot's novels, from a modern point of view, none is better than Virginia Woolf's :—

" She gathers in her large grasp a great bunch of the main elements of human nature, and groups them loosely together with a tolerant and wholesome understanding which, as one finds upon re-reading has not only kept her figures fresh and free, but has given them an unexpected hold on our laughter and tears."[1]

BOOKS ABOUT GEORGE ELIOT

George Eliot in Derbyshire : " Gossip about passages in her novels." Guy Roslyn, 1876.
The Ethics of George Eliot's Works. J. C. Brown, 1879.
George Eliot. William Morgan, 1881.
*George Eliot. Mathilde Blind (Eminent Women Series) 1883.
George Eliot : a Critical Study. G. W. Cooke, 1883.
*George Eliot's Life and Letters. J. W. Cross (Blackwood) 1885.
A useful compilation by George Eliot's husband which supplied material for later biographers, but is not an inspiring or attractive presentment of her life.
George Eliot, Margaret Lonsdale, 1886.
Life of George Eliot, Oscar Browning, 1890.
George Eliot : her Early Home. Emily Swinerton, 1892.
George Eliot. E. Lynn Linton (Women Novelists of Queen Victoria's Reign), 1897.
George Eliot. Arthur Rickett (Prophets of the Century) 1898.
George Eliot. Clara Thomson (Westminster Biographies) 1901.
*George Eliot. Leslie Stephen (English Men of Letters) 1902.
The Inner Life of George Eliot. Charles Gardner, 1912.
A Day with George Eliot. Maurice Clare, 1912.
Notes on ' Romola.' By George Eliot. Edited by P. S. Smallfield, 1921.
The Homes of George Eliot, her Characteristics and Philosophy. A. L. Summers, 1926.
**George Eliot and Her Times. Elizabeth Haldane (Hodder & Stoughton) 1927. An excellent, scholarly biography, combining background and critical appreciation.

[1] The Common Reader, 1925.

*George Eliot : Family Life and Letters. Arthur Paterson (Selwyn
   and Blount) 1928. A good study.
The Life of George Eliot. E. & G. Romieu (Cape) 1932.
**George Eliot. Anne Fremantle (Duckworth) 1933. A pleasing
   and reliable short biography in the Great Lives series : very
   good value for 2/-.

N.B.

Good essays, both scholarly and readable, on Jane Austen, The
Brontës, Mrs. Gaskell and George Eliot are to be found in Women
Writers of the Nineteenth Century by M. A. Bald (Cambridge
University Press).